A Love Big Enough to Share

Written by: Mary Beth Roedema,
Paula Elaine Huston, Pamela S. Teunissen,
Kristin Beth Oosterheert

*Dad has a
plan for your
life.
In Christ,
Pamela S Teunissen*

Create Space
4900 LaCross Road
North Charleston, SC 29406
USA

Publisher's Note: This is not a work of fiction.

A Love Big Enough to Share / Roedema, Huston, Teunissen, Oosterheert
ISBN 9781986277983

We dedicate this true adoption/reunion story
with humility and gratitude,
with expectancy and anticipation,
to Aiden, Jamey, Andrea,
Timothy, Sarah, Lucas, Marcus,
Willow, Meadow, and Ginger.

May you see that God is good and He is faithful.

A Love Big Enough to Share is the true story of four women and the surprising way their lives intersected. No one could ever have made this story happen the way it did, so in gratitude, all the praise goes to our awesome God who formed the plan and carried it out.

*Great is the LORD and most
worthy of praise;
his greatness no one can fathom.
One generation will commend your
works to another;
they will tell of your mighty acts.
They will speak of the glorious
splendor of your majesty,
and I will meditate on your
wonderful works.
They will tell of the power of your
awesome works,
and I will proclaim your great
deeds.
They will celebrate your abundant
goodness
and joyfully sing of your righteousness.*

Psalm 145:3-7(NIV)

In the past, adoption was most often "closed" and confidential. It was viewed as a social service solution, simply an event with little lasting effects. After legal confirmation of the adoption, those involved were to go on with their lives. Little attention was given to the unique needs of the members of the adoption triad: birth parents, adoptive parents, and adopted persons. In contrast, today's perspective on adoption has changed. Adoption is not simply a legal event, but is more often a more open, lifelong process for all involved.

A Love Big Enough to Share is a distinctive book that looks at real issues and explores real feelings and thoughts of the triad members. There is Paula, with an unplanned pregnancy but a deep compassion and ongoing love for the child she carries and delivers. And Mary, who became a mom by adoption, and who fears losing her 17 year old daughter as unexpected identification is made of the birth mother. And of course Kristin, who has the possibility of discovering the depth of who she is as an adopted person and what part both of her moms might play in her life.

We know from research that birth mothers do not "forget and go on with their lives." They can often have lifelong feelings of sadness and depression, resulting in the bottling up of their feelings. The reader will discover and quickly identify these emotions in Paula's story. For seventeen years, Paula lacked the opportunity to grieve openly. There was little support for her feelings of loss and grief.

In *A Love Big Enough to Share*, an adoptive mother suddenly faces the issues of an unexpected reunion between her adopted child and the family of birth. Every mother can identify with Mary's self-doubt and her fear of losing her child. Being an adoptive parent is different from being a biological parent. Mary must face and adapt to challenges that other parents do not have to face.

Kristin, as an adopted person, quite openly and honestly uses her emotional strength to acknowledge her need to repair her sense of loss—the sense of loss felt from having been separated at birth from her birth mother. Kristin, with great courage and her own fears, confronts her desire for identity and faces the questions of "Who am I?" and "Where did I come from?" In this book the reader will join Kristin in her journey to take control of her life. The reader will be able to identify the issues experienced by most adopted persons as they read Kristin's words. Her story beautifully describes the process of an adopted person who is trying to make sense of adoption. It validates the adopted person's need for human connectedness.

In *A Love Big Enough to Share,* the birth mother, adoptive mother, and adopted person let us into their lives and hearts by sharing the lifelong process of adoption and how these issues have affected them. They each grieve the losses they have experienced and they each seek to take control and come to a sense of resolution and peace out of the differences adoption has made in their lives.

The role of friendship within this true story cannot be ignored. God planned the exact moment Kristin would be recognized as the daughter of Paula. The reunion between Paula, Kristin, and Mary is unique, and the role friendship played in this process can only be found in the heart of God.

All readers will gain a sense of understanding for the issues of adoption, as well as the dynamics of the mother-daughter relationship. Each triad member's point of view is shared in the chapters she writes. Mary, the adoptive mother, deeply loves her daughter, but must let her go. Paula, the birth mother, feels deep responsibility for the welfare of her yet unborn child, and then endures the next seventeen years with persistent, hidden grief. Kristin, the adopted child, seeks to uniquely love each mother and to understand the bond she feels for each. And Pam, the fourth point of view, writes of her position as a friend who was assigned a long term, unexplained, and pivotal role.

Important to the stories of all the women in this book is their faith in God and their trust in His plan for them. His love for them called them into a circle of love—truly a love big enough to share.

- Mary Sue Kendrick

Mary Sue is now a retired, professional counselor, trained in the clinical issues of adoption. She designed and implemented the C.A.R.E.S. program of post adoption services for Bethany Christian Services, Grand Rapids, Michigan from 1989-1995. She was a state trainer for social workers and counselors with the Michigan courts and agencies in the field of intermediary services. Mary Sue has lectured and presented at trainings and conferences nationally regarding the clinical issues of birth parents, adoptive parents and adopted persons after adoption. She has also authored numerous articles addressing the post adoption issues of triad members.

In addition to her professional experience, Mary Sue is an adopted person and an adoptive parent. She experienced a positive reunion with her own birth parents and siblings in 1990. Mary Sue has also had the privilege of sharing in the search and reunion process of her adopted daughter and her daughter's birth family.

Mary Sue Kendrick and her family now reside in her home state of Georgia.

TABLE OF CONTENTS

Kristin: The Story of Me

Childhood Saturday mornings, as early as I can remember, would always begin the same way. I would go into my parents' room and find them talking quietly. I would interrupt their chat by jumping onto the middle of their double bed. A tickle-fight was sure to follow, along with hugs and kisses. My mom would slip on her robe and head to the kitchen to start breakfast.

"Tell me a story!" I would plead.

"What story?" my father would ask innocently, with a smile, pretending I didn't always give the same answer. Invariably I would reply, "Tell me the story of ME!"

We would settle into the pillows and he would begin. "Mom and I had enough love for more than two people, and we wanted to have a little girl like you in our family. So we called Bethany Christian Home and talked to one of the caseworkers there. We had to wait and wait a very long time. It seemed like forever! Finally, we got a call from the caseworker. There was a little girl who needed a mom and dad."

"And it was ME!" I would pipe up excitedly, unable to stand the suspense.

Dad's face would break into a big grin. "And it was YOU! We packed up our car and drove to Bethany, and there we saw you, Kristi, for the first time. You were so little, but you were a dandy!" And on it would go, detailing how they drove to Bethany to see me but couldn't take me home right away, how they signed court documents and told the courts and adoption agency what my name would be for the final birth certificate. They even left a little white outfit for me to wear home. Dad told how they went again and picked me up in their bright orange Volkswagen (I slept the whole way) and took me home, stopping on the way to meet my new grandpas and grandmas, aunts and uncles. What a happy introduction that was! The "Story of Me" always ended with my father's voice saying, "Before we even knew you, we loved you."

CHAPTER 1

Mary: God Sets the Stage

I've a dear little dolly,
Her eyes are bright blue,
She can open and shut them
And she smiles at me too.

In the morning I dress her
And we go out to play.
But I like best to rock her
At the close of the day.[1]

I love September! It always feels like a season of fresh starts and new beginnings.

September 1945: the whole world was celebrating a fresh start of peace as World War II had finally ended! My young parents, Maynard and Betty Bouwman, were eagerly expecting a new beginning, the birth of their first baby.

Pregnancy hadn't come quickly. Already two years had passed since their wedding, including Dad's draft into the army. But finally, I had been conceived soon after the new year began. They were delighted! The months passed, until late in September they sped to a small Michigan osteopathic hospital in downtown Grand Rapids for the delivery.

In those days, dads were not included in the birthing process, but simply had to wait in the fathers' waiting room. As my dad nervously waited, my mother experienced complications in delivery. The doctor came to tell my dad of the difficulty, "I think I can save the life of your wife or the baby, but probably not both. What do you want me to do?" With fear in his voice, my dad asked, "You can't save them both?" Then, "Please try to save my wife."

But God had other plans. I was a small 6 pound, 4 ounce baby, born at 1:18 on a Sunday morning, the last day of September. They named me Mary Beth.

Being the first born grandchild on both sides of the family, I received a lot of attention and thoughtful gifts. Dolls were my favorite. So, every Christmas I would sneak a peek under the Christmas tree, as our family arrived at Aunt Jo's house, looking to see if she had a doll-sized box wrapped with my name on it. She always did.

I grew up loving dolls, carefully tucking them in their cribs at bedtime, playing house with other girls on our front porch in the summer, and pretending I had a good husband and lots of children. As far back as I can remember, I wanted most of all to be a mom.

Besides dolls, I also grew up liking boys. Boys in grade school made tag a lot more fun, and "boys catch the girls" was especially exciting. Boys in the neighborhood brought out the tomboy in me when they invited my brother and me to play cowboys, to climb trees, or help them build forts and camps in the woods of nearby Richmond Park.

Families had a lot of kids in those days. The average seemed to be four or more. My brother, Mark, was born two and a half years after me. John came four years later. Then when I was almost ten, I overheard my mom telling a neighbor, "I'm expecting another baby." I began to watch my mom's stomach and also began to ask, kneeling beside my bed each night: "Lord, will you please give me a baby sister?" A few months after I turned ten, God gave me Jane.

Being the oldest, I was expected to mind my younger siblings. Mark and I got along well and often played together in the house, building stagecoaches out of stacked chairs and pillows, pretending we were heading West. We were both part of the neighborhood gang that played kick the can after supper till dark when Mom would call us in. When Johnny was old enough, he would join in too.

Soon after Jane was a year old, an orthopedic specialist discovered she had a congenital hip problem requiring body casts and leg braces for three years. This was a change for our family, but Mom, already a busy mother of four children, was determined Jane would NOT be spoiled. Both Mark and I were old enough to entertain little Jane after school and big enough to carry her around on one hip, cast or brace included. Meanwhile, Mom was free to do some housework or to run an errand while Dad was still away at work. There were also many evenings when I would sit by Jane's bedside and sing until she fell asleep. Later, Mom told me and Mark, "I don't know what I would have done without your help during those years."

Turning twelve was a milestone for me, marking the transition between childhood and becoming a teenager. That was the year I started junior high. Mom bought my first pair of nylon stockings with a garter belt to hold them up under my Sunday outfits. I was given my last doll, not to play with any more, but to keep special. Some neighbors on our block wondered if I might babysit their four kids now and then. It was exciting to be asked to take on such a responsible job!

Babysitting was fun whether I was paid for it or not. I often walked across the street just to ask a neighbor if I might take her little girl for a stroller ride. I found it easy to love other people's kids as I took care of them and thought about eventually having kids of my own. Sometimes I pretended they were.

My mom loved other people's kids too. Whenever we wanted to invite a friend for lunch or on a family outing, she would agree and then greet them with a hug. Many Sunday chicken dinners included extra people. Mom's motto was: "There's always room for one more."

The three years of junior high were a whirlwind of activity and fun! Besides the excitement of changing classes each hour, providing time to talk and talk some more with my girlfriends and to flirt with some of the boys who were becoming important in my life, I was also involved in a variety of extra-curricular activities. My parents had begun to sing with me and to teach me songs at an early age, and now that interest was channeled into a church trio called The Three Marys, a junior-high choir, and even a part in a Gilbert and Sullivan's musical, *The Mikado*, performed by some of the choir students.

I wasn't active in sports, but my friend Susie and I tried out for cheerleading and made the squad. We cheered for the basketball teams all three junior high years. This gave me another outlet for my enthusiasm. The teachers selected me for a Citizenship Award, an award meaning I liked people and was involved in a little bit of everything.

In contrast to junior high, the three years in high school were depressing years of declining social involvement and disappointment. I was crushed in the large Christian high school to be cut during the cheerleading try outs. I felt my self-esteem take a plunge as I allowed myself to believe that other students were much better than I was. I did have a good group of friends, but they were all girls. My growing interest in boys seemed to lead only to dead ends. The only dates I had were on the annual twirp date nights when girls could ask boys to go to a basketball game. None ever asked me out in return.

In spite of disappointments, some bright spots included my participation in the school choirs and the trio. My friendships with a few girls deepened as we matured and shared plans to go to college. It seemed that most girls who pursued an education beyond high school chose one of three careers: a secretary, a nurse, or a teacher. Since I loved kids, I chose a college prep course to become an elementary teacher.

It was at the end of my junior year in high school that all the catechism students around my age in church completed the course and "graduated" by making a public profession of faith. I didn't think I was ready for such a mass, impersonal decision, so I chose not to participate. Soon after I made that choice, I noticed God seemed to show up everywhere, getting my attention through words of songs, my personal quiet times, or words of other people. Our pastor even said to a small group of us high school kids, "Jesus wants _you!_" as he looked directly at me. Realizing the Hound of Heaven was after me, I could no longer avoid Him, and asked Jesus Christ to be my personal Savior. I was seventeen years old when I made a public commitment to the Lord in my church, with my friend, Susie, at my side.

Even though I got a job as a salesclerk at Susie's dad's Buttercup Bakery, I still continued to babysit for several families through high school and into my college years. I enrolled at Calvin College with plans to become an elementary school teacher until the time when I could marry and become a mom with kids of my own. Since few mothers worked outside the home, I looked forward to being a homemaker and caretaker of my kids. In my mind, happiness equaled marriage, which equaled lots of kids.

CHAPTER 2

Paula: The Beginnings

On March 5, 1952, a five pound, five ounce, seventeen inch, tiny baby girl was born to Pearl and Percy Roskamp in Forest City, Iowa. They named her Paula.

I was Paula, their second daughter; my sister Pat, just fourteen months older. When I was born, she had to give up her bottle. Mom said it didn't bother Pat—she wanted to give it to "dolly". My sister and I have always had a very special relationship. As we grew, three brothers were born, and our family became even closer.

I spent my childhood years growing up on a farm. Mom always said we kids didn't have it easy when we were young. We didn't have a lot of material things, but material things meant very little. We never wanted for anything. There was always food and clothing. There was plenty of love for everyone and we were never abused. Family and friends were by far the most important things in my life.

We lived in a small two-bedroom house with no running water or bathroom. All water for baths, cleaning, and cooking had to be heated on the stove. We had a pail of fresh, cold water for drinking. My sister and I and two of my brothers slept in one bedroom. Mom and Dad and the baby slept in the other. I would always wake my sister when I had to go to the bathroom during the night. She never complained and always got up and went with me. The wind was bitter cold as we tramped through the snow to the outhouse. It was even worse when we got there. It didn't take me long with the winter wind blowing around my bottom! When we got back to bed Pat would say,

"You rub my back for five minutes, and then I'll rub yours." Of course long before it was her turn to rub my back she went to sleep. I never did catch on to that. It worked for her every time!

We had chickens, pigs, and dairy cattle. Living on the farm meant there was always plenty to do, and we had daily chores helping feed and care for the animals. There was a barn, and we loved to play in the hayloft. There was a pump house, a chicken coop, and a building where grain was stored for the winter months.

There was also another small building that made a dandy playhouse for my sister and me. It had two small rooms. One room had a workbench and some shelves, which we used for a kitchen. The other room was empty, which made a perfect storeroom. Pat and I pretended that we owned a bakery. We were very well known for the quality of our baked goods. Everything was made fresh daily. There were bushes right behind our bakery with orange, red, and green berries, so we were able to decorate our pretend pastries quite beautifully.

I was about nine when my dad had his first heart attack. He was thirty-six. When Mom got up that morning and went downstairs, Dad was sitting in his chair in the living room. His face was snow white and his eyes were large and round with pain. He went to our local doctor and sometime later went to specialists at the Mayo Clinic in Rochester. It was early evening when we saw his car on the road. Mom was in the barn milking the cows when he drove up. We all gathered around the car, and Dad just shook his head. As kids, we were really too young to fully understand what the doctors told him. Mom turned around and, with her head down, slowly walked back to the barn. Later, I looked into the kitchen and saw my dad sitting by the table with his arms around my mom's waist. She held him close, and he was in so much pain he was crying. That is the one and only time I ever saw my dad cry.

After a time my parents had to sell all the animals and farm equipment because they couldn't handle it anymore. That was a very hard time for them. We moved to another farm in another small town in Iowa where we were closer to Dad's family. We just rented the house, not the buildings or the land. Even though all the farm animals had been sold, we always had at least one dog, and lots of cats.

It became necessary for us kids to be as quiet as possible because the noise and bickering made Dad very nervous. My sister and I were a little older so we understood it more, but the boys were very young and it was hard for them. We lived near a river, and Dad went fishing almost every day. It was quiet and peaceful for him there, and the fresh fish were always good. He also spent a great deal of time sitting in the car listening to the ball games on the radio.

A couple of months before my father passed on I listened to my parents talking on the way home from church. Dad said to Mom, "You know what bothers me the most? I'll never see forty. I'll never live to see my children grow up." My dad lived three years with his heart problems. He passed away when he was thirty-nine. He never saw forty.

We were all in bed that night when he came upstairs to go to bed himself. He used to puff on his cigarette to help him see so he wouldn't have to turn on any lights. From the room where my sister and I slept, I could see him and the little red light from his cigarette as he came up the stairs. When he got into bed he and Mom spoke quietly for a little while like they always did. Mom asked him how he felt and he said, "I feel like a million dollars". That made me feel good and I went to sleep.

It was about 2:00 in the morning when Mom woke Pat and me, "Come downstairs," she said softly. I walked quietly past my parents' room because Dad looked like he was sleeping so well, which he never did. When we got downstairs, Mom put an arm around each of us and said, "Dad is with Jesus."

The reality of what was going on and the finality of it didn't hit me for awhile. When the ambulance came to get my Dad, Pat and I were supposed to stay in the living room so we wouldn't see them take him out. Pat didn't see—but I did. Everyone's attention was focused on Dad, so no one saw me standing in the living room doorway. They had him covered with a sheet and strapped to a gurney. There was a very sharp turn at the bottom of the steep stairs. The only way they could get the gurney around the turn was to tip it on end. After they righted the gurney, they rolled it through the kitchen out to the ambulance. I watched them close the back doors and drive slowly away, the silent flashing lights reflected in the kitchen window. That sight is branded in my mind forever.

The first time we went to the funeral home, I stood beside Mom as she looked down into the casket. I looked up at her and then, for the first time, looked down. As short as I was, I had a very close view. I didn't know who that was, lying there. He didn't look like anyone I knew. Not until Mom reached over to fix his hair did I realize it was Dad. I stared at him for a long time, but, try as I might, I could not grasp the concept that my living dad and this man were the same person.

When it did hit me, and hit me hard, was after the funeral, at the graveside service. That was my *dad* in there, he was *dead*, and they were going to put him in that hole and cover him with dirt. I didn't want that to happen! I started to cry, and couldn't stop. Someone put their arm around me and turned me back toward the car. I kept looking over my shoulder. I couldn't believe what was happening. We had known how gravely ill he was and that he would only be with us a short time. Mom had explained it all to us, but until it actually happened I didn't think about it much. It was something in the distant future, and the future for an eleven-year-old child is virtually nonexistent. Yet the future was happening now, and my dad was gone. My mother's remarkable strength, her love for her children, and most importantly, her faith in God helped us all through that hard time.

Four months later we moved to the small town of Kanawha, Iowa. It was a very wise thing for Mom to do. It took us from the farm and the house where we lived with our dad, and where he died. It helped us, as children, to cope with the death of our father, by moving us to a totally new environment. Pat and I each had our own room while the three boys shared a room. We lived on the edge of town about a block from the grade school and high school. Mom had sisters living nearby, and it was a comfort to her to be near them. She had nine sisters and four brothers, and they were very close. We were brought up in the Christian Reformed religion and went to church every Sunday. Faith in God helped us all through many hard times. Times were tough so my mother, my sister, and I cleaned the schools and a medical clinic to help get along. We lived there two and a half years.

A year and a half after moving to Kanawha my mother met my stepfather in church. He was a widower who had lost his wife in a car accident. He was raising one daughter and three sons. My mother and Herm married on July 25, 1966, with the blessing of nine children, and our new combined family moved to a farm near the little town of Doon, Iowa. It was the summer before my freshman year in high school. It was a big adjustment for all of us. Pat had the biggest adjustment. She was fifteen and was going with a boy when we moved. It was hard on her at that age, having gotten used to town and then moving ten miles out in the country.

We three girls shared a bedroom, which was also new to us. We were all used to having our own room so it was very hard at first. The lack of privacy took awhile to get used to. My siblings and I were soft-spoken and never physically violent with each other. My stepsiblings, on the other hand, were different. Even though they were all close in age, my stepbrothers were taller and physically bigger than my brothers. One afternoon I was alone in the house, sweeping the living room floor, when my brother, Phil, came running in with my stepbrother, Doug, right behind him. Phil jumped behind me, and I immediately turned, ready for battle. When Doug got close enough, I swung and let him have it with my broom. This type of action from me was so out of character that it took him totally off guard. I guess he hadn't learned our family motto yet: "If you mess with one of us, you'll be dealing with all of us." We were fiercely protective of each other. I yelled, "You get out of this house, and don't you *dare* come back in here! Get out, *now!*" To my surprise, he did. We all had to learn our boundaries, and when we did, the trouble stopped.

Still, there was never a dull moment with six boys. What one didn't think of another one would. From trying to get a full grown horse up the stairs to their bedroom to making homemade wine and hiding it in their closet (it exploded all over their clothes). Luckily Mom came home and caught them with the horse (they only had it up three or four steps, but she wondered how in the world they would ever get it down!). They even decided to keep an alligator in the basement. Poor Mom never knew what was coming next—or from whom! We were quite a mixture, and there were many adjustments, but it didn't take long before we all became a family. My stepdad, Herm, was a farmer, and he was also one of the finest people I have ever met. He loved us like his own children, and we loved him like a father.

I went to a Christian high school. I was a sophomore when a new girl joined our school. It seemed she always wanted me to do things I knew I shouldn't do. Often she would ask, "Can you come to town tonight? There is going to be a party at the gravel pit, and my mom won't let me go alone." I knew her well enough to know there would be beer and boys at this "party".

"No. I'm sure my parents won't let me."

She would come right back with "Don't tell them where we're going. Tell them we're going to spend the night with someone. They'll never know the difference." This girl obviously didn't know my mother! I was not in the habit of lying to my mom, and even if I was, she could take one look in my eyes and know the truth.

I do have to give her credit for one thing, though. If it weren't for her, I would never have met Pam. The two of us were walking one day through Doon Park when I first saw her. Pam was short and petite with beautiful long, thick, dark hair and very pretty eyes. She was a year older than me and attended another school, yet we seemed to bond instantly. After that, when one of those "parties" came up, I would say to my new friend, "Pam, I don't want to go, do you?"

Pam would always say, "No. I'd rather do something else." Neither of us wanted her kind of parties!

Pam loved to come to my house. She said, "There's always something going on at your house." She loved all the hustle and bustle and the total chaos that was my home. "I love your mom!" she would say to me.

Our family had a couple of geese, and one in particular had a very bad attitude and liked to chase people. Poor Pam was afraid to get out of the car and come through the gate until Mom chased it away. Mom would flap her apron at them, and the geese, protesting loudly, would finally leave. When these geese got in the habit of doing their "business" on the sidewalk, the strangest thing happened, they disappeared. I hate to think that my mother had anything to do with that, but I did notice the "chicken" we had for Sunday dinner was suspiciously large.

Sometimes Pam and I would go for walks, other times we would just stay in my room and talk. We played cards and I taught her how to play rummy. I beat her two out of three games that day. I was too young to drive so going anywhere was out of the question, but, because we lived so far out in the country, Mom would let me drive alone when we needed milk. We got three gallons of milk almost every other day from a dairy farmer who lived about four miles away. Pam went with me one time in our old rusty white farm car. She got a kick out of watching the road go by under the car. The floor on the passenger side was rusted clear through. We had it covered with a piece of plywood, but it was fun watching the ground go by. She loved that kind of thing, and, when she came to my house, she was never disappointed. This stuff didn't happen at her house.

But I loved going to her house. There was just Pam and her Mom, and it was always quiet. I really liked her mom. She was so "cool". She looked a lot like Pam, with her dark hair and pretty eyes. She seemed to be able to relate to Pam and me on our own level, as teenage girls. They had a huge dog that thought he was a lap dog. It was funny watching him try to get up on someone's lap.

Pam and I felt so close to each other and had such a unique friendship that one day we decided to seal that bond forever and become blood sisters. We did not take this lightly. It was a very real commitment to us. It was also a very hard thing for us to do, as we were both scared to death of needles and the sight of blood. Still, we were determined and finally managed to squeeze enough blood to form a drop from each of our pin pricked fingers. Holding our injured fingers together, we shared a hug and sealed the bond of our friendship that would last a lifetime.

That summer we had a slumber party where we all slept in tents in her back yard. Of course no slumber party was complete without boys sneaking around and trying to scare us to death. We had so much fun. We set each other up on blind dates, some good, some awful! The best thing about our friendship was the way we could sit for hours and just talk, confiding our most private thoughts and dreams. We always seemed to know each other's heart and completely understand the other's feelings. We would talk far into the night about anything and everything. We were always there for each other, just a phone call away. This is what Pam wrote in my yearbook in 1969, my junior year and the year she graduated:

Dear Sweet Paula,

What can I say? Best of luck doesn't seem enough for someone as sweet as you, but I can't think of anything else to say: So best of luck! I really mean that too. I'll never forget all the fun we've had together or all those cool slumber parties. I'll never forget all the times I've cried on your shoulder and what a comfort it is to know that you are there, and that you will listen to my troubles. It's been really great having you for a friend. I hope we'll always be friends. Be good and keep your sweet smile and personality and you'll go a long way. Best of luck in all you do.

Your friend always,

Pam

As we got older we kind of drifted apart as all teenagers do. Pam met Anthony, moved to Michigan and got married. We had no contact, except in thought and prayer for about two years, but we still knew each other's hearts—some things never change.

During my senior year, I started seeing a young man named Mike[2]. We met through a mutual friend. He had dark hair and brown eyes, a very good-looking guy. We weren't at all serious, though, in fact I wouldn't even call it "dating". *Friends* was a better word. Shortly after I graduated from high school in 1970, Mike and I remained friends, but went our separate ways.

I had moved out on my own from the farm into the small town of Rock Rapids about ten miles from home. I had a job I loved working as a waitress at a truck stop, and I had my own apartment. At eighteen, I felt grown-up and independent.

The corner café in Rock Rapids was the "gathering place" to hang around with friends. One night at the café I met a good-looking guy named Dave[3]. He was about six feet tall and slender, with light brown hair and warm, intelligent, green eyes. I noticed him because of his good looks and outgoing personality. He seemed to be a real nice guy. He was kind and courteous and made me smile. We became friends right away, doing things and hanging around with mutual friends. Before long our attraction grew from just friends to something deeper, and we started seeing each other exclusively.

We didn't have a serious relationship at first but we enjoyed each other's company and liked going places and doing things together. As time went on we got closer and closer, more comfortable as a "couple". We liked to take long rides together. Sometimes we would stop and sit along the banks of the river. We were always comfortable being alone together without the need for small talk.

Dave was born and raised in the Rock Rapids area, the same area I had moved to. It was a place where everyone knew everyone. At times he would talk about moving away from this small town. "I want to see some of the country and live some place different," he would say in a far away voice. "I am thinking about going to Michigan." I recognized the excitement in his words, and I knew he would go. I knew I would really miss him. At that time our relationship wasn't really *that* serious, so I didn't consider going with him. Instead I stayed and he left.

Dave had a friend who had moved to Michigan a couple of months before and was able to get him a good job in a copper mine. Dave called me often. I missed him more than I thought I would. "I wish you had never gone," I told him during one of our phone calls. I had no desire to go with other guys so I didn't date at all. I looked forward to his calls, and I knew then that I loved him. We talked about love and how much we missed each other.

Then came the day he called and asked me to think about moving to Michigan so we could be together. He said, "I'll even come to get you Paula, I love you." I told him I would think about it, but my heart was pounding, and I knew I would say yes. He was older than me by a couple of years, and it all seemed so romantic: this "older guy" wanting to be with me and loving me enough to come all that way just to get me so we could be together.

When he called for my answer, I said, "Yes."

I went out to the farm to tell my folks. I hated telling my mom. I knew she would be very much against it and would tell me I couldn't go. Taking a deep breath and avoiding her eyes, I began, "Dave called. He's driving back from Michigan for a visit and to see me. He really misses me and wants me to go back with him when he leaves. I told him I would."

"Over my dead body!" she exclaimed with her hands on her hips. "There's no way! You can't just up and leave with him like that. What if something should happen? You'd be stuck there all alone!"

"Mom, I really want to go. Nothing's going to happen."

She replied, "Absolutely not, and that's final!" Our eyes met and I knew how much she would be hurt and worry about me. I also knew her words weren't going to change my mind. I loved my mother very much, and I was so sorry I hurt her. I knew she loved me and was trying to protect me. I knew she was right, but how could she stop me? I was young and in love.

I went back to my apartment. I felt awful about the disagreement with my mom, but I was confident we would be back soon to see everyone. Surely by that time Mom would realize that I was fine and nothing bad was going to happen to me. One week later Dave returned from Michigan. I was so happy to see him! He spent four days visiting friends, and when he was ready to go back to Michigan, I went with him.

CHAPTER 3

Mary: His Name Was Billy

Two roads diverged in a yellow wood,
And sorry I could not travel both
And be one traveler, long I stood
And looked down one as far as I could
To where it bent in the undergrowth;

Then took the other, as just as fair,
And having perhaps the better claim,
Because it was grassy and wanted wear;
Though as for that, the passing there
Had worn them really about the same,

And both that morning equally lay
In leaves no step had trodden black.
Oh, I kept the first for another day!
Yet knowing how way leads on to way,
I doubted if I should ever come back (1-15).[4]

Robert Frost

September 1950. Grand Rapids, Michigan. My first day of kindergarten at West Side Christian School. A room full of kids and their mothers. One teacher. An indoor sandbox, standing on legs. Two big, beautiful, blond dolls. Chocolate milk.

I was four, almost five years old on that first day of school. I was a small, shy, blond child with hazel eyes peering out from behind my mother's skirt. Another little blond girl with large brown eyes stood nearby, also hiding behind her mother's skirt. Her mother said, "Here's a new friend for you to stand by."

My mother said, "This is Mary Beth."

Her mother said, "Well, hi, Mary Beth! This is Susie."

It was September 1950, when I met Susie, who was to become my lifelong friend. She was one of a class of thirty kids who would stay together, for the most part, all through grade school, as well as through junior high, until graduation from ninth grade ten years later.

Another child in that kindergarten class was a shy, blue-eyed boy with curly, blond hair. His name was Billy. I didn't know Billy, but my mother knew his dad who was a distant cousin of hers. I had no idea Billy would one day become my husband.

Even though Billy and I were in the same classroom for ten years, I don't remember giving him a second glance. Although we also later attended the same church, catechism classes, and young people's group, our paths of interest never crossed. Billy was a sober student; I was social. Billy seemed to have just one or two friends, his cousins. I, on the other hand, had lots of friends. Billy seldom spoke; I was seldom silent. Billy didn't sing. He didn't like girls.

After high school, in September 1963, both Bill and I each enrolled at Calvin College, on the other side of Grand Rapids, but with entirely different plans. He was planning to take the Pre-Dental curriculum, focused and squeezed into two years. After these two years, he hoped to be accepted at the University of Michigan, School of Dentistry, in Ann Arbor. I began a course for elementary education so I could graduate in four years and teach young children. Since I really wanted to be a mom even more than I wanted to be a teacher, I began college with my eyes open for a good husband.

Soon after the semester started, my social life took an upward turn from the downward trend in high school. My self-confidence was on the rise, and the dating possibilities expanded as I began to meet a variety of guys from all over the country.

One young man in particular became special to me. He sat beside me in chapel and listened to me before the service started. I told him about an ended dating relationship I had been in. We became better friends and started dating steadily for a period of time. Even though he was a nice guy, I wasn't convinced that he was the person just right for me to marry. After much thought and some tears, late in my junior year, I initiated a break up with him. Consequently I enjoyed a needed summer of freedom from any steady dating relationship.

It was during that summer that several old West Side friends, who were unattached, got together on weekend evenings for cookouts at homes or picnics at the beach. One July afternoon, one of the guys saw me walking home from my summer factory job. He stopped his bike to talk, "Is it okay that I asked Bill to go along this Saturday to Lake Michigan?"

"Sure! The more, the merrier," I replied.

Even though Bill lived in my neighborhood, I hadn't seen him much over recent years. I did, however, remember seeing him that spring in the Calvin library. He was doing some research there, and we had exchanged a few friendly comments.

On the Friday night before the beach cookout, my former boyfriend showed up at my house and visited with my parents while I was out. They liked him a lot and enjoyed his impromptu visit. When I got home and heard he had visited, I felt confused. I went up to my room, knelt beside my bed and asked the Lord for a sign. I prayed, "Lord, if I did the right thing by breaking up that relationship, please let me have such a good time tomorrow that I won't even think of him once."

That prayer was answered clearly. Not only didn't I think about him at the beach, but I got to know Bill a little better, as we walked along the Lake Michigan shore with the others. Billy had grown into a handsome young man. His curly hair had sun-bleached to boyish blond and his face and arms sported a painter's tan from his summer house-painting job with his dad.

Going home that night, I ended up in the same car with Bill and some others jammed together in the back seat. As usual, I fell asleep in the car and woke up embarrassed to find myself leaning against him.

When Bill stopped by my house one evening the following week on his old maroon and cream, fat-wheeled Schwinn, my mother said, "You're not getting interested in him, are you? Remember, he's a relative."

"I know," I said and walked away to avoid any further discussion. I really didn't know how I felt about Bill, so I didn't want to go into it.

In the following weeks, Bill came on his bike a few more times to see if I could go riding with him. We would bike till dark and then sit on my screened-in front porch to eat homemade chocolate-chip cookies and sip lemonade.

Soon, it seemed, summer was drawing to a close, which inevitably meant the beginning of a new semester for both Bill and me. He would return a sophomore to the dental school in Ann Arbor while I would begin my senior year at Calvin.

I was about to do something new. During my senior year I would live on campus in one of the three-story co-operative houses, affectionately called "coops", across Franklin Street from the college. I was to be one of two senior counselors for twelve freshmen girls. I realized that as Bill and I were to part ways, I would miss our bike rides and his listening ear. I also wrote in my diary, "I feel myself falling." Before he left for Ann Arbor, I asked, "Would it be okay if I wrote you at school?"

"Sure," he said. "I would like that."

I reached up and gave him a quick "goodbye kiss", to which he looked directly into my eyes and with a stern face said, "What did you do that for?" But before I could answer, he bent down and kissed me back.

My simple request soon turned into two letters a week going both ways plus a couple of dates each weekend. Bill was already in the habit of returning home every weekend, but now he began to see more of me and less of his family. After he left for Ann Arbor on Sunday nights, I would quickly write him a letter, then another on Wednesday. He would do the same. It was fun looking forward to two letters a week from him.

Two semesters passed quickly followed by my graduation from college and a move back home. I had applied and received a contract to become one of two third grade teachers in a Grand Rapids Christian school. Both Bill and I were very busy, but we managed to maintain the same contact during that year while he was working through his junior year of dental school and I was teaching my delightful class of third graders. I told them they were the BEST class I ever had!

As my mom observed that our relationship seemed to be growing more serious, she went to her gynecologist and asked about the genetic risks of our relationship. Her doctor said, "They are very distant relatives. There won't be a problem."

During that year, Bill applied for a Co-Step program with the United States Public Health Service (PHS) for the coming summer. He was accepted and given an opportunity to serve in a PHS hospital on Staten Island, New York, beginning July 1, 1968. Even though Bill had already given me a "hope" chest for Christmas, and his plans started to sound like "our" plans, we were not engaged. Just in the nick of time, in March, he gave me a diamond ring as we were riding in Stu, his blue Volkswagen, on our way to pick up his sister, Joyce, from work one evening. He asked me to pop open the small ashtray. I did and inside was a little jewelry box containing a diamond ring! I don't think Bill ever asked me to marry him. He just assumed I would, typical of his no-nonsense personality.

I was excited to be engaged. My mom and I quickly scrambled to make arrangements for the wedding in mid-June. I would be leaving with Bill to spend the summer on Staten Island. What a romantic thought!

We were married on a warm Wednesday evening, June 19, 1968, in our church. Susie was my matron of honor. Bill's roommate, Carl, was his best man. The rest of the wedding party consisted of all six of our younger siblings—a bunch of kids all dressed up. I don't remember much about our wedding, but I do remember thinking, as we turned to walk up the aisle as Mr. and Mrs., "Now I can have a baby!"

While Bill and I were dating, we had exchanged memories from past years as well as plans for the future. I told him, "I remember you, Ross, and Jerry throwing snowballs across the street at me and Susie on our walk home for lunch."

"I remember sneaking into your back-row seat to be near the radiator and the window view while you were out with the chicken pox," he admitted. We both remembered his "Rent-a-Pen" business in junior high. I laughed as I pictured him and his cousin, Ron, with their plaid, flannel shirt pockets loaded with ball-point pens, hoping some unprepared student would rent a pen from one of them. Bill tried not to laugh and said, "What's so funny? Already back then I was a budding entrepreneur!"

Our plans for the future included immediately starting a family after marriage. We both wanted a big family, possibly five or six kids. Bill hoped to further his dental skills and to fulfill his military obligation necessitated by the Vietnam War by serving in the Public Health Service after graduation. I planned to continue my teaching career wherever we would live until we would have our first child. Then I would become a full time homemaker and caregiver for our kids. I would become a mom!

Two days after our wedding, we left in Stu, our trusty VW, packed to the max for New York City, Staten Island. We camped along the way, sleeping each night in a double sleeping bag on air mattresses on the floor of our green canvas umbrella tent. I nearly froze in my honeymoon negligee. We drove long hours each day hoping to out-distance the rain that seemed to be traveling with us. We'd finally give up around 8 p.m. Then I would still have to cook something on our camp stove, kneeling on the floor of our tent while rain continued pouring down outside. Bill thought it was cozy, but it was not quite the honeymoon I had envisioned.

Sunshine greeted us as we arrived at the building of our pre-rented apartment on Victory Boulevard. We stacked our packed beer boxes into the elevator, hoping we wouldn't be misunderstood by neighbors or the landlord, and rode up to our fifth floor studio apartment, our new home for the summer.

The summer was hot in the city. Bill took Stu before 8 a.m. to the PHS Hospital, where he worked until 5 p.m. Meanwhile, I stayed for the most part in our air-conditioned apartment with lots of free time. I passed the time by writing thank-you cards and some letters, reading, sewing some fall clothing, and tanning on our tiny fire-escape landing.

On weekends we would explore New York City. Some weeknights we ran from subway to subway so Bill could "conquer" the New York City subway system. I was never so tired in my life— also homesick for family and friends. Somehow, the time came to leave our honeymoon apartment and go back to Michigan to live in the same apartment Bill and Carl had shared before in Ann Arbor.

While Bill was working through his senior year in the dental school, he was also corresponding with PHS regarding an assignment after graduation. We were eager to see where we would be stationed to serve, hoping it would be one of our top choices: Seattle, Washington, or Anchorage, Alaska.

In the meantime, I was teaching a lively class of cute second graders in a public school in Saline, a small town outside of Ann Arbor. After school I would fix supper, eat with Bill, and then prepare for the next school day. I was finding that teaching a new grade in a new school was like teaching my first year all over again.

Since both Bill and I were very busy and involved with our own stuff, neither of us realized that our relationship was changing. It wasn't until Christmas break when I was thinking about it and wondering what was different that I realized two major ingredients were leaking out of our relationship: communication and fun.

The twice-weekly letters of the past two years were no longer written. Words of care and encouragement, it seemed, came easier on paper than in person for both of us. I was feeling lonely, even as a married woman.

Fun while dating usually meant a ride in the country, a place to talk and to hug for a while. But now, fun for me would have been an invitation to eat out at a restaurant—something we almost never did. Fun for Bill was still a ride in the country or a hug in bed. I fell asleep in both places.

Since I was the first to notice the change, I brought it up to him: "I feel lonely, even being married." When I explained it to him, he listened but couldn't really identify with me. Being a loner, he thought everything was better than ever.

Soon after the new year began, we received our PHS assignment: Gallup, New Mexico.

"Where's that?" I asked.

Bill got out a map so he could show me. "Probably warm, dry, and brown," he said. Not quite Seattle or Anchorage as we had hoped.

Bill graduated in May 1969, and drove a school bus for Ann Arbor Public Schools for a few weeks until I was finished teaching in June.

Our furniture was packed onto a large moving van, ready to begin the cross-country trip to New Mexico. Once more we packed Stu to the max for camping along the way. But first we went to Grand Rapids for a few days to be in the wedding of Bill's sister, Joyce.

After the wedding we said a tearful "Goodbye" to our families and started off on our trip to New Mexico. This would be the beginning of a three-year commitment for Bill to work in a PHS Hospital doing dentistry for the Navajo Indian people.

I had been able to get a fourth grade teaching position at Rehoboth Mission School just a few miles east of Gallup. When school started in the fall, I found my small class of fifteen students was almost an equal mix of pale-faced children of missionaries and bronze-skinned children of Navajo descent from the surrounding reservation. They were a gentle, loveable bunch of kids, but it was a challenge for me, teaching another new grade in a new location.

Since Bill and I had agreed we wanted to begin a family as soon as possible, we had done away with any birth control just a few months after we were married. By the first spring I had questioned my doctor in Michigan about our lack of success. He had given me a booklet describing timing and positions, which mainly amounted to my standing on my head in bed certain mornings of the month.

When spring came a second time after our marriage, with still no pregnancy, we decided to seriously check into our inability to conceive. Our health care in Gallup was free—part of the package of working for PHS.

When I went to the gynecologist at the hospital for an exam and consultation, he suggested, "Let's start with Bill with a simple test to determine sperm count. That's the easiest place to start." That test was the first and last one given to either of us. The results showed a count of "0". It was shocking to both of us! But the specialist held out hope suggesting a surgical procedure to determine the cause. Perhaps there was a blockage that could be corrected.

Bill was optimistic. But I began to picture cracks forming in the dream I had envisioned for so long. I began to brace myself as well as my parents for the worst by writing a letter to them. I explained what we had found out and what exploratory surgery the doctor had suggested. I felt embarrassed and humiliated to admit that something I had always taken for granted might never be.

I chose to write a letter instead of calling them because I thought I would cry on the phone. I thought that once my parents got the facts in writing, they would call me to share the emotion. I was right about them; they called. I was right about me; I cried.

It had been during that same spring of 1970, while we were still living among the red rocks in Gallup, that Bill had received his next assignment. We would be moving 100 miles north to Shiprock, New Mexico, a facility on the Navajo Indian Reservation. He would serve two more years in the PHS hospital there. It was late summer when we arrived in Shiprock, where I also would be employed, having signed a contract to teach first grade in the public school. It was a school where there was no kindergarten. Many of the kids came directly from the reservation to first grade—most with no English skills. Bill's plans were to begin his work in the hospital and soon to take a short leave to travel back to Gallup. There he would submit to the surgery which would determine the outcome of our hopes for a family, the fulfillment or fracture of my lifelong dream.

Shattered. It was September 1970 when my dream of ever having a baby was shattered. The surgery confirmed a blockage that could not be corrected. I was devastated. The words swirled around and around in my mind with no place to rest: "I will never have a baby. Never."

That September I became acquainted with the deep sorrow of grief. Grief moves into a life uninvited and takes over whenever there is a loss—the loss of a person or anything that is deeply cared about. I grieved the loss of my dream.

I shall be telling this with a sigh
Somewhere ages and ages hence:
Two roads diverged in a wood, and I—
I took the one less traveled by,
And that has made all the difference (16-20).[5]

Robert Frost

CHAPTER 4

Paula: Snowflake to Heartache

Dave and I lived in the tiny little town of Bruce Crossing in Michigan's upper peninsula for a very short time and then moved a couple miles down the road to another little town called Ewen which was close to Lake Gogebic. Michigan was the most beautiful place I'd ever seen. It was fall and breathtaking with the trees all in color and the beautiful waterfalls rushing down the rivers to the lake. We lived in a cute little one-bedroom house right at the very edge of the forest. Deer wandered freely, and sometimes we even saw a bear at the edge of our back yard. Dave worked in a mine, and I got a job as a waitress in the only café in town.

I packed his lunch every day. One evening when he got home he put his black metal lunch box on the counter as he always did. A few minutes later he said, "I didn't eat very much for lunch today. Look how much is left." I opened his metal lunch box and inside was a tiny little fluffy kitten. She was all gray except for a little spot of white right between her big green eyes. She captured my heart instantly and we named her Snowflake.

As beautiful as the country was, the winters in upper Michigan were *brutal*! Some days we couldn't leave the house because of all the snow that fell during the night. We couldn't even push the door open.

We had lived together four months when I became pregnant. I knew I was pregnant long before I should have known. It wasn't that

I felt sick, I just knew. I also knew she was a girl from the very beginning. Two emotions were at war within me. I knew what people would think and how they would gossip, especially in my small town back home. I didn't want my family to go through that.

On the other hand I was very excited. I could see Dave and myself happily married with a baby. I wasn't at all nervous about telling him because I was sure he would feel the same way. He sat down while I perched on the arm of the couch next to him. "I think I might be pregnant," I told him.

He wasn't elated but he didn't seem sorry either. He reached over and hugged me. "We'll get married," he announced with more tiredness than excitement.

Later, I went with him to pick out an engagement and wedding ring. He never really gave me the ring or asked me to be his wife. I was surprised because I knew Dave as a sensitive person who cared for the feelings of others. I had pictured a romantic proposal— perhaps we would be walking hand in hand on the beach or by a beautiful waterfall. He might begin by telling me ten ways he loved me. Instead, when we left the store I just put it on, and that was that. His indifference really hurt. I kept my feelings to myself. No wedding date was set.

I noticed he was drinking more than he usually did. When I was sure I was pregnant, the drinking became quite heavy, and he would stay out later and later. This baffled me. I thought he would want to be with me now, more than ever. Instead, I stayed home alone, listening to my own thoughts. I knew I had some serious thinking to do. My thoughts and feelings were all a jumble. I was both happy and excited, but also hurt and scared. I had an awesome and powerful feeling in the knowledge there was a new life, a new little person, being created day by day inside me. My thoughts and feelings immediately changed from what was best for me to what was best for her. It was *my* responsibility, and I already loved her more than I loved myself.

Although I wanted to call home, I dreaded making the phone call to my family. I thought of my poor mother. I had hurt her so much already. I put off calling for quite awhile, but it was always on my mind and it had to be done. At last, I dialed the number. I sat in a kitchen chair nervously toying with the plastic phone cord as Mom answered. She was calm at first but then she started to cry. To hear my mom cry broke my heart. Then she handed the phone to my sister. Pat and I were like part of each other. We were always able to tell each other anything. I told her the whole story saying, "I'm not sure about staying with Dave. His drinking worries me."

When Mom came back on the phone she said, "Come home." No matter what, my family loved me, and they were there for me. I knew I always had a home to go to. I thought about it, and I knew I would be welcome. I had no doubts about that, but at that point I didn't know *what* I was going to do.

Knowing she lived in Michigan and how close we were, Mom suggested I call my high school friend Pam and talk to her. I had never heard a better idea. Pam was just what I needed. To talk to a true friend who knew my heart would always make me feel better. I hung up with Mom and dried my tears. I washed my face in the bathroom and took a few deep breaths.

Shortly after I talked to my family Dave came home from work, so I didn't have a chance to call Pam. I didn't mention the call to my family and he didn't notice that I was quieter than usual. He got cleaned up and said he was going to go have a couple of beers with his friends. I wanted to get out, so I went with him. After we were there for a while he informed his friends, "I am tired of working in the mine and the cold weather, so we're moving to Florida." This was the first time I'd heard about that. I didn't say anything at the time. I thought and prayed about it all night. How could I go with him to Florida? I knew that Michigan was a long way from my family in Iowa, but Florida seemed like the other side of the world. What about his drinking, would it get worse? What about the arguments when he got drunk? Would he lose control one day and abuse me or, worse yet, would he abuse the baby? These were terrible thoughts but they had to be dealt with now, not later.

The next evening I called Pam. As always she was just the haven I needed. I asked if I could stay with them for awhile. Even though they lived in a small two-bedroom trailer and had a baby girl of their own, she didn't hesitate to say, "Of course. Come and stay with us as long as you want." When I was going to tell her why she said, "It doesn't matter why. I love you and you are always welcome in our home. We can talk when you get here."

I had been upset and hurt by the way Dave had announced the news *we* were going to Florida. Knowing this could very easily escalate into an argument, I gave myself some time to calm down before I confronted Dave with some news of my own. That evening I informed him, "I'm not going to Florida with you, Dave. You should have talked this over with me before you made your plans. Obviously it never occurred to you that I might not want to go. You could have at least asked me."

He seemed surprised, "Don't you want to get away from all this snow and cold? Come on, of course you want to go with me! You'll love the warm weather there. You're pregnant with my baby. We should be together. You can have the baby in Florida just as well as here, can't you?"

"No, Dave, I can't. If your mind is made up to go, you'll have to go alone because I'm not going with you. I talked to a friend of mine in Grand Rapids earlier this evening. She and her husband said I could stay with them as long as I want to. If you won't reconsider, I want you to drive me to Grand Rapids. I'll be staying there with my friends for awhile, at least until I've had the baby."

"I'm going to Florida. I'll take you to Grand Rapids if that's what you want, but you'll change your mind, you'll go with me," he said with complete confidence.

I cried as I gave Snowflake to a friend. I would miss her kitten ways and her comforting purr. We packed our things, climbed into his car and headed toward an uncertain future.

On the drive to Grand Rapids we had time to talk. I voiced my concerns to him. "We both know we're not getting along right now, Dave. What about your drinking? Are you going to slow down, or drink even more when we get there? You know how we argue when you get drunk. What am I supposed to do if you lose your temper some day and abuse the baby or me? I won't let that happen, Dave."

I could see he was getting angry, and all he had to say was, "I don't drink that much."

"Please, Dave, stay with me in Grand Rapids until the baby is born," I pleaded. "Let's have the baby, and then see how things are going before we make such a big move."

"No, I'm leaving," he said. "I'll take you to your friends. You can either stay there or go with me. It's up to you."

I cried as I asked him one more time to stay with me. I saw my "happily ever after" picture shatter in my mind as I realized this was the end of our wonderful seven month relationship. Something had gone terribly wrong. I wasn't sure either of us knew where or when the beginning of the end had started, but it had begun. I found myself being driven from my happy dream toward a very uncertain future. I knew he really did want me to go with him, but something was warning me that it would be a terrible mistake.

The rest of the long drive continued in silence. He stared straight ahead at the road, one hand on the wheel and the other arm leaning against the door. I watched the beautiful winter countryside grow brighter from the passenger window, and I cried.

I don't think he really believed I was going to stay until we arrived at Pam and Anthony's and got my things out of the car and into their trailer. After the introductions they thoughtfully went to the bedroom to give us some privacy. Dave sat down by the kitchen table. As I was walking past him to sit down myself, he pulled me down onto his lap and put his arms around me. We went through the whole thing again, only this time his attitude was entirely different. He said, "Please go with me. I'll get a good job and everything will work out, you'll see. Please go with me. I love you!"

"I just can't go with you. What if we get to Florida and you can't find a good job? What if things don't work out? Please stay here in Michigan with me. At least until the baby is born. I need something stable right now, something safe and secure. Something I can count on. Why can't you understand that?"

"Think about the baby," he said, "That's my baby, too."

I took a deep breath around the lump in my throat, "If you don't love us enough to stay with us then no, she's *my* baby." It was a difficult moment. It was like facing a fork in the road, not knowing which one to take. There were only two choices, and both were hard. Either one would affect the lives and futures of so many people. As I lost the battle with my tears, I knew I could only go with my heart. When Pam and Anthony heard me crying they came out of the bedroom and Anthony told Dave to leave. I stayed and he left.

He called me several times in the next month or so. These phone calls were very hard on me. One day I was in tears while talking to him. I had mentioned to Pam how I wished he would just quit calling. On this particular day Pam said loudly enough for Dave to hear, "Tell him not to call here anymore!" The calls stopped, for which I was thankful. If he wasn't going to change his mind and come back to me there was nothing more to say. Pam and Anthony said I was under enough pressure as it was and didn't need the added stress of the calls that were getting us nowhere at all, except for more tears. They were right.

Meeting and getting to know Anthony was very easy. I couldn't imagine how anyone could know him and not love him. He was sweet and kind and sincere and very intelligent. It was wonderful to see how much they loved each other. They opened their home to me. They stood behind me in my decisions and listened to my indecision. They never once said, "If I were you . . . ." Pam held me close and cried with me, and I knew I was not alone.

One late night, just Pam and I stayed up to talk. We sat quietly for awhile, then Pam asked, "How are you, Paula? Do you want to talk? If you want to be alone just tell me, and I'll leave you alone."

"No Pam, please stay with me for a little while." There was a companionable silence for a few minutes. "I don't know what I'm going to do, Pam. I just don't know what to do."

She sat next to me on the couch and put her arm around me. "You will make the right decision, I know you will. So far you have. You didn't go to Florida with him. That was definitely the right decision. I wish I could tell you what to do, but I can't. Only you can make this decision. I feel so helpless, but you know I will *always* be there for you! I love you, Paula, and with God's help you will make the right decision. I know you will. There's a lot of time yet to think and pray about this. When the time comes, you'll know what to do." She always knew how to soothe my mind, and help me to think rationally again when I was feeling overwhelmed.

I knew what I wanted to do, but was it best for her, my baby girl? I conceived her and would give birth to her. My decision had to be for her, not for me and my desires. It seems kind of peculiar to say that I loved her so much I couldn't keep her, but that is exactly how I felt. I wanted her to have so much more than I could give her. God knows how much I wanted to be selfish and keep her, but deep down inside I knew what was best for her. I knew what I should do, but it was the one thing I couldn't do. There was so much pain involved in trying to make an impossible decision. I thanked God for Pam. She was always there to listen and help me talk things through. After those first few months my decision was far from being made.

Tracey, Pam and Anthony's four-month-old daughter, was a real joy. I helped take care of her and babysat with her whenever I could. She was such a sweet-natured, beautiful baby. I would hold her and talk to her and think about the baby growing inside me. I thought about how wonderful it would be to hold my baby in my arms and wondered if I would ever be able to. I knew I couldn't give her up, and I knew I had to. It would make my decision harder when I saw Pam and Tracey alone, and saw the love in Pam's eyes for *her* baby girl. Then I would see her with both Pam and Anthony, and that would make my decision somewhat easier. Tracey had a mother and a father, a family—the things I wanted for my baby.

Staying with Pam and Anthony was the right thing for me to do. I was with my best friend and this was now my home. I was safe and surrounded with love. Pam and I shared every feeling just as we always had.

What I needed to deal with now, and right now, was prenatal care. I told Pam, "I have to take care of myself, and, more importantly, I have to take the very best care of my baby that I possibly can." She agreed, and we both would do all we could to make sure this baby was healthy. My baby *would* be born healthy. I would see to that! The problem was: I had no money. Pam and Anthony would have gladly helped me, but, as it was, they were struggling to put food on the table for the three of them. My family also would've helped if they could, but they were raising six boys at home. I knew I would have to find another way.

Pam and I discussed it and decided the only option open to me was Social Services. As much as I disliked the idea of being on welfare, it was my reality, and I would do it. I would be able to get the proper care I needed for my baby, including pre-natal vitamins, and also to receive a very small check, which would at least help Pam and Anthony pay for groceries. Their love and support were free.

Social Services sent me to a clinic. I went at least once a month. Pam drove me to my first couple appointments, and after that I went by myself. There was no need to get Tracey all bundled up and take her out in the cold.

Although I did appreciate the clinic and received good care, it was a terribly depressing place. It reminded me of a hospital emergency room.   There was one large room partitioned off into curtained cubicles.   There was very little privacy and, although it was clean and sanitary, it was very impersonal.   No one greeted me by name or asked how I was really doing, and I never saw the same doctor twice. Each visit, a new doctor would come in, say hello, examine me, tell me everything was fine, and then leave.   I would make my next appointment at the desk as I left.   I was always grateful to get home after those visits.   Pam always reminded me to take my vitamins each day, and she made sure I was getting enough of the right foods.

Pam and Anthony had been married over a year, yet Pam didn't have a diamond ring.   I wanted to give her the one Dave had given me, but I didn't know quite how she would take it.   I decided to talk to Anthony about it first.   It was a beautiful ring but I knew I would never wear it again.   I asked Anthony what he thought about giving it to Pam.   His first concern was about me, how I would feel seeing Pam wear it.   Also, when Pam got a diamond he wanted it to be from him, and I understood that.   I assured him that it wouldn't bother me, and he could pay me for the ring if he wanted to.   He agreed and planned to save the ring until their second anniversary.

I shall never as long as I live forget what it felt like the first time my baby moved inside me.   We had ordered pizza and I went to get it. I was sitting on a wooden bench waiting for our order when I felt a soft little fluttering movement.   My heart jumped and I put my hand on my stomach.   It was like the whole world froze, and I sat absolutely still and waited for it to happen again, and it did.   I believe bonding starts in the womb before birth and I think at that very moment our bonding started.   That little fluttering movement was my baby girl!   I felt a fierce protective love flow through me.

Soon the soft little fluttering movements grew stronger and stronger.   She was very active, and as she grew and moved I could feel her little hands or feet or knees or elbows, like she was trying to stretch and get comfortable.   I would softly rub the little protrusion and she would settle right down.   I rocked her all the time, and I talked to her in my thoughts and sometimes out loud. When she would wake me in the night kicking, I would rub my stomach and promise her I would never let anything hurt her.

I loved being pregnant. It was as if my baby and I were one person. I could feel the bond between us growing stronger as my pregnancy continued. I took good care of myself and didn't gain a lot of weight, so I didn't get too big and cumbersome. I loved every little movement she made. I spent a lot of time with my hand on my stomach rubbing and touching her, loving her. She knew who I was. She heard me when I talked to her, and she knew I loved her. I also knew she loved me. I didn't want these feelings to end. I kept trying to block from my mind what lay ahead for us.

I tried not to think about the decision I would have to make. I wanted everything to stay the way it was. I thought about what it would be like to have a husband at my side to share this wonderful time, someone else to look forward to the baby's birth and the years to come. I knew these things were not in my reality. How I cried for things that would never be.

CHAPTER 5

Mary: A Road Less Traveled

When upon life's billows you are tempest tossed,
When you are discouraged, thinking all is lost,
Count your many blessings, name them one by one,
And it will surprise you what the Lord has done.[6]

I knew in my mind that when God closes a door, He opens another way of His design. But my heart, my emotions, hadn't caught up with my mind. I felt like I was drowning in waves of grief. During the day I would hide behind busyness and smiles as I met the challenge of a large class of first grade Navajo children trying hard to be bilingual. Then I would come home after school to cry in the privacy of our own house. I felt very lonely in Shiprock, another new location for me. I knew no other woman there with whom to share my intimate grief.

The finality of the word "never" haunted me. I was tempted to linger on thoughts of "what if . . ." and "if only . . .". *What if* I had found this out before we were married, what would I have done? *If only* I had married someone else, this wouldn't be happening. I had to work at keeping my mind in order, to remain faithful to Bill in my thinking. It was hard.

I also thought about what the gynecologist in Gallup had suggested. He had mentioned the possibility of a relatively new procedure called artificial insemination with a sperm donor. I knew that wouldn't work for me. Who would the sperm donor be anyway?

How could I bear a child whose father was not Bill? I knew I was too selfish and would be too possessive for that to work.

Meanwhile, Bill, who shows little emotion, looked and acted as solid as a rock. He quickly accepted the closed door and began to think of alternative ways to have a family. He was sympathetic toward the deep feelings of loss I had, but said, "There's nothing more we can physically do right now, Kid. Let's see what our options are in starting a family before we waste more time."

The previous spring, while we still had been living in Gallup, we had been mailed an annual report from Bethany Christian Home, an adoption agency in Grand Rapids, Michigan. The report to contributors, which included an update on the work and finances of the agency, had included a phrase that had caught Bill's eye, "adoption on a nationwide basis".

In mid-October of 1970, only a few weeks after our infertility was confirmed to be permanent, Bill quickly typed a letter to Bethany requesting information on adoption, hoping that "nationwide" might really include Shiprock, New Mexico. I was glad he was taking the bull by the horns, that he was strong and assertive, because I was still weak and hesitant.

It wasn't long before the letter of reply came, stating: "As was indicated in our report, we do extend these services on *nearly* a nationwide basis." It went on to say that their involvement with us would require their reliance on the Social Services Department of New Mexico to help them in the evaluation process, as well as post placement supervision. Perhaps waiting would be advisable or perhaps exploring local resources would be less complicated. Also, we would be asked to make at least two visits to Grand Rapids. Before Bethany could make any commitment, we were asked to inform them of our present and future plans and locations.

Not to be deterred, Bill quickly wrote a reply, outlining our long-term plans to return to Ann Arbor, Michigan, in July of 1972 when he would begin a two-year dental specialty program. Our short-term plans included a visit to our parents' homes in Grand Rapids over the coming Christmas holiday season. He also assured them that future trips to Grand Rapids would not be a problem. Bill didn't tell them he had recently earned a private pilot's license, had purchased a small private plane, and was more than eager to put both of those to use.

A visit was scheduled at Bethany on December 22, 1970. We were excited and hopeful that perhaps this was the plan God had in mind for us to have kids.

We got up very early Saturday morning, December 16, to drive the thirty miles from our home in Shiprock to Farmington, New Mexico, where our four-seater Cessna 182 was tied down at the airport. Barring any stormy weather, we were hoping to fly northeast out of New Mexico, across the Midwest, to Michigan all in one day.

Bill filed a flight plan and we took off just in time to watch the sunrise. There was good visibility and the flying was smooth as we began our cross-country flight. But as the short winter day progressed and as we headed east toward the later time zones, the conditions began to change. I had packed a lunch but neither of us ate it. Bill was too busy; I was too tense. So we both sucked on large salty stick pretzels. As time went on, it became obvious we could not make the whole trip during daylight hours. We decided that with darkness falling quickly and a strong head wind, it would be best to stop for the night at a small town in Indiana.

Being unfamiliar with the small country airport, Bill circled a few times trying to make radio contact with the airport personnel on the ground, but we received no response. Bill went down without radio guidance and executed a stiff cross wind landing. He made contact with the ground with the down wind wheel still high in the air, just the way it should have been done! I was scared skinny! We rolled to a stop, safe, near the end of the runway, then turned toward the small terminal building.

The man who was in charge of the airport came running out to greet us. He told us he could hear Bill on his radio, but couldn't seem to get through to us. Our radio must have been acting up.

Thankful to be down on the ground, we asked the man if he could give us a ride somewhere to spend the night. He agreed and took us to an old hotel in town so we could be near a restaurant.

The hotel looked like it came straight out of a Western movie set. As far as we could tell, we were the only guests staying there that night. We didn't go to a restaurant but ate the lunch I had packed for the flight and went to bed.

In the morning we found the desk clerk drunk, lying on the floor behind a chair in the lobby. No one else was stirring, so we put our money on the desk and left.

It was still early that winter Sunday morning, so most people were still not up and about. Bill had just suggested we hitch-hike to the airport. But there were no moving cars or people to be seen. Then we saw one man down the block, standing by his pick-up truck. We walked over to him. Bill explained our situation and asked, "Would you be able to give us a lift to the airport?"

He agreed, so the three of us jumped into the front seat of his truck.

"Where'd you stay last night?" he asked as we started off.

When we told him about the old downtown hotel, he said, "You kids should never have stayed there! The owners of that place are always in jail for one thing or another."

Bill had carried the airplane battery with us to keep it warm overnight, but when he tried to start the plane, it wouldn't start. Our kind friend jumped it with his truck, and soon we were taking off toward Michigan.

The rest of our flight was uneventful until we heard over the radio that it was snowing in Grand Rapids. We decided to land at South Kent, a small airport south of the city where it was not yet snowing. We came down fast and long—too long for the runway. Our plane stopped abruptly, nose down in a pile of snow at the end of the short runway.

In sheer emotional exhaustion, I began screaming. It was the only time in our marriage, before or since, that my husband yelled at me, "Shut up!!!"

We managed to get out of the plane. No one was around, so we went into the small building to phone our parents for a ride. My folks wouldn't come. They were miffed that we were flying on Sunday, and, besides, they were eating Sunday dinner. We called Bill's family. I don't think they were real thrilled with our circumstances either, but they were glad we were there and were safe. Bill's dad and brother, Ken, came to get us and helped Bill get the plane back on its wheels.

After a few days of settling in and making peace with everyone, including my folks, who really were glad to see us, Bill and I borrowed a car from his dad to go to Bethany. We went seeking approval to begin the adoption process. By now I realized there wasn't much that rattled Bill, but both of us were a little nervous, not knowing just what to expect. We met with a caseworker who put us at ease by his quiet confident manner. After some conversation, he gave us an application for adoption to take with us to fill out at home, as well as two medical report forms, and a request for service from the inter-state coordinating agency.

Bethany also asked us to complete two family-history sheets, and we were told that they would like the New Mexico agency to have their study completed by the next November. We were thrilled to realize that we were approved to begin taking our first steps on another path to have a family.

With that completion date in mind, I did not sign a new teaching contract in the spring of 1971. I would not be able to continue teaching first grade in the Shiprock School System because Bethany expected adoptive mothers to have no work outside the home. That gave me the hope of being a mom before the next school year ended!

In May, 1971, the medical exams and forms were to be completed. Our interviews with the state of New Mexico began in June, which required additional information sheets, other medical reports, a floor plan of our house, and pictures of both of us. Letters of reference were asked for and submitted from three separate families who knew us. Finally, in December 1971, we were asked to make a final trip to Grand Rapids to tie up loose ends, to submit yet another formal adoption application, and to compose a joint statement of our faith.

Finally, after what seemed like having every inch of ourselves and our situation scrutinized, we received a letter of approval for adoptive planning in February 1972. That meant that we would be considered each time a child came to Bethany's attention for adoptive placement. We wondered eagerly just how long or short the time would be before we would get that life-changing call from Bethany.

In the meantime, Bill's sister, Joyce, and her husband, Steve, had announced their first pregnancy. Their son was born in February, the same month we were approved. How simple it seemed for them to have a baby compared to the investigation we had just gone through. In spite of our hope through adoption, I still felt jealous and longed for the private intimacy of conceiving and giving birth to a child.

Since I was not teaching school, I kept busy by volunteering my time at the PHS hospital. I held and rocked premature newborns in the nursery. I visited a young Navajo boy whose appendix had ruptured. He didn't have the comfort of his family because they lived a long distance from the hospital on the reservation.

I also joined the women's morning Bible study group at our church and taxied older, cheerful Navajo women dressed in colorful native dress to and from the weekly meetings. They would laugh while I struggled to clasp their seat belts in our cramped orange VW Fastback.

I became involved with other PHS wives, but soon realized that most conversations with women revolve around kids. I began to avoid situations that would stimulate my grief or self pity. Instead I started to focus on encouraging other people whose situations were less fortunate than mine.

Bill told me that one of the maintenance men at the PHS hospital had a wife who was dying of cancer at their home just around the corner from us. I decided to spend some time with her each week until she passed away. I sat quietly beside her, working on a baby cross-stitch project for our future baby's room. Sometimes we talked—when she wanted to. Other times we shared companionship in silence. I think I blessed her with my presence, but the Lord also used that time to begin healing my soul.

Bill and I also took opportunity to travel that spring. We drove to Mexico City and to California, using up the vacation time he had accumulated. In my spare time I worked on a baby quilt, a baby cross-stitch project, and a baby girl's crocheted sweater, just in case our first baby would be a girl.

Always, I was preparing mentally for the child that would one day be ours. Sometimes the uncertainty of it all would cause fear to rise in me. I learned to think about God, who knows all and sees all. I often prayed, "Lord, please protect the little child You are preparing for us. Keep it safe. Please keep the mother from using cigarettes, alcohol, or other drugs, so her child will be strong and healthy."

The 1971-72 school year came and went without having a child join our small family, but we trusted God for the right child at the right time. We began to make moving preparations since Bill's military obligation would end on June 30, 1972. We left Shiprock, New Mexico, still childless, and drove across the country to a three bedroom ranch style house we had purchased in Ann Arbor, consoling ourselves with the thought that it was probably easier to move without a baby.

CHAPTER 6

Pam: A Trailer Called Home

It was cold winter when Paula came to stay with us. She arrived early in the morning. Her boyfriend Dave waited in the car as Paula knocked on the door. After greeting Paula with tears and hugs, I introduced her to my husband, Anthony.

Paula was about five foot, five or maybe five foot, six inches tall. It's hard to judge other people's height when you are short yourself. To me, everyone seems tall if they are over five foot, three inches. Paula always lightened or darkened her sandy brown hair according to whatever "phase" of her life she was in. She was in the "blond phase" when she came to live with us. Paula had beautiful eyes. They were almost blue, almost gray, and almost green, depending on the day. Most important to me, they were the eyes of friendship. She had long, thick eyelashes and wore glasses well, like the girls in the magazines.

Today her eyes were green and filled with sadness. Paula's eyes searched mine, and I knew what she was going to say. She took a deep breath, "Pam, I have something to tell you. I'm pregnant."

I took Paula's hand and did not look away, "That doesn't matter, Paula, what matters is that you're here."

"No, just listen a minute, Pam. Let me say this. If you don't want me here, I'll understand." She took a ragged breath and continued, "but I sure hope you do because I don't know where I'll go if you don't."

Tears were running down her face as I held her close, "Paula, it's okay. Our home is your home for as long as you need it."

Paula motioned to Dave and he brought the first of her things inside. She quickly introduced us. This was the man who was making my best friend cry, and the less I was around him the better. Anthony and I went to our room to give them a private moment to say goodbye. Our tiny two-bedroom trailer already housed Anthony, me, and our four-month-old baby Tracey. But friendship ran deeper than convenience, and Paula became part of our family.

We fell into a routine easily. Each morning Paula would clear her bedding off the couch and put it away. She helped me with dishes and housework, and we spent many happy hours with Tracey. Since Anthony and I were barely scraping by and couldn't afford the luxury of a babysitter, Paula would often take care of Tracey while we went to the grocery store or just out for a drive. Even in the winter, gas was cheap so a drive in the country was affordable. The three of us stayed up late playing rummy. Anthony would invariably end up sleeping, and Paula and I would see who really was best at this game. It was usually Paula.

When Sundays rolled around, the four of us would be off to church. Anthony and his three girls, or "Anthony and his harem," was the kidding he took at church.

Paula was undecided as to what she would do when the baby was born. One morning, I entered the living room to find Paula sitting on the couch. She was deep in thought, staring out the window. "A penny for your thoughts?" I asked.

Paula brushed her hair away from her face with a trembling hand, "Pam, I am so mixed up, I can't even think straight. I miss seeing Dave and hearing his voice, even though things were bad between us, and yet I know I need to put the baby ahead of my own feelings. Trying to decide what to do is going to be hard."

I walked over and placed my hand on her shoulder, "Just take your time in deciding. You have plenty of that. I'm here to listen to you anytime."

Paula reached up and squeezed my hand, "I know, and it means more than you realize."

This was only the first of many hours we spent talking of what options she had. Anthony and I continually assured Paula we didn't want to influence her and would support her no matter what choice she made. Her pain was so great. If a heart could bleed from the pain of a decision, Paula would have bled to death. I held her, and she cried. I told her, "Whatever you do for this baby, Paula, I know that you are doing it out of love."

That night I looked upon the sleeping face of my Tracey and knew that Paula was stronger than I. I couldn't even consider giving up my baby. As I watched my child sleep in her darkened room, Paula's pain became my pain. I was reminded of it each time Tracey smiled or laughed. Even Tracey's cries made Paula's pain my own. How could Paula give up her baby? Yet how could she not? I knew Paula truly had a mother's love by the choices she was considering. Who else but a mother could put her child's needs first and foremost, knowing that in doing so she was breaking her own heart?

Pregnancy looked good on Paula. She was slim and didn't look pregnant at all for quite some time. When she did start to show, it looked like someone had slipped a small basketball under her shirt. Her outward appearance did not reflect her inner struggle. Her eyes glowed when she spoke of the baby. As the baby became more active, Paula would often smile, put her hand on her stomach and say, "I know you're there. I love you and we're gonna make it through this just fine."

Some women complain about their babies kicking at night, but not Paula. She would get up in the morning smiling, "I know this baby is a girl—I can just feel it. She kicks like a girl. I think a boy would kick harder. I am sure she is doing gymnastics in there, not playing football."

"I know what you mean," I laughed. "I knew Tracey was a girl too. I don't know how I knew; I just knew."

Paula and I talked while we did dishes, made beds, did laundry and cooked. Our conversations came as natural as breathing. They became part of us, and we became even more a part of each other. We talked with our hearts. How can I explain how my heart sounds when it beats? That's how our conversations were: constant, steady, and at times intense, like a heart pounding on a dark scary night.

We sat at the table having coffee one morning when I looked at Paula and waited for her eyes to meet mine. I noticed her eyes seemed more blue than gray today as I asked her the question I had been thinking since last night, "How are you feeling about your decision?"

"It's hard to say," she sighed. She sipped her coffee and I waited for her to continue. "One minute I feel like giving her up is the right thing to do, the thing I have to do. The next minute I just want to keep her. It's hard to think of her taking her first steps for someone else or smiling for someone else and not for me," she explained, her hands leaving her cup and resting under her chin. "When I think of those things, I can't let her go. Then when I think of the importance of her growing up in a home with two Christian parents instead of one, and the security that would give her, I know I have to give her a chance at that. I have to. I love her too much not to. I had that, and you know she deserves it too." I could tell Paula believed every word she said by the intense look she had on her face. Then I heard the uncertainty in her voice, "Do you think she will know how much I love her?"

"Yes, she'll know. How could she not know? You are making such a selfless decision. It's not like it's the easy road to take."

"I know, believe me, I know. She was awake again most of the night. We had quite a talk, baby and I."

"What did you talk about?" I asked.

"I told her how very much I love her. I told her that we are survivors, she and I, and that we'll make it through this."

I went over and hugged Paula. "I know you will. God will help you. He'll be there to watch over her when you can't."

Paula began to cry. Her pain was so great, I could feel it as I held her.

"I know He will, Pam. It's just that I love her so much. I want her to know that, to know that above everything else I loved her. I'll always love her."

"She'll know, Paula. Don't ask me how, but she'll know." By this time I was crying too and we pulled away, each of us wiping the tears off the other's face. Paula's right, I thought. She and that baby are survivors.

Spring brought a visit from Anthony's Aunt Bertha from California. She was staying at Anthony's folks' house and called us up to see if we wanted to go to Lake Michigan. It was a sunny day and Paula and I were always ready for an adventure. Anthony and I had only one car, a small white Subaru. Since Anthony had a progressive eye disease that left him unable to drive, he took the bus to work, which left the car for Paula and me. We packed up Tracey's baby things, loaded up our tiny car, and away we went. We arrived and found a good spot for our blankets and towels on the sand. Paula and I sat down while Aunt Bertha held Tracey and walked down by the water. The wind off the lake was cool, and Paula and I relaxed and squinted out over the view. I looked over at Paula. She was sitting with her knees pulled up against her. Her stomach was in the way, and it looked awkward. "Are you comfortable sitting like that?" I asked her.

"Yes, I can feel the baby better this way. It's almost like holding her."

Tracey was excited seeing seagulls for the first time, and I heard her laughter as Aunt Bertha pointed them out to her. I looked sideways at Paula, "It's kind of sad, you know—I mean, our children may never know each other. They won't be able to spend the day at the beach like this."

Paula looked sad and twirled her hair around her finger, "I wish things could be different, but I have to do what's best for her." She stroked her stomach, "I don't know what to do."

We sat in the silence of comfortable friendship, each feeling what the other was feeling. No more words were needed as we watched the waves roll in.

Paula found out about Bethany Home through the phone book. They were a Christian adoption agency and would find a home for Paula's baby. The two trips we made there were agonizing for both of us. It somehow felt so final. Watching Paula wrestle with the decision to give up her baby was almost like watching someone with a terminal illness get worse and worse. It seemed the trip there was fifty miles away, when in reality, it was only fifteen. I didn't want to meddle or influence Paula's decision. I was there to support her no matter what she decided to do in the end. The first time I took her there, I pretended to read while I waited. Time passed slowly. Finally, I glanced up from my magazine for the third time and there she stood. She was pale and trembling. I wanted to wrap my arms around her and rush her away from there and never take her back again. Instead I swallowed hard and said, "Are you all right?"

"I will be," her trembling voice replied. "Let's go, shall we?"

We rode the first few miles in silence. We each needed time to process all this.

"Well, what did you find out?" I finally asked.

"They can guarantee that they'll put her in a Christian home."

"Well that's good," I replied, and there was more silence.

"I can change my mind. Even after she is born, I can change my mind. There is a waiting period before the adoption is final."

I reached over and touched Paula's hand. I felt her pain flow through me like a cold wind off Lake Michigan, and I was silenced by it.

We made one more trip to Bethany. This was a group meeting for unwed expectant mothers. We both dreaded to walk through the door to the reception area. Again I took up my vigil among the waiting room chairs and magazines. I wanted to be with Paula, but I knew she must face this without me. When she emerged this time, her outward appearance was stronger than before. Almost as if she was bracing herself for what she must do. We waited until we were in the car to talk. I spoke first, "Well?"

"I can give birth at a place called Booth Memorial Home. It is a home for unwed mothers. They live there and go to school there. The Salvation Army runs it."

"Are the girls who live there giving up their babies?" I almost added "too" at the end of the sentence, but I caught myself. I didn't want Paula to feel locked into the decision she'd made so far.

"Some are, some aren't. They have their babies right there at the home. They have a doctor on call twenty-four hours a day."

"Will you take classes then? I mean to get you ready and to let you know what to expect? Anthony and I did before I had Tracey. It helped some." I didn't want to go into the details of Tracey's birth because it had been a very difficult one. I didn't want to scare Paula more than she already was.

"The classes are only for the girls who live there. They have them during the day, right along with their other classes."

"Oh well, I'll be there to help you through it. You'll be okay, it's not so bad." I refrained from adding "It's worth it in the end." I couldn't imagine going through the pain of childbirth and then giving my child to someone else to raise. Once again, I was awed by Paula's strength.

She glanced out the window and took a deep breath, "I had to fill out a paper giving some background information about my family. I wrote that both my mom and myself want her to be raised in a Christian home. I also included my hobbies and so on. I wonder if she will ever know those things about me."

"Oh, Paula, this is so hard for you," I answered as my heart hurt. "Remember it's not final right now. You still have time to change your mind."

"Don't remind me. I have to do what's best for her. I love her too much not to."

She stroked her stomach and stared out the window. We finished the ride home in shared silence.

Paula's mom called weekly to see how Paula was doing and to offer encouragement. When I would answer the phone, Pearl would ask me how Paula was really doing. I tried to be honest with her, knowing that if it were me, my mom would want to know too. "It's hard, Pearl, really hard. She's trying to decide what is best for her baby."

Paula and I agreed that we wouldn't call her mom and stepdad until after the baby was born. Paula didn't want her mom to see her go through labor and delivery only to give up the baby for adoption.

Paula's baby decided to make her entrance into the world three weeks early.

CHAPTER 7

Paula: Labor of Love

I had been with Pam and Anthony for about four months when my mother suggested I contact Mike, the young man I had been seeing before dating Dave. She felt I needed to talk to someone who was completely out of the picture, someone who wasn't emotionally involved in any way. I decided to call. After talking for a short time I told him where I was and about my situation. He was home from college for the summer.

"Would it be all right with you if I come to Michigan and spend some time?" he asked. "I can drive you back to Iowa, if that's what you decide to do later."

I hadn't called him with the intention of having him come to Michigan. It was his suggestion. I said it was fine with me. I was glad he was coming. Pam's life as a mom was structured around nap-time and other baby details, and with Mike there, I would be able to get out more, and Pam and Anthony could also have some much needed privacy. He came and rented a small trailer nearby. Mike was a nice looking man with dark hair and eyes. He was always rather quiet and soft-spoken.

We spent a lot of time together. We both enjoyed going to the zoo so we went often. We especially liked watching the monkeys. The little ones were always swinging on the bars, chasing each other around and chattering. There were always at least a couple of mothers sitting quietly off to the side, watching their children play and cradling their newborn babies in their arms. It amazed me how much like human beings they were; just like mothers taking their children to play in the park. As my time drew nearer, we would sit on a bench and watch the monkeys play and the people go by. We also liked watching the polar bears getting in their water to cool off. I was amazed to think these huge animals that looked so docile were actually so savage.

One morning in late June Mike came over and asked if I would like to go to the zoo. I said sure. When we got there it was still too early for the monkeys to be out, so we wandered slowly to where the polar bears were kept. There were a few out, lazily moving around, getting ready for their day.

"Let's sit down over here," Mike said. We sat for a little while on a small wooden bench, and I noticed he was nervous. Finally he said, "I really wanted to ask you this by the monkeys, but we like the polar bears too, even if they are second best. I love you, Paula. After the baby is born, and we're back home in Iowa, will you marry me?"

"Yes," I answered immediately as I thought of the three of us. I pictured what it would be like to have a family—a husband and a child. A burden was lifted from me. I no longer faced an impossible decision. My baby and I could be together. She would have a Daddy. When I shared the news with Pam and Anthony, they too were thrilled for me. I was so happy! I could stay with Pam a little while longer. She would be able to share my happiness and to hold and love my baby girl.

A couple of weeks after he asked me to marry him we went for a walk. We were talking about how much longer it might be before my labor started and my baby was born. "We may have to stay here until my baby's first checkup, just to be sure we are both healthy and strong enough for that long trip," I said. After my little daughter's first checkup, the three of us would travel back to Iowa. Mike and I would get married, and when it was time for him to go back to college, we would all go, and our little family would settle in Iowa City.

He looked surprised, "No, not both of you, just you and I will be going back. I could never raise another man's child."

My initial reaction was shock and disbelief. Although I didn't say anything more about it at the time, I felt confident he would change his mind when he saw my baby. After all, he knew I was pregnant from the first phone call, yet he wanted to come. I assumed he was staying until after the baby was born because he had offered to drive me, and I thought my baby, back to Iowa. When I realized Mike's proposal didn't include my baby, I was crushed. I found myself right back where I had started, and knew I still had difficult choices ahead of me. How could I leave her behind? If it was only as simple as deciding between Mike and my baby, my baby would win hands down. She had no competition there. I would never give her up in order to simply have Mike as a husband. I had to keep my mind focused on my baby and what was best for her. I knew she needed a family—a mother and a father who loved her.

In addition to the viewing areas for the monkeys and polar bears, Mike and I also had a favorite place in the park where we spent a great deal of time talking or playing cards. That was where my labor started about four weeks after our conversation. I wasn't sure, I didn't have any pain yet, but I knew something was going on. I asked him to take me back to Pam's. It was mid-afternoon and the evening progressed with no major changes. I had some cramping feelings, but I didn't mention them to Pam or Anthony yet. I was getting nervous, but I wasn't due for another three weeks. We all went to bed, but I didn't get much sleep that night. I did a lot of praying, and I did a lot of talking to my baby and rubbing my stomach. I treasured her every little movement because I knew this would be the last night I would be able to feel her moving inside me, so I prayed and talked and rocked. She was ready, but I wasn't.

When Pam got up the next morning she found me sitting on the couch. When I told her the pains had started she said, "Oh my, oh my! How are you? How far apart are the pains?"

I told her they weren't regular yet, and she said "Oh my, oh my." Knowing Pam as well as I did, I could almost see her mind working, trying to figure out how to keep me busy, how to keep my mind occupied with something else. She suggested we play rummy. She would say, "Are you having a pain? Was that a pain? How are you Paula? How do you feel?" Every time I had a pain, she said, "Oh my!"

I didn't know where Mike was, I didn't even know where Anthony was. It was just Pam and me again. Just like always, knowing each other's mind and heart. I could see her concern and love for me in her eyes, and that helped so much. No words were needed between us.

When the pains started getting closer together Pam took me to the hospital. The drive to the hospital was uneventful, although I do believe Pam was in worse shape than I was. After being signed in and prepped, I was encouraged to move around and walk a little.

I walked slowly down the hall. One gal asked me if I had had a boy or girl. She thought I had already given birth—I hadn't gained much weight. I saw other girls and heard them talk about what they were going to do once they delivered. I thought they sure seemed indifferent to the very thing that was the most important thing in the world to me. One asked me what I was going to do.

"I am giving her up for adoption." It was the first time I said the words aloud.

"Why?" she asked.

"I can't think about what I want." I told her. "I have to make this choice for my baby. This little baby depends entirely upon me to make sure she has the very best life I can possibly give her, even if it's not with me." These words, although spoken to her, were the words my heart had been saying to me for a long time. My decision was finally made by answering the question of a total stranger. Adoption was the best thing I could do for my baby. It made my heart ache. It also seemed to make the other girl think, and I believe she took her decision more seriously. I hoped so.

Pam fully intended to stay with me during my labor, and I wanted her there with me—but they wouldn't let anyone except family in the labor room. I knew Pam would put up an admirable fight about this. She's little but very tenacious, and I knew when she wasn't there it was no fault of her own. It was the middle of July and there was no air conditioning in the room. There was just one bed, a small bedside table, a window fan in the only window, and a big round clock high on the wall across from the bed. It was so hot and I was so scared and alone.

I hadn't had any classes about childbirth so I didn't know what to expect. I didn't know about breathing or changing positions or if there was anything I could do to help ease the pain. I thought there would at least be a nurse there to tell me these things and check on me regularly. The pain was terrible. When the pains came one after another and I was pushing, I finally called for a nurse. They hadn't looked in on me for hours. The look on her face told me I had "bothered" her with my call, but she said, "Well, how are we doing in here?"

"Could you please give me something for this pain?" I asked. "I can't handle this much longer."

"Let me check you first to see how you're doing. Then I'll get you something, okay? Are you breathing with the pains? We can also turn you to your side and put a pillow between your legs to help ease some to the pressure on your back. Weren't you taught these things at your childbirth classes?"

"I didn't have any classes," I answered through the pain.

She seemed a lot more sympathetic after I told her that. When she checked me, her hand was covered with blood up to her wrist. She found that I had only dilated to three and then ripped. Things happened a lot faster after that. I suddenly had everyone's attention.

She kept saying, "Don't push! Don't push!" They called for a doctor STAT and helped me out of bed. They helped me walk to the delivery room trailing blood behind me. She said she could have called for a gurney but there wasn't time. The doctor didn't have time to wash his hands. He just put on gloves. They strapped me down, and a nurse held my hand. When they finally told me to push, my baby girl was not long in coming. That she was a girl was no surprise to me. I knew that all along.

I had decided not to see her, thinking if I didn't look at her or know anything about her, maybe it would be a little easier for me. As the nurse walked by me with my baby, she turned her back to me, as arranged, so I couldn't see. But I couldn't take it. I had to look at her. I said, "Please, wait." She looked at the doctor and he nodded. She turned toward me with my tiny little crying bundle. My baby was so tiny and so beautiful. I wished there were words to express my feelings at that moment. She was small but she was strong and healthy for which I thanked God. The nurse turned away again, and my heart broke as she walked through the door of the delivery room. Only then did I realize the doctor was talking to me.

He told me there were a few things I needed to know. I needed to know how much injury had been done and that she only weighed five pounds, six ounces and was seventeen inches long. If I ever had another baby it was very important that I tell the doctor these things because I would never be able to deliver a baby any bigger than she was.

I wanted so badly to hold her. The incredible physical pain I was in no longer mattered. I was now trying to deal with the stabbing emotional pain that was coming from my heart! I had just given birth to my baby girl. She was my daughter. I was her mother! My final decision wavered. I was completely exhausted both physically and emotionally. Someone had finally given me something for the physical pain as they worked on me, but my tears were from the emotional pain, and there was nothing they could give me for that. I turned my head into the pillow and cried.

I didn't know how many stitches I had, but it took twenty-four inches of stitching thread to repair the damage. The doctors called me "the brave little girl with all the stitches." I had been in labor for twenty-six hours.

After the delivery room and the recovery room, I was put in a room very near the nursery. Even worse than the physical pain was the emotional pain of lying there in the dark listening to the babies cry. I had free access to the nursery. Strength given by God was the only thing that held me in that bed. I wanted so badly to go to her and hold her close to me so she wouldn't cry anymore. It broke my heart to think of her lying there crying when I was so near.

I wouldn't let Pam call my parents until after my baby was born. I didn't want them worrying about me when they were so far away and couldn't be there. But they came from Iowa to the hospital as soon as they were called. I happened to be walking down the hall when they got there. They came through the doors. Mom headed straight for the nursery. When I called, "Mom!" she immediately turned and came to me instead. I didn't want them to see her. I knew it would be harder for them if they saw her, and they respected my wishes. She held me tight for a long time. It felt so good to have my mother holding me!

"My poor little Paula," she said, "you've had such a hard time!" I looked into her eyes, and through our tears I could clearly see the anguish she felt for me, and, more importantly, I could clearly see her love. My stepdad was standing right beside her. When Mom and I finally let go of each other, he leaned down and hugged me close to him; and when I looked up at him, there was love in his eyes too.

The day after she was born, a woman came with some release forms for me to sign. She left for awhile, and when she came back I still hadn't signed them. She explained that these weren't the final papers. These were forms giving my permission to release her from the hospital when the time came. I still had time to change my mind. One of the forms asked if I had named her. I thought about this for a long time. In my mind I would have named her Kendra Dawn. I wanted very much to put that name there. There are two reasons I didn't. I thought it might be easier on me emotionally if I didn't officially name her. Also, I wanted to give that very important privilege to her adoptive parents. I didn't want them to think of her by any other name than the one they chose for her. I knew how much that choice would mean to her adoptive mother.

God always has a purpose, and I believe he helps us make the right choices. I have always felt I made the right decision. Knowing God had helped me and led me to that decision gave me some measure of peace. He chose me to give birth to this tiny, beautiful baby girl, and I knew the parents he chose were somewhere waiting for her. This had been His plan for all the years of our lives, and now, at the moment of her birth, another part of His plan had been fulfilled.

Even so, I cannot describe the terrible heartache of signing the final adoption forms, knowing that my name on those forms would take her away from me. There were two things I wanted assurance on, and I would not sign the papers until I had gotten it. I wanted my baby girl raised in a good Christian home, and I wanted her to know I loved her—always. The lonesome, empty longing to hold her in my arms seemed more than I could take. By signing those forms I may have given up my legal parental rights, but never the deep emotional love that only a mother can feel for her child. Already I was envious of her adoptive mother. She would be the one to hold her, feed her, cuddle her, and just stand by her crib watching her sleep. I loved my baby and I wanted those things so much!

CHAPTER 8

Pam: Part of Paula's Heart

When her labor started, Paula seemed pretty calm. I, on the other hand, was a wreck. I'd never been an observer in this scenario before. I prayed I would be able to help. The foolishness of Paula's not being able to attend a birthing class suddenly hit me as I drove. Anthony and I had attended all the classes we were supposed to and had seen the movie about childbirth. How would Paula even know what to do? I would just have to coach her through it. That shouldn't be so hard— but why was I so scared? We left Tracey at Anthony's folks, and it was just the two of us again.

On the way, I just kept asking Paula, "Are you okay?" If she was having a contraction, I knew she wasn't okay. It made me want to drive fast, but my driving usually worried Paula anyway, so I just concentrated on the road as much as I could. When we walked into the Booth home, it was like walking into a wall of heat. The building was not air-conditioned and the labor rooms were on the upper floor where it was even hotter. Paula signed herself in and I gave her a hug. "I'll be there in just a minute. I want to call Anthony at work and let him know what is happening." She nodded, and I thought about how sad she looked as I hurried to make my call. After the call, I went immediately upstairs to the desk.

"I'm here as Paula Roskamp's labor coach," I said.

"Are you her sister?" the woman asked.

"No, I'm her best friend. I'm supposed to be her labor coach."

"I'm sorry. Only relatives are allowed beyond this point."

"You don't understand," I explained as calmly as I could, "we arranged this in advance. She has no family here. She is my best friend. I'm supposed to be with her and help her."

The woman at the desk looked half-heartedly through her papers. "I'm sorry. It's not written here anywhere. Relatives only, sorry."

No matter what tactics I used, (I even said I was Paula's sister, after all we were blood sisters) the woman still would not budge. The only thing I was able to accomplish was to get them to make sure she had a fan in her room because of the awful heat. It seemed Paula was on her own once again.

I kept checking with the woman at the window every ten to fifteen minutes until finally she disappeared altogether. Now, I knew nothing. Time passed and it grew hotter and stuffier. I tried the door that went back to where I thought she was, but it was locked.

Finally a doctor came hurrying through. I tried to talk to him but he had no time. He knocked on the door impatiently. It opened and he disappeared inside. There was still no one at the window.

I paced and leafed through magazines for another hour and finally the woman came back. I rushed over to the window. She opened it before I knocked. "Your friend had a baby girl," she stated.

It was no surprise to me. Paula knew she was having a girl. I was most concerned about how my best friend was doing. "When can I see Paula? When can I see her? Is she all right?"

"You can't see her yet. I'll tell you when," she answered, and then she was gone.

I paced. I sat down. I got up and paced some more. At last the locked door opened and the woman from the desk stood there. "You can go in now, but you can only stay five minutes. Your friend is very tired."

I nodded, afraid that if I said anything she would slam the door in my face, and I wouldn't get to see Paula. I went through the door into a wide hallway. To the left was the nursery. I looked in and there, off to the right, was a tiny bundle with a red wrinkly face. It was the tiniest baby I had ever seen except for one in an incubator. I knew without looking at the tag that she had to be "Baby Girl Roskamp". My eyes filled with tears. Paula's daughter. I wanted to linger, but my need to check on Paula was greater. Paula's room was at the end of the hall. I noticed the shades were drawn as I walked in and the room was hot in spite of the humming fan near the bed. Paula's eyes were closed, and her hair clung damply to her head. I walked over and brushed my finger on her cheek. She was so white. Paler than I had ever seen her. Tears were running down my face. She opened her eyes.

"How are you?" I asked softly.

"I'm okay," her reply was weak.

"I'm so sorry I wasn't here to help you," I sobbed. "They wouldn't let me in. They couldn't find that paper. They said only relatives could come in. I told them I was your blood sister. *That* didn't count."

"I know, Pam, it's all right." Paula held my hand, "She got born okay. It was hard and I bled a lot. I walked to the delivery room, holding her little head in. There wasn't time for a stretcher, but she got born. Is she okay? Did you see her?"

"Oh, yes, she's okay. She's beautiful, she looks . . ."

Paula held up her hand to stop me. She was crying. "Don't tell me, Pam, don't tell me. I can't bear to hear it. I couldn't even hold her. I knew if I did, I wouldn't be able to part with her. Please don't tell me."

I bent down and hugged Paula, and we cried. The nurse came, "Your 5 minutes are up."

"I will call your folks, and I will see you tomorrow."

When I walked past the nursery, Paula's baby girl's isolette was empty. I could see they were weighing her. I lingered a moment to watch and thought of my sweet baby Tracey waiting for me. My arms suddenly ached to hold her, yet I knew that was nothing compared to the ache Paula was feeling.

When Paula's parents arrived the next day I took them to the hospital. While they visited with Paula, I walked to the nursery and there was the baby, that precious baby, her dark blue eyes open. I marveled at how tiny she was, how perfect, and how much she looked like Paula. I grieved because I would never see her grow up. I grieved even more that Paula would not see her grow up. How could Paula stand to not see her, to know she was so near, and not let herself hold her. The thought ripped my heart out.

After three days, they said Paula could go home. Her mom and stepdad picked her up and brought her to our trailer. She was still walking slowly because of all her stitches. Other than that, she didn't look like she had just given birth. I embraced her as she came in the door, and we cried together.

"Oh Pam, I had to sign a paper saying I gave her up. It was so hard, but it's not final. I can change my mind. I can change my mind. They said I could. I wrote that on the paper before I signed, just to make sure."

We cried harder. What could I say to her now? I had my child and she had none.

Paula's folks left the next day. They didn't want to leave, but they had a farm in Iowa to run and a large family to care for. Paula hated to see them go, but Mike, a former boyfriend that had reentered Paula's life, was still in Michigan. He could drive her back to Iowa when she was ready to go.

In the coming days, Paula walked around like a zombie. Words were few, and we choose them carefully, not wanting to open up the flood of pain she was barely holding back. She spent much of her time with Mike, away from us and the trailer. It hurt me to feel her pull away from me, yet I knew each time she saw us with Tracey it was a vivid reminder of what she had given up. Of what she would never have.

Two or three weeks after her baby was born, Mike took Paula back home to Iowa. She needed to escape, to grieve, to heal, and to put distance between her and her baby girl. Saying goodbye was hard for both of us. I held Paula close and promised to always be there for her. We were both crying as she left.

One of Anthony's relatives was a foster parent. Through this informal network I learned Paula's baby was in a foster home until the adoption was final. The baby had a blocked tear duct and was having a lot of matter in her eyes, but they thought the tear duct would open soon and all would be fine. The baby was slow in gaining weight because she had been early. According to the family source, the baby was being adopted by a dentist and his wife, who had been a schoolteacher. The wife had quit her job and was going to be a full time mom now.

The information seemed both good and bad to me. I was happy Paula's baby would have a good home, yet almost angry that someone else besides Paula was going to be called "Mommy" by this child. After all, didn't Paula deserve that? Wasn't she the one who had loved her child enough to let her be adopted? Still, I couldn't help but rejoice that the baby would have the kind of home Paula wanted her to have. The adoptive couple had no other children, so they had lots of love to give this baby. I shared what I had found out with Paula, hoping it would help ease her pain. She was grieving so for her baby, for giving her up. It was as if a part of Paula had gone with the baby, a part of Paula's heart.

Anthony and I were almost ready to celebrate our second anniversary when Paula left us. Anthony had been going to college when we got married, so there had been no money for an engagement ring or fancy wedding band. An inexpensive set of matching silver bands had to do. For our first anniversary, Anthony bought me a pearl ring. He knew I had always wanted a diamond, but at that time, he also knew that our first baby was due in a month and there was no money for a diamond.

Paula had the matching wedding band and engagement ring that Dave had bought for her. Unbeknownst to me, before Paula left, she and Anthony struck up a deal, and he bought the set from her, and presented the rings to me for our second anniversary in August. He was worried I would be hurt because it was a second-hand diamond. I didn't see it that way at all. I was touched by the love Paula showed to each of us by selling it to Anthony.

The rings not only came to represent my husband's love for me, but also my best friend's love for me as well. How many women have a wedding ring set that holds all of that meaning? I would look at my rings often and always know they represented a deep, deep love and commitment from two people instead of one.

Paula and I kept in touch. Even after she and Mike got married and made their home in Des Moines, we stopped to see them on our yearly visit to my parents in Iowa. Mike didn't like Paula to talk about the baby, but Paula and I were both still grieving. Her grief was much worse than mine. We needed to talk about it, to wonder, to hope, and to dream that this child had a wonderful home. The home that we knew God had chosen for her.

CHAPTER 9

Mary: Guess What, Kid? You're a Dad!

Jesus loves me! This I know,
For the Bible tells me so;
Little ones to Him belong,
They are weak, but He is strong.[7]

We celebrated Bill's twenty-seventh birthday during the hottest week of the summer, the middle of July, and worked on all the things moving and settling in requires. We had moved back to Ann Arbor where Bill hoped to earn a specializing degree in Prosthetic Dentistry. Bill was busy finishing our unfinished basement into which his brother, Ken, would be moving toward the end of August. Ken also had chosen dentistry as a career, and together we had plans for his living with us during his four years of dental school.

One morning in mid-August Bill left to buy building supplies, while I made arrangements for a bike ride with one of my new neighbors. Before I left, the phone rang and the voice on the other end identified himself as our caseworker from Bethany. As my heart began to beat wildly, I heard him say, "Mary, we have a little girl for you. She was born on July 18, so she will be four weeks old this week. She weighed five pounds, six ounces at birth, so she's a tiny one. She has brown hair, blue eyes, and a rosy complexion."

I was so excited I could hardly think. I managed to agree that we would come to Grand Rapids a few days later, on Friday, August 18, to see her. We would bring some clothes and come with a name so the adoption placement could legally proceed.

The short bike ride seemed to last endlessly since I was riding on a bubble of joyful news that I didn't want to share with my new neighbor. I wanted Bill to be the first to hear. When I got home, I paced the house saying, "Thank you, Lord! Thank you, Jesus!" I could hardly contain my excitement until Bill finally came home. I met him at the door and said, "Guess what, Kid! You're Dad to a baby girl!"

With tears in his eyes, he hugged me tight and said, "Considering that, Kid, you look great!"

It was a warm, summer day that Friday as we drove our orange VW Fastback from Ann Arbor, 120 miles to Grand Rapids, to meet our first child for the very first time. I had gathered together some clothes: a tiny white dress with pink smocking and a matching panty, a hand-knitted pair of pale pink booties with white fuzzy angora insteps, a T-shirt, some white flannel diapers, plastic pants, and a white flannel blanket with tiny pink and blue flowers.

Months before we had decided on a name for both a boy and a girl since we weren't fussy about what gender our first child would be. We had chosen Kristin Beth for a girl's name, thinking Kristin was the pretty name of a young friend in Gallup; Beth was my middle name.

Butterflies danced in our stomachs while fear and excitement traded places in our hearts as we drove into Bethany's parking lot that morning. We were welcomed into the office of our caseworker. I listened carefully while Bill took notes of an abbreviated description of our new daughter and her birth families. Among other things, we were told that both the birth mom and birth grandmother wanted to be sure the baby would be placed in a Christian home. Next we were escorted into a small room in which there stood a little white wicker baby basket which held a very tiny baby girl. She was dressed in a pale pink dress and white booties. Her soft brown hair showed just a hint of auburn. She was sleeping soundly on her back and she didn't even stir when we entered the room. I whispered, "She looks like a little pink rosebud."

We each held Kristin carefully and quietly, since she continued to sleep contentedly. We shed tears of joy that this child was ours, tears of wonder knowing the magnitude of what was happening while she slept unaware through it all.

That day we had to leave her to return to her foster care family for one week while legal matters were processed. An appointment was made for 11:00 a.m. the following Friday for the homecoming event. We could hardly wait!

During the interim week, we showed Polaroid pictures we had taken to everyone who was or wasn't interested. Most couples have nine months to prepare for a baby. We had one week. We bought a used baby bed with a white cotton lace canopy, as well as a car seat and a few other necessary items. The night before we were to take Kristin home, my friend, Susie, quickly gave a baby shower for me with a few friends. All the relatives knew about the new baby. Some planned to stop by the following day at one of the grandma's houses where she would be on display. The excitement was running high.

On August 25, 1972, Kristin Beth was given into our care. That day she weighed six pounds, six ounces and was nineteen inches long, almost the identical weight and height I was at birth. She was still unusually small for a baby already five weeks old. The Lord blessed us with a tiny doll, my heart's desire. We prayed, "Thank You, Lord, for this precious baby, a gift from You to love."

Friends and relatives came to take a peek and some pictures. My dear grandma came to hold Kristin and immediately took off her pink booties, exposing her tiny feet saying, "It's way too hot for booties today!"

Even though Daddy Bill had very little experience with babies, he acted like a pro giving her eye drops with one hand while cupping her little head in his other.

Already I felt like a protective new mom saying, "Be careful with her, Kid!"

We stayed in Grand Rapids until 4:30 p.m. when we began the two and a half hour ride home to Ann Arbor. Kristin slept most of the time in the midst of the hubbub. In spite of her sleepyhead response, she still must have gotten worn out because she went right to sleep in a small bassinet in her new bedroom. She slept till five o'clock the next morning, drank a bottle, and slept again. I wondered if all babies were this easy.

CHAPTER 10

Paula: The Other Side

While on one side of an adoption there is great joy and happiness, on the other side there is great loss and sadness. Although I could imagine the gratitude her adoptive parents felt for their baby, I felt great loss and sadness.

As I said goodbye to Pam, Anthony and Tracey, I felt another knife in my heart. I loved these people so much! We had been through so much together. It was difficult for all of us. I kissed Tracey goodbye, and Anthony gave me a big hug. I was losing the battle not to cry. Pam and I clung to each other. It was extremely hard for us both. Pam, knowing me as she did, understood why I had to leave. Our hearts reached out for each other, and we cried as we said goodbye.

When we left Pam's home, Mike held my hand while I sobbed for everything I was leaving behind. It was hard for me to believe that I could feel so miserable. Physically I was still in extreme pain from my baby's birth, and the emotional pain was tearing me apart. How could I leave the little trailer that had become my home and the wonderful warmth, support, and love of the people who lived there? How on earth could I leave the place my tiny daughter had been born? It was only days since I had signed those final, horrible forms so I knew she was still there. The bond I felt for her was so strong it was almost physical. I wasn't ready to leave yet. It was too soon. I needed more time. I didn't want to go, but I had to. I knew I still had time to change my mind, and staying would only make it more difficult to abide by my decision.

As we drove, Mike's mood became lighter and lighter while mine grew darker. To him it was all over. There was no need to talk about it now, or even mention it in the future. It was done. We drove further and further from Grand Rapids while I held her in my heart and cried. My heart was broken. There was no going back. I knew I would never be completely happy again until my daughter and I were together. Only she could fill that empty space. All it held now were my tears.

After I was back with my parents in Iowa, I received two very difficult phone calls. The first was from Dave, my baby's father. I was glad Mom answered the phone and talked to him. Although I believed he had a right to know, I had no desire to talk to him. I'm not sure I could have. Mom picked up the phone, "Hello."

"Can I talk to Paula?"

"I don't think she wants to talk to you," Mom replied.

"Did she have the baby?" he asked.

"Yes."

"May I know what it was?"

"A little girl," Mom said softly.

"What did Paula do?"

"She gave her up for adoption," Mom told him. "It was her decision."

"I know," he said, "Does Paula know where her baby is?"

"No," Mom answered.

My protective mother then asked him, "Where are you calling from?" I don't know what his answer was, but my mother said, "Stay there." And he said, "I will." I know my mom would have told me where he was if I asked, but I didn't. I didn't want to know. My dad was very upset over the phone call, but I told him Dave had a right to know. That was the last contact we ever had.

The second phone call was from the adoption agency to tell me she had been placed with her adoptive parents. I was told a little about her adoptive parents, a little about what they looked like, their occupations as a dentist and a school teacher, and that they were Christian Reformed. That was all I was allowed to know. It was a comfort to know these things. Even so, the reality of that last call from Bethany really hit hard. It was done—she was gone. The decision was made and carried out. I knew she would be well taken care of and loved, but I didn't know where she was and probably never would. When I hung up the phone I told mom about the call. She needed to know that her little granddaughter would be okay. Then I said I wanted to rest and went to my room.

My mother so accurately describes this time of our lives as grieving. She told me it took all her willpower to stay where she was and not come to me and comfort me, but she knew I wanted to be alone. She said she could hear me weeping in my bedroom and she was weeping as she ironed clothes in the kitchen. I was grieving for my daughter and she was grieving for her daughter and her granddaughter. If I hadn't had my mother and sister to help me and love me and reassure me, I don't know what I would have done. The right decision was very hard to accept. I tried to hide as much of my emotional pain as I possibly could from my mother and sister. They knew what I was going through. It was far easier to deal with my physical pain.

I still had a low-grade temperature when they released me from the hospital. They never should've released me because a temperature is a sign of infection, but I had to get out of there. To walk down that hospital corridor and leave my baby behind was the longest, hardest walk of my life. After I had been home for about two weeks I still had a lot of pain and cramping. I knew something was wrong. Mom drove me to my doctor's appointment. He said the trouble I was having was not normal even with all the trauma I had been through. He wanted to put me in the hospital and do a D & C. When I told mom on the drive home she started to cry, "Haven't you been through enough?" she asked. I went into the hospital and had the surgery. There had been some placenta left from her birth.

After the surgery, at least physically, I began to feel better. Mentally I knew I never would. My mind knew I had done the right thing, but my heart didn't. I wanted to know where she was. I wanted to run back to her, take her in my arms and never let her go. I wondered if this terrible emotional pain would end. Would it ever get easier?

CHAPTER 11

Mary: Child of the King

My Father is rich in houses and lands.
He holdeth the wealth of the world in His hands.
Of rubies and diamonds, of silver and gold,
His coffers are full, He has riches untold.

I'm a child of the King, a child of the King,
With Jesus, my Savior, I'm a child of the King.[8]

By September 1972, our little family size had doubled. Kristin came home to live with us on a Friday night, the last weekend in August. Bill's younger brother, Ken, arrived on Sunday night that same weekend, to start dental school.

I loved being a mom! While Bill and Ken were gone all day at school, I had this new little person to care for and talk to. There was one negative thing I soon noticed, however. There were no recess breaks. The realization dawned on me that we were responsible for Kristi 100% of the time with no time-outs. As I became tired from this new baby schedule, Bill offered to get up with her during the night for her feeding. He had often told me, "I like waking up in the night so I can go back to sleep!" So, hey! Here was a perfect chance for him to do something he liked and also spend a little more cuddling time with the baby. I was grateful!

I felt like Kristi's small size was a special gift to me from the Lord. Since adoption was our way to have children, I had thought my hopes of ever having a small baby, like I had been, were out of the question. We would never have a newborn. But she was so small that I gave Kristi her first baths in a round, plastic dishpan in our kitchen sink. As she grew, she stayed small for her age. Her weight nearly matched her age in months, so that by the time she was two years old, she only weighed twenty-three pounds. Daddy Bill nicknamed her "Small".

Kristi was a good baby, a very contented child. She learned to sit alone when she was five and a half months and didn't bother to crawl until she was nine months. She would sit so long in one spot on her little Raggedy-Ann quilt on the floor, playing with a few toys, that we asked our caseworker if this was normal. He laughed and said, "Don't worry about her. She's just one that takes time to smell the roses."

Just before Kristi began to walk, a week before her first birthday, a friend from church asked me, "Have you started taking her to the library yet?"

I grinned and said, "No."

"It's not too early to start, you know."

So, off the two of us went to a small branch library near our home. Kristi would ride in a stroller or in a child's seat behind me on my bike. I would choose ten books at a time to keep us busy for a week or so, pack them into a blue denim book bag, and we would hurry home to begin looking at them. Kristi learned to love looking at books or listening to them read by me or Bill, cozied up together on the couch or in a big chair.

Both Bill and I thought Kristi was a precocious child. She was talking clearly by the time she was eighteen months old. By twenty months, she could count to ten.

Her favorite book was *Good Morning Farm*. As soon as one of us would begin reading, "Good morning farm!" her little low-pitched voice would chime in, "That's what I say every morning of every day." Then as we read through the book, she would finish off every page from memory.

Kristi was not only talkative, she was also very friendly. She smiled a lot and always greeted strangers with a friendly, "Hi!" at the grocery store as she sat in the cart. During the summer when she turned two, we took a cross-country camping trip to Colorado in our Fastback, with our small blue pop-up trailer behind. She jabbered all the way over and back, often reviewing her colors with large plastic beads. "He'ya go, he'ya go," she would say, naming the color as she held out a bead to me in the front seat from her car seat in the back.

One day, while we were in Colorado, waiting in line to tour a dam, Kristi suddenly disappeared. She was brought back into view a few scary seconds later by an older woman holding her hand. Shaking her head, the woman warned us, "You are going to have to watch out for her. She's so friendly. She would probably go with just about anybody."

We thanked her profusely, saying, "She is pretty sociable!"

Since I liked music and singing, I bought and borrowed records for Kristi to listen to. I also taught her to sing. When she was three years old, she could sing well with a good sense of pitch. She could even stay on tune singing, "The wise man built his house upon a rock . . ." while she turned the handle to her Jack-in-the-box which was playing "All around the mulberry bush, the monkey chased the weasel . . .!"

Besides "Jesus Loves Me", one of the first songs my parents had taught me was "A Child Of The King." Because Kristi was adopted, there was never a question about to Whom she belonged. Early on I taught her "A Child Of The King" as well.

Sometime in January 1976, when Kristi was three, we adopted a baby boy we named Brian, again through Bethany. He had bright blue eyes, blond hair, and had weighed nine pounds, seven ounces at birth! He was even bigger eight weeks later when he came to live with us— quite a big contrast to the tiny baby Kristi had been. Brian was about as loud as he was large, so he demanded my attention. My one-on-one time with Kristi was reduced considerably, but we still managed to read books, bake cookies, or do something fun together while he napped or sat in his high chair beside us.

Kristi loved God's creatures of any size. Since Bill and I weren't fond of pets, she had to be content with collections of potato bugs or garden toads. I nick-named her "Bugs". Whatever she collected, including stones, she always took time to carefully name each one.

How soon it seemed that Kristi turned five years old and started kindergarten at St. Paul Lutheran School. Our first baby was already going to school! She posed with Brian for her first-day snapshot on our back patio. She smiled confidently, her rosy complexion now accented with a smattering of freckles across the bridge of her little nose, her short brunette hair shining in the early morning sun as she held her new school bag over one shoulder. She looked ready and eager for school to begin.

Kristi learned to read in kindergarten, so her love for books grew. My love for reading also increased. It seemed I would always have one book or another in progress.

At the same time, I was also forming deeper friendships with several women from our church who were encouraging my spiritual growth through Bible study, seminars, and personal reading. As I read Christian authors and interacted with my older friends, I began to realize there was something missing in my spiritual life. There was something they had that I didn't, but I didn't know just what it was. There seemed to be a stirring, a hunger in my soul.

A few of these godly women discerned my need and began to pray for me. Then in the fall of 1977, they encouraged me to enter into a curriculum of my own: the study of the person, work, and power of the Holy Spirit. After more reading, prayer and consultation with our friends and pastor, both Bill and I surrendered to the Lordship of Jesus Christ. We prayed together to specifically ask the Holy Spirit to take complete control of our lives—a prayer that marked the beginning of a lifelong transformation.

It was that same year that Bill and I began to pursue Bethany for still another child. Since we had already been given two infants, the agency asked us to consider other options: perhaps an older child or one from another country. We carefully thought about the options they presented, but we both felt an infant would be the best for the four of us.

Then, nearly a year after our original request to adopt a third child, our caseworker called Bill at his office one day in December, 1978. "Bill, would you consider an infant with a Dutch-Hispanic background? We have been working with a couple of cases like that. Would you be interested if either of these babies is released?"

Knowing I had my heart set on another baby, Bill answered, "We sure would! But would you call Mare at home and ask her, so she can enjoy the excitement of hearing this good news directly from you?"

When I heard the caseworker's voice on the phone and then listened to what he was asking, I eagerly answered, "Yes! Oh, wow! Another baby! Just what we wanted!"

He called back a week later, on Brian's third birthday, just before Christmas, to say one of the babies had been released. He described a five-week old, dark-haired, brown-eyed, beautiful baby girl. We would name her Susan Joy.

All four of us went to Bethany the day after Christmas, eager to meet Susie. Susie came home to live with us only a few days later, the day after Kristi was a flower girl in her Aunt Linda's wedding. It was certainly a big week for a six-year-old! Big sister Kristi was the first to get Susie to smile.

By the time we had three children, Uncle Ken had graduated and no longer lived with us. Bill had finished graduate school and was now working as a teacher at the School of Dentistry. Bill was busy, but he always took time to cuddle up and read books to the kids after supper.

Being a student at the Lutheran school required Kristi to recite a weekly Bible passage from memory. Bill usually helped her with that while I helped the younger kids get ready for bed.

Just about every Saturday morning, Kristi would come into our bedroom and climb into our bed with her Dad, as I got up. She would say, "Tell me the story about me, Dad." Then he would slowly begin the story of how we had wanted a baby so badly and how God had arranged it so that she could be our first child. Then he would add: "And remember this, Kristi, you were adopted twice, once by us, but also by God. You're His kid, and don't ever forget it!" She never tired of that story.

CHAPTER 12

Paula: Be Happy, Little One

Mike never wanted to talk about her. I should have heard a warning in the words of his proposal, "After this is all over and we are back home in Iowa . . . ."

Another warning flag appeared when he came to see me the day after she was born. I asked, "Have you seen her?"

"No, why?" he asked.

"She is so beautiful." I started to cry.

"When we leave here and get back to Iowa you'll feel better. Being in totally different surroundings will help you put all this behind you. It will all be in the past and you can start to forget." He was sitting on a chair next to my bed watching people walk by in the hall. "Once I finish college and we are married, I'll be able to get a good job. After a couple of years we can buy a house, and then we can think about having children." He sounded like he was talking to himself, like it was a terrible thing for me to have to go through, but it was over now. In the past. All emotions and feelings would be left behind in Michigan, as if they wouldn't exist in Iowa. In Mike's mind, simply not talking or thinking about it would be like it never happened. I guess that was why he wanted to leave Michigan as soon as possible after my little daughter was born. To him the final papers I signed were a release form, a conclusion. We were now free to leave it all behind. We could breathe a sigh of relief and head back to Iowa where no one knew except my family. A new beginning toward a new future. Life to Mike seemed to be a series of beginnings and ends.

Coming to Michigan to be with me was a beginning for him, and leaving Michigan to go back to Iowa would be the end to that beginning. To him, what had happened in the past year had no place anywhere in our future. I knew nothing was further from the truth for me.

She was all I thought about. I was only me on the outside. I appeared like the same person to everyone else. Only the people who really knew me the best, my mother and my sister, could see the truth inside me. I also could see it when I gazed in the mirror. Although my outward appearance looked like me, I was changed. Inside I was totally numb, empty, drained. Nothing mattered to me. I went along with everyone and everything because I just didn't care anymore. I followed along with whatever happened. Truthfully, somewhere way back deep in my mind, I wanted to blame Mike. After she was born I wanted him to come to my room and tell me I couldn't possibly give up that beautiful baby girl for adoption. I wanted him to say he loved us both and that he wanted to marry me and he would be her father. Of course, that didn't happen. It was a beautiful dream, but it was just that, a dream. I didn't blame him really. He never once said, or even hinted at anything of the sort. The decision was totally mine to make, and the decision I would make would be right. Terribly hard, but right. I could talk to my mom and my sister. I always had an understanding shoulder to cry on, even if it wasn't Mike's.

I do believe he loved me, and I said I loved him. I couldn't picture myself with anyone else. I guess, because he had been there, he was a link to the past I couldn't let go. Instead, I followed numbly along. I met his family, all wonderful people. I was very comfortable with all of them, especially his mother. Mike and I got engaged when he gave me a ring, even though he had first proposed to me in Michigan. Then he headed back to Iowa City for his last year of college. Mike was a very intelligent man, graduating in just three years. His majors were accounting and finance. He loved politics and following the stock market and wanted very much to have a career in either state or federal government.

It was a beautiful fall day in mid-September, a Tuesday, when he called, "I'm planning to come home this weekend," he said. "I really miss you. Do you think we should wait until after I graduate to get married?"

"I don't care." I answered truthfully. "It doesn't matter to me."

"I'll be home Friday afternoon. Shall we get married Saturday? I really want you to go back to Iowa City with me Sunday." He sounded eager, and I knew he really did want to be with me.

"Okay, that's fine." I replied.

Once again I was giving my poor mom shocking news. Pat's wedding took months to plan and prepare for. We had four days. Mom said "What about a dress?"

"Let's go get one," I answered. We came home that afternoon with a dress. A lady Mom knew put together some flowers. The church and pastor were available. I wore my sister's veil and, as my maid of honor, she wore my prom dress. We got married on Saturday. We had a small reception at a very nice local restaurant. The next day we went back to Iowa City together. Mike looked nervous as we got married. I wasn't at all nervous, nor did I have second thoughts. It was only a couple of months after my baby's birth, and I didn't really care what happened. To me this was no big deal. I existed in a world of unreality.

After he graduated, we moved to Des Moines. He had been offered a very good job working for the state of Iowa. We bought a beautiful house with all new furniture. He started his job, and we settled in. I had no great expectations of married life. To me it was one of the required steps to having a baby. A couple of months later I said to Mike, "You finished college, we're married, you have a good job. We bought this beautiful house. We're well off with no financial worries. Now let's talk about having a baby, okay?"

"I'm not ready," he replied. Nothing more and nothing less. Just, "I'm not ready." I thought perhaps he wanted to be more secure in his job. After all, he had only been there for a short time. I decided to wait a little longer before I brought the subject up again.

I didn't work for quite awhile. This was a mistake on my part. Alone at home all day, I wondered and worried about my baby. What did she look like now? Where was she? Maybe Des Moines? Would I see her with her adoptive mother on the street? Was she okay? Had she developed some disease, and because she was so small, couldn't fight it off? I thought I was losing my mind.

The period of time between buying the house and going to work seemed especially hard for me. I sat alone all day in this beautiful three bedroom split-level house, but it was just that, a house—not a "home". My "home" was still a small two bedroom trailer filled with warmth and love, tears and compassion. A place where I could talk about my feelings freely to people who listened and truly loved me. It was so cold and lonesome there in my beautiful new house.

Financially I didn't have to work, but when a neighbor who worked at Des Moines General Hospital told me they needed part time help I jumped at the chance. The first day at work they asked if I could work all day for a week or so. I was there almost six years.

Every summer Pam and her family traveled to visit her mom in Doon, Iowa. She always arranged to stop on their way. I was so happy when Pam and Anthony came. I noticed Pam was still wearing the ring Anthony had given her. That made me feel good. Conversation was strained and uncomfortable around Mike, as he was still ignoring the past like it never happened. I needed desperately to talk about my baby girl. It was so hard to keep it all inside. Pam and I had to take a walk so we could talk freely to each other. "I wonder where she is, Pam." I said. "I pray she's a happy, healthy baby and that she is okay. I wonder what she looks like. Oh, Pam, I love her and I miss her so much."

"I think she must look like you, Paula." Pam replied, "I know you are hurting and the pain you carry deep inside is terrible to bear, but always remember, Paula, you did the right thing. God will take care of her. He will take care of us all." As always, Pam not only heard my words, she heard the pain in my heart as well. She felt how unhappy I was. I didn't need to tell her. It was wonderful to release the emotions and feelings only she could know. I could feel her heartache for me as we held each other close, and her words, "I love you, Paula," came straight from her heart.

After about a year and a half of marriage, Mike decided it was time to have a baby. When we had no results after a year, we decided to see a doctor; there must be something wrong. With all the problems and trauma I had undergone in the past, it was natural for the doctors to assume the problem was with me. When all my test results looked fine, Mike was tested. The problem was with him. What was tragic news to me didn't seem to bother him at all. As ironic as it seemed, we couldn't have children. The precious baby I had given up for adoption would be my only one. I was devastated. I had been on both sides now—the pain of giving up a child, and the pain of not being able to have a child. I knew adopting a child was out of the question. His words, "I could never raise another man's child," echoed in my memory. After thinking long and hard about the situation, I realized it really wasn't "a" child I was yearning for. I didn't really want "another" baby, I wanted her. There wasn't any substitute for her. After that understanding came to me, I was okay with not having any more children.

After four years of marriage, we finally admitted to each other that neither of us was happy, and this marriage wasn't going to work. Mike and I were nowhere near compatible. To me the most important thing in the world was family and friends, not money. If I had money I would much rather use it to help someone else who needed it more than I did. To Mike there was nothing more important than money. This man, who was by all standards rich, hated to spend a dime. I just could not understand that. If I went shopping and bought something, I would put it on and show him. He always had two things to say: "How much did it cost?" and, "Can you take it back?" He never wanted to go anywhere or do anything, and I didn't want to sit at home all the time. I joined a bowling league with some girls I worked with, and it was a lot of fun. Also on weekends I enjoyed going shopping with my cousin, Loris, mostly just to get out of the house. But Mike didn't care for that because I was likely to spend money.

One Saturday Loris and I planned to go to the mall. It was my turn to drive. Mike, as usual, was angry about my going.

"I don't plan to spend any money," I told him.

"You're not taking my car," he replied angrily.

I didn't say anymore. I called Loris and she picked me up. Our first stop was a car dealership. When I got home that afternoon I no longer needed to take his car. I drove my own.

We had separated for a short time once before, but had decided to give our marriage another try. It didn't get any better. One evening after dinner Mike and I were sitting in the living room watching television. He sat on the couch reading the newspaper, and I sat across the room in my recliner thinking about our relationship. It was getting so bad we were arguing about what to have for dinner. It was time to do something. I couldn't live like this any longer. "We need to talk," I said to Mike.

"Yes, I think so too," he answered quietly.

"Are you happy?" I asked.

"No," he answered, "are you?"

"No," I sighed. "It's not getting any better, is it?"

He put his newspaper down and looked at me, "No."

I was close to tears, "I just can't do this anymore." I left the room and packed a few things in a small suitcase. As I walked to the door he warned, "If you walk through that door, you're not coming back."

"I don't plan to," I answered and closed the door behind me.

I moved in with a friend from work, Cathy. When I called and told Mom, she wasn't surprised. She knew Mike and I had been separated, and she knew we had tried. When I told her she said to me, "How can I be happy if you're not?" Again, my mother's love and concern was there for me. I stayed with my friend for a short time and then got my own apartment.

Des Moines General Hospital, where I worked, was having some duct work done. One of the sheet metal workers was John Huston. It soon became apparent that John and my friend, Alice, had "eyes" for each other. One evening they had plans to meet at a local club. He didn't know for sure what time he could be there, and she didn't want to wait alone, so Alice asked me to go with her, at least until John got there. Knowing he was going to be later than he thought, he asked his brother, Kenny, to sit with us. Kenny and I took an instant dislike to each other. He was incredibly handsome, with dark hair, brown eyes and a beautiful smile. It was obvious he had no trouble meeting women. It was also obvious that he knew it. I thought he was self-centered and arrogant, so after the introductions, I pretty much ignored him and centered my attention on other people in the room. I'm sure that's why he thought I was a snob. For that evening at least, we were both right.

Another very good friend of mine, Candy, was going through the process of a divorce. We had worked together at the hospital for nearly four years. We had become really close friends, to the point of knowing each other's thoughts and feelings. God had blessed me again with a lifelong friend, and we decided to share my apartment. After her divorce was final, she started seeing one of Kenny's best friends, Jim. By that time Kenny and I had seen through arrogance and snob and really liked what we saw underneath. Learning more about Kenny through his brother, John, and watching him interact with people completely changed my opinion of him. He was extremely compassionate and generous. He was divorced and had custody of his three children, Shawn, age thirteen, Teresa, age twelve, and Michael, age eight. He and his children lived with his mother. We enjoyed each other's company and spent as much time together as we possibly could.

During the time Candy and I shared an apartment, she became pregnant with Jim's baby. They were planning to marry but hadn't picked a date yet. Though this pregnancy was unexpected, it was a very happy time as her doctor had told her it was unlikely she would ever have children. She and I lived together through her pregnancy.

At this point no one knew about my daughter. I had her safely tucked away in my mind and my heart. I carried her with me every day, but I would not share her with anyone, not even Candy. My baby was mine alone. Even though I never told her, I did know what Candy was feeling physically day by day, and the emotions she was feeling. There was never a question in her mind. Candy knew she would keep her baby. I was not at all jealous about that. Her circumstances were one hundred percent different than mine had been. Jim loved Candy and wanted to be as close to her as he could throughout the pregnancy. He wanted to be her husband. This baby was an unexpected blessing for her and Jim. Candy's decision never made me doubt my own. I knew I had done the right thing.

When Candy was in labor, Jim and I took her to the hospital. Now I was on the other side of the birthing process as Jim and I stuck it out in the waiting room. I learned what it was like on the father's side of that door. It was bad. A lot less painful, but bad. I knew what she was going through and the pain she was in, and Jim and I were worried about her health and the health of the baby. Candy finally gave birth to a perfect little baby girl, Melissa Christine. I was so happy for her. Although Kenny and I were just dating, I was proud when Jim and Candy named us as Missy's godparents.

Around the time Missy was born, Kenny and I were getting pretty serious in our relationship. I knew before things went much further I would tell him about my little girl, but I just wasn't ready yet. My oldest brother, Phil, took the decision out of my hands. He was in Des

Moines visiting for a couple of days. I was in my apartment, and he and Kenny were down by the pool. Phil was being exactly what he was, my brother looking after me. He was making sure all was well with me and making sure Kenny's intentions were clear, and making sure that my having a baby made no difference in his feelings for me. Phil also assumed I had told him.

I didn't know about this pool side conversation until that evening when Kenny and I were alone. He just out of the blue said to me, "Why did you give her up for adoption?"

I was taken completely by surprise. "Maybe someday I'll tell you about it." I walked out and stood on the balcony. After a little while he came out. He put his arm around me and we just stood there in silence for a long time. When I finally got my emotions under control enough to talk, I told him all about her.

"Why didn't you tell me before?" he asked, "Why haven't you talked to anyone about this?"

"It's too hard for me to talk about. I don't want to share her or anything about her with anyone. I would have told you when I thought the time was right." She was the one thing I loved most in the whole world, and she was mine. She was a very important part of my heart. That evening she became a part of his heart too. That is where we kept her, sharing her with no one else, not even with his children.

At first I was very upset with my brother. Then I realized he had only done what he did because he loved me. He loved me enough to take Kenny aside and make sure his sister was not going to be harmed in any way by this. I have always loved my brother. After this I loved him even more.

Kenny's children were very important to me. In a very short time I loved them all. They were a part of Kenny, and I wanted them to be a part of me also. When we started talking marriage I had to be sure the kids approved. One evening after Kenny had left for home, his son Shawn called me at my apartment. "Dad told us he asked you to marry him," he said.

"Yes he did," I answered, "but I want to know what you kids think."

"That's why I'm calling you. We talked about it and we want you to marry him." Well, that was good enough for me! Kenny and I got married on October 22, 1977. Candy stood up for me, and when she and Jim got married about a year later, I stood up for her. Kenny and I bought a real nice four-bedroom house and the five of us moved in. I was twenty-five years old and I finally had a home and a family. Knowing the kids loved me and approved of our marriage and having had stepbrothers and a stepsister made being a stepmom a lot less scary than I thought it would be.

I knew Kenny had had a vasectomy many years before. He told me when we first started seeing each other. I knew there would be no children. Even so, I found myself irrationally thinking about having a baby. Kenny often said he also wished we could have a child. I cried on his shoulder often. At one point he told me he would have a reverse vasectomy if it meant so much to me. My stepdaughter Teresa told me later that she had heard me crying while Kenny and I were talking in our bedroom.

"I thought you wanted a new baby because you didn't love us," she admitted.

"I didn't mean to sound like I wanted a baby because I didn't love you," I explained. Because I did love you, and I still do. Very much!" I looked right into her big beautiful brown eyes, "Teresa, if I didn't love you, I never would've married your father." She understood then and we shared a hug.

Kenny was thirty-five years old and I knew a vasectomy reversal was not the answer. It was just like before, I wanted a baby, but not just any baby. I wanted my baby. She was in my heart and mind, and my empty arms still ached for her. I could not picture her as a five-year-old child. She was still that tiny beautiful baby girl that I had only briefly seen and had never even held. After a while I got a grip, by remembering my thoughts and feelings when Mike and I were faced with the fact that we would have no children. Once again I was trying to replace something that was irreplaceable. It couldn't be done. I loved Shawn, Teresa, and Michael and they loved me. They were beautiful children, inside and out, and I was proud to be their mom.

Shawn had blond hair and brown eyes. He was always rather quiet and more reserved than Teresa and Michael. He tended to hold things inside and deal with them himself. I could relate to that. He played baseball, and he was very good. Kenny and I stood in the stands and screamed right along with all the other parents. It was always amazing how stupid the referees could be when they were calling a play on our son.

Teresa was a beautiful little girl. She was petite with big brown eyes and long dark hair. She was very "domestic", always picking up after her brothers, doing dishes, laundry, and even cooking. She was a tremendous help to me, always willing and eager to help. She was happy to have her own room and kept it neat and clean. She had one of the downstairs bedrooms. It was easier to have the boys upstairs where we could just shut the door.

Michael was the very image of his father, with his dark hair and eyes. He was outgoing and good natured. He had never had his own room so it took some time for him to adjust. He had the bedroom directly above ours. There were times when I heard him crying late at night, and I would go to him. "It's okay Michael, I'm right here." I would say. He never admitted that he was scared, but he would say "Mom, will you stay with me until I go to sleep?" Which I gladly did. I would lie beside him, and in a few minutes he would fall asleep. He loved contact sports. He played soccer when he was younger, and wrestling and football in high school. I learned how terrified a mother could feel seeing her son lying motionless on the football field!

Every year on my daughter's birthday I cried. No matter where I was or who I was with. To not know where she was or how she was or even what she looked like was torture. Every year I prayed that

God would bless her and keep her safe in His hands. Every year I would say "Happy Birthday, little one. Be happy. I love you."

Time went on and the years passed.

CHAPTER 13

Kristin: The Story of Me

Childhood Saturday mornings, as early as I can remember, would always begin the same way. I would go into my parents' room and find them talking quietly. I would interrupt their chat by jumping onto the middle of their double bed. A tickle-fight was sure to follow, along with hugs and kisses. My mom would slip on her robe and head to the kitchen to start breakfast.

"Tell me a story!" I would plead.

"What story?" my father would ask innocently, with a smile, pretending I didn't always give the same answer. Invariably I would reply, "Tell me the story of ME!"

We would settle into the pillows and he would begin. "Mom and I had enough love for more than two people, and we wanted to have a little girl like you in our family. So we called Bethany Christian Home and talked to one of the caseworkers there. We had to wait and wait a very long time. It seemed like forever! Finally, we got a call from the caseworker. There was a little girl who needed a mom and dad."

"And it was ME!" I would pipe up excitedly, unable to stand the suspense.

Dad's face would break into a big grin. "And it was YOU! We packed up our car and drove to Bethany, and there we saw you, Kristi, for the first time. You were so little, but you were a dandy!" And on it would go, detailing how they drove to Bethany to see me but couldn't take me home right away, how they signed court documents and told the courts and adoption agency what my name would be for the final birth certificate. They even left a little white outfit for me to wear home. Dad told how they went again and picked me up in their bright orange Volkswagen (I slept the whole way) and took me home, stopping on the way to meet my new grandpas and grandmas, aunts and uncles. What a happy introduction that was! The "Story of Me" always ended with my father's voice saying, "Before we even knew you, we loved you."

I was the first grandchild of my mother's parents, and the second of my father's. I grew up loved, surrounded at every conceivable "occasion" (birthdays, Christmas get-togethers, holidays, and summer sleepovers) by a dozen aunts and uncles and, eventually, sixteen cousins. When we weren't having fun with our extended family, we had our own fun at home.

We sometimes watched shows on our small black and white television in the living room. One commercial in particular always caught my attention. It was a jingle about whole wheat bread, and included a cartoon character that I liked named "Mr. Bread". Later, while mom cooked dinner and did dishes, I decided to make a picture of him. I climbed into my chair and sat where I often sat while I colored or painted—at our kitchen table with my back to the sliding glass doors that led to our patio and backyard.

Mom always tried to encourage my creativity. She was creative herself. "Momma, I need brown paper," I told her. "Mr. Bread is brown, so I need brown paper." We didn't have any brown paper in the house, so she handed me a grocery bag. Brown paper. It worked for me. "Thank You! Now this is what my friend Mr. Bread looks like," and I gave him a blue sweater and yellow hat.

Mom and I did everything together when I was little. We wore her handmade aprons to bake cookies and cakes, always sampling the dough and licking the bowl. We took long walks, Mom pushing me in my stroller, to the schoolyard "park" down the street or to the library where we would take out ten to fifteen books at a time. There was a pet store along the way that I loved to stop at and admire the talking parrot and gaze longingly at the squirming kittens. We didn't have a pet while I was young, but there was a good reason: we were campers.

Every summer before I went to school or as soon as school let out we were off, heading west, usually, sometimes east or north, but always camping! We went to the Grand Canyon, Nova Scotia, Florida, World Expo in Vancouver, and other faraway places. We stayed for a while on a dairy farm, and I played with the barn cats, tasted whole milk, and watched the birth of a calf. Sometimes we stayed closer to home, like Green Lake at Interlochen, or Muskegon State Park. I loved every trip because I loved nature—from rocks and rivers to bugs and the thousands of thirteen-striped ground squirrels that populate the western states. Each evening, my dad would pull out whatever Chronicles of Narnia book we were on and read a chapter or two by the dim trailer light while we lay in our sleeping bags and imagined C. S. Lewis's magical world. When we camped in the mountains, and the sky was especially clear and bright with stars, my dad would wake me up and carry me out in my pajamas to show me the beauty of the constellations. I loved dipping my hand into the clear, ice-cold mountain streams, and drinking the fresh, sweet-tasting water. I loved camping—relaxing, reading, swimming, exploring, spending time outdoors, and especially Turtle Hunting.

No magnet ever drew children like a "turtle hollow". It's the murky end of the lake, swarming with dragonflies and mosquitoes. It's the boat trapping place, shallow and dense with lily pads and tall reeds, and ringing with the cries of indignant red-winged blackbirds. Once I learned the joy of capturing my first turtle, leaning far over the side of the rowboat with my net, my father holding tight to the back strap of my bright orange life preserver, I was forever hooked. I found it humorous to compare my parents' hunting styles—my mom's excited "There! Over there! Turn to the left, Bill! Quick! Kris, grab the net!" to my father's ever-calm "There's a turtle. On the right. Just went down." He never raised his voice or got excited, but he caught more than his share! Almost every summer, it seemed, we came home with three or more turtle-pets. They lived in a baby bathtub on the back porch, received daily feedings of worms, flies and bologna, and were released in the creek when fall arrived. If we didn't bring home turtles, we at least had a good turtle adventure story to share!

When it was too cold to camp, my mom and I made snowmen and angels in the snow. She read me countless books that became favorites—*Good Morning Farm*, *The Velveteen Rabbit*, and *Charlotte's Web*. We had tea parties with my dolls and animals over a cardboard box table on the back patio. She taught me to use my natural talents in art and to be creative. I drew pictures, sometimes of the characters in the stories she read, like Curious George. I cut out magazine pictures and glued them to construction paper with macaroni accents. I painted pictures of my family and our blue tent trailer while she fixed dinner for my dad and Uncle Ken. My mother was appalled by the fact that when her back was turned, Uncle Ken let me watch the "Three Stooges" on TV with him. She was mortified at what a terrible influence they would be on young, impressionable me. I loved them!

Mom and I listened to records over and over again until I knew hundreds of songs by heart. I especially enjoyed songs by Evie. *The Music Machine* and *Peter And The Wolf* were also favorites. Even in the car on our way to the grocery store, we would sing together.

> *Little children, little children who love their Redeemer*
> *Are His jewels, precious jewels, His loved and His own.*
> *Like the stars of the morning, His bright crown adorning,*
> *They shall shine in their beauty, bright gems for His crown.*[9]

Another favorite was "A Child Of The King." My mom always told me I was a child of the King. By example and encouragement, she taught me the wonderful expression of song.

When I was three and a half, my brother Brian was adopted into our family. Three years later my sister Susie arrived. We got along as well as most siblings, playing "house" or "rocket ship" in the basement, or climbing the monkey bars and building matchbox car villages in the sandbox. My mom's time and attention were no longer exclusively mine. I began to enjoy spending time alone. Maybe it was when they came that I began to pull away a little. Maybe it was just that I was at the age of becoming, reasoning, and beginning to think for myself.

We had a birthday tradition around our house when we were little. Not only the birthday child got presents, but the other two kids received small gifts also. Mom and Dad would hide the gifts in different rooms and then write up small clues, which would send us careening through the halls, with flashlights, in search of treasures. It was a race to the first present, and the clue there would tell us where to go to find the next one. We always had cake and ice cream, and every year Mom would make some creative shape with our cake. One year I had a butterfly with yellow coconut wings. My brother had a clown with a red candy nose, and my sister's teddy bear cake had a bright bow tie. The inside was always chocolate or marble fudge! Our family would sit down to dinner, and my Dad would pray for us on our special day—thanks for the safe and happy year past, for the fine kids we were turning into, and asking for continued blessings in the year to come. I would feel pride and a quiet awe as he would always add, "Be with Kristi's birth mother on this day. We don't know where she is but we thank You for her. Bless her this year too, and thanks that Kristi is in our family. She's a special kid, and we love her. And we love You, too, God. Amen."

I had many good friends, including Julie, Jenny, and Michelle. I spent much time playing with each of them, cooling off in the little plastic pool we set up in the backyard, finding pretty rocks to polish, playing dolls or Barbie on the sidewalk, watching cartoons, reading and writing little stories. It didn't come up too often in my younger years, because it really didn't matter, but most of my friends knew I was adopted.

Our adoptions were never hidden from others, but they weren't overdone either. Sometimes people knew within twenty minutes that I was adopted. Sometimes they were astounded after three years. It was a comfortable subject for my family to discuss, but it wasn't something we needed to talk about very often. If it was pertinent to the person or the conversation, we freely discussed it. If not, it didn't come up at all.

I never really knew what a true "blood" sibling was, or if I would have been closer to mine if we were really "related". My brother and sister and I never had major fights, and in our younger years we played together well and often, but I never felt very connected to either of them. I looked at my friends, a family of six sisters who got along amazingly well. They never argued, and seemed close enough to read each other's minds. They had a special bond with each other. For a while I thought I was an awful person because I could feel such irritation with my brother and sister. It took me years to realize that a blood relation doesn't necessarily mean automatic love, closeness or fondness.

To me, my adoption made me someone different. It was something that set me apart from all of my friends and neighbors. I understood that it meant that I came from "somewhere else", and I took pride in the fact that while everyone else was the same, I was unique. I stood apart with a special secret, and though the specifics of it eluded me I could see the difference between others and myself.

I did help create that distance. I set myself apart, waiting for that "missing piece" to fall in. I retreated, and as I came of age to know myself, I backpedaled into myself. I didn't want to be like everyone else. I wanted to be different, and adoption was my way.

When I was nine, we moved to the Grand Rapids area. It was summer, and I would begin fourth grade in the fall in a new school. That same year my Grandma died, my mother's mom. The move separated me further from my friends and established relationships. I burrowed deeper into my own world, and rediscovered the joy of reading. Books were a safe fantasy world. I could step out of my reality, and into another life. I could get involved with no risk. I could be anywhere. I shut out the shouts and laughter of my brother and sister playing outside on their bikes with their new neighborhood friends, and devoured book after book upstairs in my room. Five years after we moved into our house, our next door neighbors were shocked to hear my brother mention me, saying, "We never even knew you had an older sister!"

I wanted to see myself behind a shield, needing no one. I was shy, but convinced myself I was tough. In my mind I stood apart, untouched by those around me. Mom and Dad paired off, my brother and sister played together, and I lived, content, in my own quiet world.

When psychologists talk about adoption, they often mention the "empty hole" or "missing piece". I wondered about my origins. "What made me me?" I was contemplative, analyzing everything, half the time denying that the adoption and my missing past were part of what had made me strong. Because my past—which I believed formed a person– -was gone, I needed to form myself. I wanted to be strong, needing nothing. Needing no one. Perhaps subconsciously I was saying I didn't need her, my birth mother, the one who chose to leave me. One of my favorite poems was called "Comes The Dawn," author unknown. I liked how the poet said to plant your own garden, and decorate your own soul, instead of waiting for someone else to bring you flowers. I was decorating my own soul. I was me—I was enough.

I did think about her, though. Occasionally people would ask me how I felt about being adopted, whether I thought I would ever meet her, or if I even wanted to. It forced me to wonder, and I was never sure how to answer. Usually to their questions, I would shrug my shoulders and say, "I don't know. I've never been 'not adopted'." I knew someday I would meet her again, but I couldn't explain how I knew, so I would just say, "Maybe, someday. I'd like to."

I always wished I had a twin. I wished someone were there set aside with me, someone who could read my mind and understand me, someone who looked like me and felt like me. Growing up I often heard "You look just like your mother!" which would cause us to chuckle and would confuse the complimentor. I did resemble my mother, our hair color and size were similar—but we didn't really look the same. We didn't see ourselves when looking at each other. I did love the idea that there must be someone out there who has my eyes, and if she looks like me and is related to me, she must see and think and feel like me. She was the bonded soul mate, the person/piece I was missing, but she wasn't my twin.

I never thought I needed another mother. I had a wonderful, loving, tenderhearted, compassionate mother right where I was. We had the usual struggles growing up, but I never once considered her less than my mother. We had a special bond that comes with honesty, a love born not from my physical birth, but from commitment, the "getting to know you". I loved her and appreciated all of the books read, games played, time spent, and honest conversations we had.

As I headed into my teens I used her less and less as a confidante. I believe this separation occurs in almost every mother-daughter relationship in the growing up years. It's the growing up itself. It's the becoming you. For me, this separation was probably wider, because I wanted so much to be self-sufficient, on my own.

During these years, I consciously put my birth mother away, planning to deal with her later. I didn't picture her as a parent. I saw her as a young unwed woman. Even when she must have been thirty-five, I saw her as eighteen. I expected her to still be eighteen. Sometimes I wondered where she was, if she was married, if she had any other children. I simply didn't know anything about her. Did she remember me often? Was she happy? She might be in pain somewhere, still dealing with having to give me up. It made me uncomfortable to imagine her hurting for any reason, but there was nothing I could do, so I tried not to think about it. I had enough to deal with—growing up. I still answered any questions airily, "Oh, yes, I'm sure someday I will meet her again." In a way, it was like anticipating a vacation—the more you dwell on it, the longer it takes to get there. I chose not to dwell on imaginations of meeting my birth mother because I had years before it could happen anyway.

The oddest part was that I really did know I would meet her again someday. Maybe she promised me so in that first hour of my life, or even earlier, as I kicked her awake at night before I was born. Maybe I could feel our twin-link-thread still connected—I quietly, confidently knew we would someday reunite. I was biding my time, going about the business of becoming me. When the time was right, we would be together again.

CHAPTER 14

Mary: The King's Kid

Jesus said,
"Let the little children come to me,
and do not hinder them,
for the kingdom of God
belongs to such as these."

Luke 18:16 (NIV)

Since I had been the oldest of four children, I had not spent much one-on-one time with my mom while growing up. I decided I wanted that to be different with my kids and me.

As Kristi got older, our friendship grew. She was a wonderful mother's helper and since we both loved books, music, and creative projects, we found many activities to share. However, even though we were growing closer together, I always had a haunting thought in the back of my mind: somewhere out there was another mother who might someday enter our picture.

Articles of birthparent/adopted person reunions were showing up more and more in the newspapers in that world of confidential adoptions. Both birth parents and those adopted were becoming more assertive in their desire to meet each other. Also, a friend of my brother Mark had recently searched for and found his birth mother.

My mother said, "I'm wondering if you might have that happen with your kids someday." She encouraged me to allow it to happen.

With the possibility of reunion in mind, I had purposed from the start to be prepared. I had put together not just one family photo album, but also an individual album for each child. I thought that if I were a birth mom, I would be eager to see what my child looked like and what he or she did through the growing up years. Also selfishly, I thought if a reunion ever did occur, the family album wouldn't leave the house or need to be dismantled.

In the spring of 1980, when Kristi was still only seven years old, I was asked to do a book review at church for the Adult Education Class. The book I reviewed was *If I Die at Thirty* by Meg Woodson. The book records fifteen conversations between the mother, Meg, and her daughter, Peg, as they faced the possible reality of Peg's early death from cystic fibrosis.

In preparation for the review, I found myself relating in two ways: as a daughter but also as a mother. Since my mom had recently been diagnosed with breast cancer, I identified closely as a daughter with the threat of an early death of my mom and the beauty of open, honest communication which was beginning to blossom between us. I also empathized with Meg, as a mother, who thought about how protective of herself she had become, never really allowing herself to get too emotionally close to her daughter, guarding her heart from a future loss. I realized then that although I didn't think about separation by death of a child, I did think about the possibility of separation from Kristi or one of the other kids by a possible reunion with one of their birth parents. I realized I was failing to live intimately today because of my thoughts and fears of "what ifs" for tomorrow. I resolved from then on to try to be God's best mom I could possibly be for Kristi and our other kids.

About this same time, Bill and I became aware of the Lord's gentle leading to move back to the Grand Rapids area. Bill had been called by a couple of different dentists asking if he might consider starting a private practice there. We prayerfully investigated the possibility and Bill found some oral surgeons and other specialists who had imminent plans to build an office complex in Grandville, just outside of Grand Rapids. They thought a prosthodontist, like Bill, would be a welcome addition to the group. With mixed feelings of sadness to leave our close friends in Ann Arbor as well as eagerness to live closer to our relatives, we began making plans to move in the summer of 1981.

While thinking about moving, I wondered if any of our kids' birth parents might be from Grandville. I called our caseworker at Bethany to ask.

After a quick look at the files, he answered, "No, Kristin's birth mom was from Iowa. No problem there. The other two were from the west Michigan Lakeshore area."

I felt relieved because I could just imagine us moving next door to one of the kids' parents or grand-parents! We both thought the kids were all too young for mixed loyalties.

Our move from Ann Arbor to Grandville in July was a relatively smooth transition in spite of the fact that Bill had to commute between the two cities the year before as well as the year after the move. He did that to gradually let go of his patients in the small practice he had begun in Ann Arbor while slowly building up his practice in his new location.

Kristi was about to celebrate her ninth birthday soon after our move. She was eager to live closer to both sets of grandparents. My mom had been declared cancer-free in the previous January after undergoing chemotherapy and radiation following her mastectomy. Our family never had lived near any of our relatives, so we were all looking forward to it.

But my hopes for time with my mom barely materialized. My mom was able to share the joy of the move in July, but by Labor Day, the cancer had reappeared, having moved to her liver. She became very sick, and by mid-January 1982, she was gone. Kristi and I both suffered loss and grief in her passing, compounded by our recent move. We both missed the shelter of old friends.

By then, adoption had become a common word in our family, but the implications of adoption issues were not really fully known to us—not even to Bill or me as parents. We simply explained adoption as God's way to enable us to have a family. We told Kristi, and later the other kids, that she did not grow within me before her birth, but instead grew within another woman, her birth mother, who for certain reasons was not able to take care of a baby right then. We told her that her birth mother loved her so much that she chose to give her to a family who could care for her and give her the love and attention of two parents. That seemed sufficient.

Birthdays were a big deal at our house. We would celebrate with a favorite meal, a special cake and ice cream for dessert, and a treasure hunt for the hidden birthday gifts. But I would always think of the birth mom the week of the birthday and would pray, "Lord, help her to know that she made a good choice. Give her Your peace." Bill would give thanks before the birthday meal for the gift this child was to our family and for God's blessings on the birth families who were remembering.

In her grief, Kristi had become, in general, a quiet, private child. She asked very few questions and kept her personal thoughts to herself. She continued to enjoy reading and buried herself in books in her room at home or in the car. Wherever we went, Kristi would have an open book in her hands. One particular evening, however, not long after our move, she rode along with me to the grocery store. I was parking the car when she asked me a question: "Mom, what do you know about what happened when I was born?"

Since the information we had was minimal, I simply told her the details I knew while we sat in the car in the darkened parking lot:

"Your birth mom and dad were planning to be married, but when your birth mom got pregnant with you, he left her to face the birth alone."

Kristi began to weep softly and said, "I'm sad that he would do something like that."

I hugged her with tears rolling down my own cheeks and said, "Me too, honey. It must have been really hard for her."

After that brief conversation about her birth parents, she didn't ask anything more about them. We did tell her that Bethany had told us that both her birth mom and birth grandmother had specifically asked that she be placed in a Christian home. We talked regularly about her being a child of the King.

One spring Sunday evening, Kristi asked me how to invite Jesus into her heart. With me as her witness, she prayed, "Dear Lord Jesus, thank you for dying on the cross for me. Please come into my heart today."

She showed the fruit of that decision in specific ways as she grew older and began to mature into a delightful, godly young woman. She and I participated in a mass choir for Alive '85, a revival meeting in the Grand Rapids area. In junior high, Kristi met Jodi, a new friend who also enjoyed singing. The two of them began to sing duets and were asked to sing together in church and chapel services now and then. Kristi's face always radiated joy when she sang in public.

In the summer between junior and senior high school, Kris asked Jodi to spend a week with her at Cran-Hill Ranch, a Christian camp. Both were excited and eager to go. I was finding, however, that letting go of this girl-woman was hard for me. I got a lump in my throat just thinking about her being away from home for a week. To help myself, I wrote her a note the night before she was to leave and left it beside her bed to be found when she woke up. The conclusion of the note read:

> I want you to know that Dad and I will be praying for you this week, for your protection, your friendship with Jodi and others, and especially for your spiritual growth. Just remember whose you are—a child of the King!
>
> Love, Mom

CHAPTER 15

Kristin: The Year My Life Began

I was fourteen the year my "life" began. I first noticed the advertisement in our church bulletin as I sat in the service next to Mom:

> ATTN: High school students. Youth for Christ singing/drama group is seeking members to minister through singing and drama in a group called MAGI. Auditions now being held.

"Mom, I want to be in this group." I whispered decisively, pointing out the announcement in the bulletin. Mom's hazel eyes turned to me with a surprised expression. Given my shy, low-risk personality, Mom and Dad hadn't expected me to "go for it," but I did.

I had been singing duets throughout junior high school in our church and school choir but I was still nervous as I auditioned later that week. Mom played piano while I sang "Be Thou My Vision" in my clear soprano voice. After a few questions, the audition was over. Within a week, the director called, and I had made the group.

MAGI began that year with a musical called *Surrender*. We sang two to three Sundays a month at local churches with practice sessions in between. I made new, older friends (I was the only freshman in this high school group). My mother was nervous. Although she wanted me to make new Christian friends, I had never ventured out so completely and unexpectedly on my own before, and she was concerned for my tender heart.

Being a member of MAGI entered me into a whole new world. Youth for Christ was linked with Campus Life, an outreach into area public schools. I was suddenly busy with a new peer group and new interests. MAGI was giving me a chance to be someone different from the Kristin I was in school. I could suddenly be fun, friendly, and confident. It was a new start, and another chance to be me. I began to come out of my shell and get involved with others more than I ever had before. MAGI gave me a chance to share my talents and do what I loved best besides reading—singing! I grew stronger spiritually and emotionally. I even fell in love for the first time. My life blossomed!

In April, 1987, shortly after I started in MAGI, Youth for Christ sponsored a trip to a Christian music festival in Kentucky called *Ichthus*. Several well-known Christian bands would perform there. My new friends, who had attended similar festivals, talked it up, and I could hardly wait to go. After a little convincing, my parents agreed.

I had become quite close with two young men in my group, Tony and Dennis. Not everyone in MAGI went on the trip, but these two friends did, and to my Mom's dismay, I wanted to travel with them.

"Aren't there any nice girls in MAGI?" Mom asked. I only smiled and nodded, afraid she might change her mind and say no. Instead she simply asked me to finish packing and soon I was on my way to the blue-green mountains of Kentucky.

Tony, Dennis and I traveled with our MAGI director and several other Campus Life teenagers from our area, most of whom I had never met before.

Wilmore, Kentucky was a quaint small town that had been invaded by young people. We all stayed in tents and walked in happy droves to see our favorite Christian musicians perform on the huge outdoor stage set up in a green field. Colored blankets and tarps were spread out over the outdoor area like a crazy quilt while we clapped and cheered for our favorites in the glow of the purple and blue stage lights. Our group's blanket was near a pink lawn flamingo some ingenious teen had brought to make finding their place easier. As we traveled through the crowds eating pizza and drinking soda, we batted at a blue and yellow beach ball circulating the field and hunted for our landmark. When other teenagers asked where we were, I would say, "Two tarps left of the pink flamingo."

It was an awesome, exhilarating weekend and I was happy. We got sunburned and bug-bit and loved every minute of it. My feelings for my friend Tony were growing. At fifteen, a year older than me, he was tall and good looking, with dark hair, and incredible blue eyes. He called me beautiful and held my hand. My heart pounded whenever he looked into my eyes. It was the first day of the festival when he introduced me to Tracey, one of the girls from Michigan traveling with us.

Tracey was almost a year older than me with a shy, yet friendly smile. Her hair was shoulder length and dark compared to my sunny brown curls. She had deep-set green eyes and at five foot, ten inches, she stood five inches taller than me. I thought she was a beautiful girl, but she obviously didn't realize it, and that was part of her beauty.

After about three minutes we were over the usual new-relationship wariness. We quickly sensed a friend in each other and by the second day we were spending most of our time together.

When we walked into town to buy squirt guns, we had to pass by several boys who were rating the girls on a scale of one-to-ten. Tracey was completely insulted that they were "rating" us. We walked quickly by while I appraised them myself and she gave them dirty looks. Ignoring Tracey's visual daggers, they called out their numbers as we passed. I was thrilled. "I got an eight!" I told her as we walked on and she started to laugh at the delighted grin on my face. We bought squirt guns and got in water fights, always "us against them." It was Tracey's idea to race behind the group of boys who were still rating girls and douse them with water. "Now you're a ten!" she told me as we escaped into the crowd.

We walked together to the concerts, and she listened while I talked of Tony and my confused heart. She seemed to understand me right away. She nodded sympathetically when I didn't know how to explain my feelings, "I just—you know?" And she said, "Yeh. That I do know."

She knew Tony from Campus Life before the trip and saw immediately how much I liked him and his blue eyes. She also knew him to be a heartbreaker. She thought I seemed too sweet to notice, and because she liked me, she was immediately determined to steer me away from any hurt my young and yet unbroken heart might suffer. I was fast falling head over heels in love with the wrong guy, and at just that moment in my life I had met the friend I needed most, Tracey.

Due to a fortunate (or unfortunate, according to Tony) bus breakdown, Tracey and I rode home together. The hours in the crowded van cemented our friendship as we shared interests: reading, art, and horses. I taught her to play "Hand and Foot," a card game like rummy, and she beat me 1000 to 200 her first game. We discovered we had a lot in common, including where we lived.

I grinned at her quiet comment and the look in her green eyes, "I meet you in Kentucky and we live only four miles apart." She shook her head, "Doesn't that seem a little . . ."

"Ironic?" I answered for her and we both laughed. It was only the beginning.

It was summer, 1987, and we packed it full—riding bikes to the mall, eating countless hot fudge ice cream cakes at Elias Bros., playing cards, watching movies, and taking walks. We were determined to visit Mr. Fables until we had sat in every booth. I spent hours at her house and got to know, quite well, her mother, father, and Holli, her sister. Her mother, Pam, only five feet, two inches tall, but full of spunk, said we were two of a kind with a special kind of friendship. She laughed at me, listened to me, and told me I reminded her of her best friend when she was fifteen. I felt like family.

I had never had a friend like Tracey. We shared everything—clothes, secrets, books, library fines, and innermost feelings. We saw each other through our first, second, and third boyfriends. She was right all along about Tony and comforted my heart, with only one "I told you so" at just the right moment. We were like sisters, even twins, only closer.

On one summer day, by candlelight, we poked our fingers, promised undying friendship, and became blood sisters in my bedroom. It was a solemn meaningful time.

"You now have a drop of my blood inside you to help you out on the hard days when I can't be there for you," Tracey told me. We shared dreams for the future and decided that when we were old we would be roommates in the "home." It was as if Tracey knew me better than I knew myself, and I knew her the same way.

She was there the night I got my first kiss from Jimmy at McDonalds, knowing what had happened simply by the shine in my eyes before I even told her. Our hearts knew each other before the words even started.

I told her our friend Ryan liked her, but she disagreed. She called me immediately after he asked her out. "How did you know?!" she asked.

"I know you," I had told her, "I'm your twin." When Ryan told her they needed some time apart, I hugged her close and cried with her over her first broken heart. Much as I cared for Ryan, I was angry enough to want to shake him. I hated to see Tracey hurt.

We shared a stronger link than I had ever experienced with another person. I told her the story of my adoption as we walked one evening, and she understood my feelings and accepted me, as she always had, without question.

"I'm sure part of the reason you were adopted was because God knew I needed you for my best friend," she said softly that night as we walked slowly through my neighborhood. When I spoke, she heard my words and listened to my heart.

Tracey told me Jimmy and Tony weren't good enough for me. She laughed at my jokes and strange verbal expressions. She told me I was a great singer, and came to my MAGI concerts where she held up "Smile" signs from her place in the front row. She always said she couldn't sing well, and I told her I would sing for her. She was my best friend and my number one fan. We were inseparable. We had found a soul mate in each other.

Her mother became a second mother to me. Pam was also a friend who remembered what it was like to be a young teenage woman and did her best to help us get through it. I valued her honesty, input and advice. She wasn't afraid to share personal stories of her own. She asked questions about me and seemed genuinely interested in the answers. She watched me a lot. After Tracey told her of my adoption, her casual questions became more specific. When was my birth date? What agency was I adopted through? What did I know about my birth mom? And the usual questions: Did I think I would meet her again, and did I want to?

I was used to the questions and answered them the same as I had all of my life. Still, a seed was planted somewhere in my subconscious when she tossed off the remark, "My best friend Paula gave up a baby in 1972—you could be her daughter. Wouldn't that be something?"

School began again—I was a sophomore and Tracey a junior. Our moms had become friends also, after carting us back and forth and conspiring about curfews all summer. We couldn't get them to drive us as often during the school year, so we had to resort to long letters and even longer telephone calls. To maintain privacy from listening ears (our sisters and moms), we developed a detailed color code to use when speaking or writing. We were the only two who knew that Tony was blue, Ryan was red, silver meant love and chartreuse meant happy. It drove her mother Pam absolutely crazy when we used it within her earshot.

"No more code! I mean it!" she would say. Tracey and I could talk for an hour, and our conversation would consist mostly of colors: colors for people, for feelings, and for actions. After we ran out of colors, (using a box of Crayolas for inspirations like mahogany, sepia, periwinkle and melon) we graduated into flowers—rose, carnation, orchid—and smells—mint, evergreen, cinnamon, etc. Whole situations and conflicting feelings could be translated easily into one color. It seemed we could say more with our own private code than with regular words.

I would tell her, "Gray silver Blue," while my sister gave me strange looks from her place on the stairs, looking through the spindles at me.

"Yes, but Blue is khaki and cinnamon Gray." Tracey would reply with concern, "Turn pink to purple."

I would sign off, "Later," and hang up.

Through that winter and the next summer we used the color code to discuss the most influential young men and women in our lives. We used it camping with my family, at the beach with hers, antiquing, canoeing, and riding the roller coasters at Cedar Point.

I spent hours, days, and weeks at Tracey's house, and she at mine. We baked and ate hundreds of chocolate chip cookies. I slept at her place over my sixteenth birthday, July 18th, and she baked me a chocolate cake with chocolate frosting. Together we decorated it with M&Ms in the shape of a flower. We ate the whole thing, drank a two-liter of Mountain Dew, and watched Ghostbusters three times in a row. Her mother stood in the doorway at 1:00 a.m. watching us recite the lines with the actors. She shook her head, "I think you two are crazy," she said.

"You were once a teenager," Tracey countered.

"You're right, and I guess Paula and I did our share of crazy things too."

"Best friends will be best friends," Tracey stated as if to explain everything. With one last, "Happy Birthday," and, "Goodnight," Pam headed upstairs.

I was almost too busy then to think of my adoption. I was young, I was in love, and I was in over my head in almost everything.

About this time, my mom and dad reminded me that since I was sixteen we could send for non-identifying information about my birth parents. They said the adoption agency kept records of information the birth mother had provided and we could have access to them if we would write and ask. In two years I would be eighteen, the age I would be legally able to find, or at least search for her. I had put it off long enough. There were only two years left of my excusable childhood innocence. Maybe it was time to start considering if, or how, I would search for her. Maybe I should examine my feelings, start dealing with any unresolved issues I might have concerning her. I wanted to be a whole person, wanted to have my mind organized and under control. Maybe it was time to prepare myself and learn more about this woman I would one day meet face to face.

After I came down from my sixteenth birthday sugar rush, my parents wrote to Bethany Christian Services requesting information. I wondered about what I would soon know.

On July 28th, the white envelope that I knew contained answers to at least some of my questions finally arrived. I took it up to the sanctuary of my room where there would be no interruptions. With a deep breath and more curiosity than anxiety, I opened it. There were three pages detailing my birth parents' statistics and medical histories. It noted that the information was quite dated, as they had no contact with either since July of 1972, the same month I was born. I was especially interested in my birth mother, and read those paragraphs carefully. I learned that her hair was blond and her eyes were blue. I discovered her height, weight, and Christian Reformed Church background. "Already she seems like me," I thought as I read the pages intently.

My birth mother had one older sister and three younger brothers. When she was young, her father had died of heart trouble and her mother remarried, adding one stepsister and three stepbrothers to the family. I sat on the floor with my back to the bed, wondering what it had been like to discover she was pregnant. How would that feel? Was she scared? I would've been. For the first time, I seriously wondered what I would've done if I had been in her situation. I looked at the pages in my hands and kept reading.

The information intrigued me. She was like me in so many ways. She loved the outdoors, reading, drawing, and cooking. We were similar in height and weight. Since she liked the same things as me, I reasoned, she must look and feel like me. I read further. She had loved me much, but decided it would be best if I grew up in a Christian home with two parents. She was not going to marry my birth father.

What stood out the most to me was that she had given me up out of love for me. Not because I was an inconvenience in her life, but because she had loved me, and wanted what was best for me. Even then, I was loved. That knowledge made me feel so special. I was surprised to realize I had tears on my cheeks. I sat on the floor with my head on my fingertips and felt. I felt pain, the beginning stirrings of the loss I had experienced. I felt pain also for her—young, afraid— how would I feel in her situation? What would I do? Could I make the decision to give up a child because it was best for her? I didn't think I could. I thought it would hurt too much. I hurt for her as I imagined her feelings.

I wondered where she was now. My stomach twisted with excitement and nervousness. It was a big deal, a glimpse through the door into the future. I didn't know if I was ready to know her or not. I sighed and shook my head. What if she wasn't what I expected her to be? What if I wasn't what she expected me to be? What would finding her mean to my life? I could never go back. What would it mean to the only mom I knew? In one way I was glad I had some time before I had to face those hard questions. I could hold onto "not knowing" and live in my comfort zone a while longer. I didn't have to make the choice to find her today.

On the other hand, I did want to find her someday. I wanted to reestablish that lost connection I had with her and no one else. Knowing she loved me patched a hole in the dike of my heart—it eased my fear of ultimate rejection and made me feel safe knowing she was still out there for me somewhere. I felt sorry for her—missing and loving me all those years. I wanted her to know I was okay and happy. I glanced toward the window at the bright blue sky outside and I wondered if the sky was blue outside her window.

Whenever I heard the song, "Somewhere Out There," I thought about the words and how fitting they were for me. How someone out there was sleeping under the same big sky, maybe wishing on the same bright star. Maybe we could find each other in that big somewhere . . . .

Knowing our similarities reinforced the invisible bond I felt between us and established another link in my belief that we would one day find each other again.

After several moments, I pulled myself from my reverie and brought the non-identifying information pages downstairs to my parents. I wanted to see what their reactions would be, so I asked my dad to read them aloud. He did, slowly, and Mom listened carefully. It was all very interesting, and Mom mentioned that it was like reading a description of me. Dad handed the letter back, and I took it upstairs and read it over once more. Then, I filed the now-precious papers in a safe place in my desk and in the back of my mind.

In January of 1989, I started dating a senior named Lee. He was tall, handsome, and had wonderful green-brown eyes. We met at Zondervan's, a book store where I had been working since I turned sixteen. He happened to go to Tracey's school, and, in fact, was in a few of her classes. Because of me, they formed a friendship and occasionally ditched class together to come visit me at my school.

Lee understood as much as possible about my adoption and my feelings regarding it, and he just listened to the rest. He was a great listener and cared very much for me. He was a Pentecostal believer and opened my Christian Reformed eyes to a whole new style of church and worship. I began attending his youth group at First Assembly of God church, and my spiritual life became stronger yet. He was a great student of the Bible and could talk for hours explaining the history and meaning of a text, often telling me how a word came from this Greek or Hebrew word, and what that meant. I learned a lot from him and we grew very close. He was an artist and a romantic and always treated me well. At times we discussed marriage, but we were too young to seriously consider it yet.

Tracey and I burned Polo-scented candles in my room (against the rules). We collected business cards and souvenirs from everywhere. She steadily added to my camel collection. We were Student Leaders in Campus Life and went on retreats together, abandoning our tent and sleeping under the stars. We attended the same early Saturday morning Bible study and grew even closer. We did so much together that we would surprise and confuse our friends when either of us went somewhere without the other.

We broke a few hearts and had our own broken. We boxed up and duct-taped memories from heartless men, only to dig them out and cry together over them later. We shared our first attempts at poetry, sharing some of them with Pam, another writer-at-heart who shared some of hers with us.

Before Tracey's grandparents came up from Iowa for a visit that summer, Pam told me, "Wait and see. The first thing my mom will say is 'Doesn't she put you in mind of Paula?'" She did.

More and more around that house I heard Paula's name. Pam said I looked like her, smiled and laughed like her, and moved my hands the same way when I talked. According to everyone who knew us both, we shared a sense of style and humor.

Even Tracey's dad, Anthony, who is legally blind and does not distinguish facial features, told me, "Your hands are so soft. I never felt hands as soft as yours except for Paula. She had soft hands just like yours."

Anthony's parents who saw me rarely and always referred to me as "that girl, that Kristin girl" said my smile looked just like Paula's. Pam had lost contact with Paula some years ago, but often mentioned how my friendship with her daughter reminded her of the closeness she shared with Paula.

"You and Tracey have a special closeness that only happens once in your lifetime. It was the same way with me and Paula, and even though I haven't seen her in years, that closeness will always be there. We could not talk for months and then just pick up where we left off. There are so many similarities between your friendship with Tracey and mine with Paula, even the little things. You both love to read, and talk. You are a year apart, one goes to Christian School and one goes to Public School. You first met when you were fourteen and Tracey was fifteen-years-old. I'm a year older than Paula and we met when she was fourteen and I was fifteen. We stayed up all night talking like you two. Paula was and always will be my soul mate."

Several times she mentioned Paula's baby, and she almost always cried when she told us how Paula lived with them before she gave up her little girl for adoption. She told how they had stayed up nights, playing cards and talking about the agonizing decision Paula had yet to make about the baby she carried and how hard it was to decide. The bizarre possibility grew in my imagination and tantalizing thoughts of "What if?" began. The odds were too great, weren't they? I couldn't be Pam's best friend's long lost daughter, could I? Once, when we were laughing and imagining if it were true, Tracey ran up to her room, dug through her vacation souvenirs and brought down Paula's graduation card.

"Here," she said, tossing it at me. "I found this in my Grandma's basement. It's for when you want to find your mom." It was fun to imagine, to dare to speculate, but there was just no way. It was unheard of for an adopted child to be recognized as their best friend's mother's best friend's daughter. In best-selling fiction maybe, but not in real life. Not in my life!

I put the small white card away, but its printed letters stayed with me. I put it in the same place in my desk as my birth mother information sheets, along with a note I wrote about Paula—what I knew about her. She had given up a baby. In 1972. To Bethany Christian Services Adoption Agency, to a dentist and his wife. I didn't tell anyone, didn't let the seed of hope grow. It was just too bizarre, too strange, too crazy to believe for a second that it might be true. I hid the card away, in the desk and in my heart, for a year.

CHAPTER 16

Mary: My Daughter, My Friend

Packing up the dreams God planted
In the fertile soil of you
Can't believe the hopes He's granted
Means a chapter in your life is through
But we'll keep you close as always
It won't even seem you've gone
'Cause our hearts in big and small ways
Will keep the love that keeps us strong

And friends are friends forever
If the Lord's the Lord of them
And a friend will not say never
'Cause the welcome will not end
Though it's hard to let you go
In the Father's hands we know
That a life-time's not too long to live as friends
No, a life-time's not too long to live as friends.[10]

Michael W. Smith
Deborah D. Smith

Both Bill and I had grown up in families that had gone camping for summer vacations. We both believed families that camp together grow close. So we started going on annual two to three week camping trips as soon as Susie was three years old and could handle long distance travel.

In the summer of 1986, just before Kris entered high school, our point of destination on our annual trip was Washington State and Vancouver, British Columbia, which was the site of the World's Fair that year. Our travel plans included a driving goal of 500 miles a day for five days. After that, we hoped to arrive at the Stremler Dairy Farm in Lyndon, where we had made arrangements to camp while we visited the World's Fair. The fair was good, but, if the truth were told, we all enjoyed the farm more. It was June, so several of the cows had recently given birth to calves. There were also cats with new kittens in the barn's hayloft.

The first morning on the farm, we were awakened to the sound of mooing. At 6:30 Kris was the first out the door of our pop-up tent trailer to watch the milking. Brian, who usually had trouble waking up, slept with his wristwatch around one ear so he wouldn't miss his early alarm.

Another morning Susie woke up and slipped out first only to come running back to the trailer calling, "Hurry! A calf is being born!" We all quickly pulled on our jeans and ran to the barn to watch Casey, a recent widower, assist the first-time mother to deliver her calf. What an education!

Since Casey was trying to adjust to living alone in the farm house, he was eager to spend a little time with us. He invited us to share hamburgers and ice cream at the local Dairy Queen one evening after our long, hot day at the fair. We, in turn, invited him into our camper for a breakfast of grilled cheese sandwiches and Cheerios.

Our five-day stay came to an end all too soon. It was a sad parting for us all, ending with hugs, tears, and a promise to see each other again.

On our way home, we drove through Iowa and camped in a small city park in Sioux Center. It was Sunday, so we went to a combined area church service at Dordt College. Bill and I talked together remembering that Kristi's birth mom was from Iowa, but we didn't know the exact area. We decided not to mention Iowa to Kristi until we felt the time was right.

September seemed to come quickly that year with mixed emotions of our oldest already beginning high school. We were eager to continue watching Kris mature, but we also knew that high school would introduce a whole string of opportunities for us to learn to let go—something I knew would be difficult for me because Kris and I were close friends.

About a month after school started, there was an entry in our church bulletin under "Requested Announcements" which had been submitted by Youth for Christ. The announcement was addressed to high school students who might be interested in auditioning for a small singing-drama group called MAGI. A phone number for information was given. Kristi leaned over and whispered to me, "I want to try out for that group." I was surprised, but smiled and whispered back, "That sounds like fun."

By the time we got home from church, my protective mother-mind was hoisting red flags because I was thinking: This will mean new friends, boys, new experiences, boys, older friends, boys . . . .

I told Bill what Kristi had said in church and what I was thinking. "Don't worry, Kid," he said. "Kris is so laid back, she probably won't do anything about it."

The next week I drove her to the audition. Since Kris was still very petite for her fourteen years, I wasn't prepared for what I saw. The other kids in the group all looked like giants! The girls were well developed and looked much older than Kris. The boys were grown men who sang tenor and bass. One had long blond hair.

Kris and I came home together and gave our reports to Bill who was wondering. I rolled my eyes and said, "Kris did a great job, but you should have seen the other kids in that group!"

Kristi's face beamed as she told her Dad, "I think I made the group, Dad! The director will let me know for sure after she hears all the auditions."

Sure enough, Kris did receive a call confirming she made the group, so the next week I drove her to the first practice. The next day, I wrote in my journal:

> I have been in a real struggle about this group. My protective side whispered that I didn't know any of these kids or their families. My prideful side said, "These kids are a bunch of misfits!" The devil tapped me on the shoulder and filled me with a ton of fears. Through the struggle, the Lord reminded me that He looks at the heart, not outward appearance. So, I think the Lord is saying, "Give her wings and trust Me, Mary."

MAGI practiced for a few months before they were ready for their first public performance at an evening church service in January. They had prepared a musical called *Surrender*. Its message encouraged total surrender to the power of the Holy Spirit. They did a terrific job! We were especially proud of Kristi, of course.

After the service, an unfamiliar man came up to me, introduced himself and asked, "Is one of the singers yours?"

I proudly pointed her out and said, "Yes, Kristin."

"Oh yes. Kristin Roedema, 3739 Basswood," he replied. I must have looked really surprised because he quickly added, "I'm your mailman."

Later, when I told Bill about our mailman, Bill commented, "I wonder what our mailman thinks of our outgoing mail lately," referring to Kristin's letters to her movie-star crush, Ralph Macchio.

Later that evening on the way to a church fellowship group, I said to Bill regarding our daughter's crush, "I think Kris must be losing her mind!"

"Don't worry about that," Bill answered. "It won't be long before we'll have more than her mind to worry about."

Bill was right. A couple of weeks later Kris came home from MAGI announcing a Youth for Christ (YFC) music festival in Kentucky called *Ichthus* which would be coming up in April. She wanted to go! But only two kids from MAGI were going, Dennis and Tony. No problem. She would go with them.

"Oh this is great! Probably staying in a tent with boys. I don't think so!" I said to Bill. After much discussion, we decided to let her go. We had been watching Kris drift from one friendship to another with girls at her Christian high school, never settling on one best friend. After having had Susie as my best friend all through school, I really wished for a friendship like that for Kris.

When April came, I waved goodbye to Kris in a van full of high school kids including Dennis and Tony as well as several other guys and girls from other groups. Bill and I let her go, praying specifically: "Lord, will You help Kris to find a Christian girl on this trip for her to hang out with over the weekend?"

When Kris returned from the weekend, we learned that our prayer had been answered. She not only met a new friend in Kentucky, but the girl knew Tony and Dennis and had been in the same van with Kris. She lived in Wyoming, another suburb of Grand Rapids, only about ten minutes from our home. Her name was Tracey. She was one year older than Kris. She attended a public high school, and she went to a Wesleyan church. Kris was very excited about this new friend. She told us, "We have a lot in common!" Bill and I were as guarded and cautious as we were with all new friends of our kids.

In May, MAGI was scheduled to give their last performance of *Surrender* in a Reformed church on the other side of Grand Rapids. I thought it would be fun to surprise Kris by inviting three or four of her friends from school to go to the musical with us and then have them over to our house for dessert. Not knowing I had invited these girls, Kris told me she had invited her new friend, Tracey. She was to show up at the church if she could get a ride from her Mom. I doubted that she would show up.

Our family had gone to nearly every performance of MAGI that season. Kris had always looked pleased, grinning widely when she saw us. As we entered the church, I looked around wondering if Tracey was there. Since we had not met her, we didn't know what she looked like. Walking toward the front of the church with our family and the girls, I saw no one I knew except one handsome young man sitting with his parents. His name was Scott. He had been our neighborhood paper boy when we had just moved to Grandville.

We hadn't been seated long when MAGI walked in and took their places up front. We saw Kris look around, spot all of us sitting in a front row, and instead of breaking into her usual broad smile, she looked directly at me and glared. If looks could kill, I would have been dead.

That performance was probably the longest one I ever sat through. Afterward Kris came over to us, gave her friends a cool shoulder and hissed into my ear, "Why did you invite them? I told you Tracey was going to try to come!"

Tracey was there alright. She emerged from the back of the church, a tall, thin girl with long dark hair. We all climbed into the van and rode the "long" ride home across town.

I mechanically served dessert to the table-full of girls, as I tried to make small talk. Kris and Tracey sat on one end of the table, the other girls on the opposite end, the two groups barely speaking to each other. After dessert, Bill proposed taking the school friends home. Tracey would go home later.

As soon as Bill and the girls left, I sat down at the table with Kris and Tracey. I explained what I had tried to do—to surprise Kris. I said, "Kris, I am really sorry for making things so uncomfortable for you. Will you forgive me? Tracey, will you forgive me?" They both said they would.

What a traumatic introduction to Tracey, the friend God sent in answer to our prayers! Unknown to us, He was also continuing a work He had already begun which would be much more than we had asked or ever imagined.

Neither Kristin, as a sophomore, nor Tracey, a junior with a September birthday, had a driver's license during the summer after they met. They had to be satisfied in their growing friendship with phone calls, letters and their mothers' taxi services.

I was still guarded about Kristin's new friend the first time I met Pam, Tracey's mom, on their driveway. She was an attractive, petite woman with beautiful dark brown hair. The next time the girls got together, I went outside to greet Pam on our driveway. She rolled down her car window and said, "We like our daughter's choice of friends."

I thanked her and smiled but thought guardedly, I hope we like our daughter's choice.

As Kris and Tracey's contacts increased and Tracey began to call me "Mom", my guard began to drop. When the notes and letters to Kris came in the mailbox from Tracey, there would be a little, "Hi, Mom!" on the outside of the envelope or a tiny scripture reference tucked into the corner of the envelope: Phil.4:13. I began to realize, Wow! This really is a Christian friend that we had wanted for Kris! Tracey was winning my heart.

In September, Kris invited Tracey to go on our annual Labor Day family canoe trip. We had only been on the river a few minutes when the girls' canoe tipped over plunging them both into the cold water. Undaunted, they both righted the canoe, checked with each other to make sure they still had their contact lenses, got in and went on their way down-stream. Bill and I laughed as he commented, "I guess those two *are* a lot alike."

As autumn progressed into the holiday season, Kristin became more involved with Youth for Christ and Tracey. Tracey was becoming her best friend.   In fact, their friendship was growing so strong, that I felt our mother-daughter friendship was threatened.

I decided it was time to make work of an idea I had earlier.   My idea would hopefully maintain positive communication and encouragement during the growing-up years of the kids, when communication might dwindle down to negatives or nothing.

I had realized that most of my positive thoughts came while they were away at school and I was home alone.   At times, I had written little notes to them on scraps of paper left here or there around the house, but those would be tossed away or lost.   So, I bought three small cloth-covered journals and put one in each of the kid's rooms.   With these I could communicate and encourage them in a lasting way.

After the new year began, while Bill was gone on a two-week medical-dental mission trip to Honduras, I felt lonely and wrote in my journal:

> I wrote a note to Kris asking her forgiveness for something I said.   The reason I did what I did was because I'm jealous of her fond attention given to Tracey and her mom and hardly any given to us.   Then I was convicted by Proverbs 10:19 (NIV), "When words are many, sin is not absent, but he who holds his tongue is wise."   I asked for forgiveness.

Kris was also becoming interested in boys at Youth for Christ. Her latest interest centered on a young man who attended Alcoholics Anonymous meetings regularly.   She was becoming more and more secretive about herself and her friends.   In fact, Kris and Tracey developed a color-code language to talk on the phone so no one could interpret their conversations.

Since we were not accustomed to adolescent behavior and the sudden changes that occur, in February, I wrote with concern in my journal:

Kristin's personality is changing from submissive to rebellious, seemingly not only to us as parents, but also to God, from a cheerful disposition to one of moodiness, from contentment to a lonely reaching out to whomever is available, girls and boys. Lord, help us to parent her with wisdom and love and to trust You for direction and guidance.

The following week was a real downer as I wrote:

Who would have thought that three kids spaced three years apart would all hit adolescence at the same time! Lord, help me to hang in there today!

Living with adolescence the first time around is not easy for the parents or the child. Being parents that some might describe as "helicopters", we had trouble letting go of the control. We wanted everything to be done as we would do it. Neither of us really understood personality differences and how they play out in life styles and choices.

Being our first child, Kris had to make her way through the high expectations often placed on first-borns. We were all feeling the strain.

On March 15, 1988, I wrote in my journal:

It is very difficult to stand firm and wait patiently while watching a daughter in teenage foolishness thinking herself to be the example of wisdom. Still the message the Lord seems to be consistently saying to me and Bill is: "Back off. Let Me handle it." It's hard, Lord. Increase our faith and trust.

A week later the Lord gave us a gift to enable us to see more clearly and to back off. We were invited to a YFC banquet. It was the best time I'd had at a social gathering in a long time. We sat with Tracey's parents, Pam and Anthony, which enabled us to get to know them. We were impressed with their caring, sincere attitude and a strong relationship with Jesus Christ. The whole evening was eye opening. I realized that YFC was a real gift to Kris and not a threat to us. I thanked the Lord for His help to change my attitude.

As the months of spring came, we continued to watch Kristin's emotional withdrawal from us as parents and her growing attraction to her friends.

One evening when Bill picked Kris up from YFC, they talked together about friends and wise choices. Somewhere in the conversation Kris blurted out, "Who knows? My birth mom might have been a prostitute!" Bill told her he knew that wasn't true, but the comment was insightful for us. Perhaps a low self-esteem motivated some of her choices.

In May, while Bill and I were at my brother Mark's fortieth birthday party, we talked to Mark's friend who had previously searched and found his birth mother. He told us about an adoption conference coming up the following week at Hope College, about thirty miles from our home. He suggested we go there to see if we could gain any insights into adoption issues and acting-out behaviors of adopted children.

We took his suggestion and it was at that conference that we began to learn about adoption issues in children as well as in birth mothers and adoptive parents. We were not familiar with issues of grief and loss or other adoption issues and had not given any thought to these things before.

It was late in the afternoon, near the close of the conference, when we were in an open forum including representatives of all three angles of the adoption triangle. We did not know any of the conferees nor their relationship to adoption. As questions were asked and feelings were shared, it became clear that two of the women in the room were birth mothers who had released their children for adoption eighteen and nineteen years previously. Neither knew where her child was.

With tears streaming down both faces, one of them asked, "What do adoptive parents tell the kids about us?"

Until then, no one knew for sure which angle of adoption Bill and I represented. At that point, I spoke up and said, "I'll tell you what we tell them. We have three adopted children. We tell them that you loved them so much that you chose life for them and that you gave them the gift of two parents, a family to love and care for them."

I stood up from my chair and walked over to these two hurting women. I now had tears in my eyes as I hugged each of them. One of the women dried her eyes and spoke, "I wish you were my son's mom." We quickly compared the ages of her son and our Brian, but determined it couldn't be possible. Still, I was touched by her genuine love for her child.

On the way home from the conference, Bill and I talked together about our kids and about adoption issues we had learned that day. This was the first time Bill and I became aware of the intense pain of the opposite side of adoption. It was during that conversation that the words of a familiar poem came to my mind. I said, "Kid, do you remember that little poem that says something like 'If you love something, set it free'?"

He nodded. Then with his voice choked by emotion, "I think we need to give the kids permission to search for their birth parents. We need to set them free."

My voice, also choked, was barely audible as I agreed, "Me too."

It was at the dinner table that evening when we brought it up to the kids. We told them what we had learned that day, what we had heard and seen, and what we had decided on the way home. We promised them our encouragement and help to search for their birth parents if and when they wanted to do it. Each of their responses was different. Kristin, who was fifteen, nonchalantly said, "If it happens, it happens;

if it doesn't, it doesn't.." Brian, a middle school twelve, responded, "I'm not interested!" And Susie, who was only nine, but who already had been thinking about her birth parents, said, "Can we start tomorrow?"

The next month our family traveled west and then south toward the Grand Canyon. We planned to hike down and camp overnight at the bottom. Kris was not really eager for these family trips anymore, but since this one was quite unique, she agreed to go, but declared for the future, "This is the last trip I'll be going on."

As we traveled through Iowa, we stopped for lunch at a rest area. Kristin checked the phone book for "Grandma Iowa," Tracey's grandma on her mother's side, who lived in Doon, Iowa.

After we ate lunch, Kris and I were still sitting together at the picnic table, when I said, "Kris, I think your birth mother was from Iowa."

She looked at me in amazement and said, "You mean—I'm a farm girl?" I chuckled at the look on her face, and said, "It could be."

When we arrived home from the Grand Canyon early in July, we did two things to try to understand Kristin better. First, we took her to a counselor who assured us that she was working through adolescent issues typical to her age. The counselor said, "Adoption is not a problem for her."

Second, we called Bethany Christian Services and asked them to send her non-identifying information surrounding her birth and adoption. We had some notes that Bill had scribbled down when we were at Bethany years before, but now we requested a typed information letter so that both Kris and we might better know her roots. Since Bethany's policies regarding information had relaxed over the years, they were eager to respond to our request as they were already doing with other requests by this time.

When the information arrived a few weeks later, addressed: "To the parents of Kristin," we gave her the choice to first read it alone or with us. She took it upstairs to read alone. Later she came back down and asked her dad to read it aloud to the three of us. By the time Bill finished reading the letter, Kris looked interested but unemotional. She looked over at me and asked, "Why are you crying, Mom?"

I answered, "Oh Kris, these are happy tears. That information is a picture of you!"

I had been doing much thinking and some reading about adoption lately. Many things I read were discouraging and frightening. Adoption seemed to bring few rewards. It seemed to me that pain from loss was part of the picture for all involved. I was afraid of the "what if's" in the future. Writing my feelings and thoughts in my own journal usually helped me to think straight, so I wrote:

> Last night my mind was spinning with thoughts of the past, present, and future. My emotions were involved with grief and fear. I believe that the things I've read about the world's statistics need to be followed with the words, "But God . . . ."
>
> This morning a verse from the Psalms encouraged me. "But you, O God, do see trouble and grief; you consider it to take it in hand. The victim commits himself to you; you are the helper of the fatherless." Psalm 10:14 (NIV)

"Sweet sixteen and never been kissed." I didn't believe she had never been kissed, but Kris was becoming sweeter again as she began her junior year in high school. The summer had brought many changes in her life—a driver's permit, a new hairstyle, a special boyfriend, and a growing relationship with the Lord, including a new confidence and joy.

Her self-image had changed and with it her attitude and behavior improved. Even teachers at school saw the difference and wondered what had happened to her over the summer. We told them, "We think Kris is beginning to discover the wonderful person she really is."

She had applied for her first real job at Zondervan Christian Bookstores and was quickly hired. She became a salesperson selling books and music, two of her favorite things. Kris proved to be a diligent employee and was appreciated by the other employees so that just before Christmas I wrote in her encouragement journal:

Dear Kris,

I am so proud of you. I went into your store today. Karolyn was at the front desk. She said they were just waiting for you to come in. She said everyone wants you to work with them. What a special honor to be considered such a valuable worker!

The same day I wrote on another subject:

Also I cried this afternoon—tears of joy. Focus on the Family played a series of Christmas messages from their listeners today. One which touched me was from a birth mother from Iowa who gave her daughter for adoption.

She was calling to remind her daughter and her adoptive family that she was placed in just the family God wanted her to be in. And she hoped the family would know God's peace and His love during the Christmas season.

I don't know if we are the family that message was intended for, but I heard it and I praise God for giving you to us.

I'll love you always,
Mom

The holiday season brought another change. Kristin's dating relationship with Tony seemed to be cooling, but at the same time she was becoming more and more interested in another young man at work. Lee was introduced to our family on Sunday evening, New Year's day. Like Tony, he was tall, dark, and handsome. He had a winsome personality and also answered Bill's interview questions confidently, so his became the familiar voice on the telephone calling for Kris.

During the second semester of Kristin's junior year of high school, as plans turn toward graduation and afterward, I began to have sad, sentimental thoughts of having our first child leaving home. I heard a panel of women speak on the radio about "The Empty Nest," and I cried along with them identifying closely with their words and feelings. I shared some of those feelings with Kris in her journal in February:

Dear Kris,

I know this will sound quite sentimental. I guess it is. Still, I wanted you to know how much you bless my spirit when you play the piano in the shadows of the living room. Last night I got tears in my eyes thinking about how short that time will be until you're gone to college or on your own. That's just one of the ways I'll miss you.

Love,
Mom

Winter melted into spring and with it the track season began with Lee being a track team member at his public high school, the same school Tracey attended.

One beautiful April day, Tracey and Lee skipped out of their school early, picked up Kris from her school and headed out to a track meet across town where Lee was to participate. They never reached their destination. Instead, I got a phone call from Lee: "Mom, we've had an accident on the expressway. Tracey's car is totaled, but we're all okay. The Lord took care of us. Could you come to get us?"

The phone call was shocking. The accident had been serious, but the Lord had spared all three of them from serious injury. Obviously the Lord wasn't finished with any of them yet.

The following month I attended an annual spring women's retreat where a woman named Lee Ezell was to be one of the featured speakers. My friend Kathy and I were particularly interested in what Lee might share because we had read that she was a birth mom who had a reunion with her grown daughter whom she had released for adoption as an infant. Kathy too was an adoptive mother—of six children.

That Saturday afternoon, Lee Ezell shared her story as well as some slides showing look-alike pictures of herself with her birth daughter. Both Kathy and I were moved to tears picturing future images of reunions that might become part of our children's lives. As we walked back to the dorm room where we were staying, I said to Kathy, "I have a feeling God's preparing us for something."

Summer of 1989 seemed to drag by. It was the first summer since 1982 that we did not take a family trip. Kris had lost interest in going. Bill and I had no interest in going without her with a steady boyfriend in the picture.

Kris turned seventeen in July and managed to find time to get her driver's license just before she would have had to retake her road test. She had postponed getting a license for a year by getting rides from Lee, Tracey, and other friends.

Her relationship with Lee was still intact, but she was showing some signs of restlessness. Both Tracey and Lee had graduated from high school and were making plans to start college. Lee was enrolled in the community college. Tracey would be leaving for Indiana Wesleyan.

I knew that since Kristin's friendship with Tracey had grown strong, having Tracey leave would be hard on Kris. Still I was confident that as she had matured in the Lord, He would see her through.

The summer ended with a week of camping in northern Michigan with some of our relatives. Kris came along for a few days and spent quiet time reading, playing her guitar, and taking walks with me. Our friendship was regaining strength after the stress of adolescence. It was good to have a growing friendship, woman to woman, as we faced her senior year, her last year at home with us.

CHAPTER 17

Pam: Saving Them Up In My Heart

Tracey was fifteen in the summer of 1987. She had been involved in Campus Life for about six months. Campus Life was different than any group she had ever been part of. Some of the kids that I saw when I dropped her off on Monday nights looked rough. Some even stood outside and smoked. That concerned me, yet I could see that Tracey was challenged toward Christian growth and commitment in ways she hadn't been before, and better yet she was meeting the challenge. When her Campus Life group was going to a Christian music festival called *Ichthus* in Kentucky, her dad and I agreed to let her go. Little did we know what an impact this would have on all our lives. She came home from *Ichthus* thrilled about a new friend she had met there. Her friend's name was Kristin and she lived nearby in Grandville. Tracey was rather shy and reserved so it was unusual for her to go on and on about a friend, especially one she had just met. I heard all about how Tracey and Kristin were on the same wavelength, how they thought alike and even had the same quirky sense of humor.

Tracey's words made me remember times with my best friend when I was fifteen. I smiled as Tracey continued, "You'll love her Mom, she's great." It didn't take us long to see that she was right. Less than a week after Tracey got home from Kentucky, Kristin's mom, Mary, dropped Kristin off to spend an afternoon with Tracey. Mary introduced herself to me and checked to make sure the girls would be in a supervised setting. This got points for Kristin right away. Her mom was like me. She wanted to know where her daughter was, whom she was with, and what she was doing. As Mary and I talked, it was obvious Tracey and Kristin tuned us out completely.

When Mary left, I met Kristin and was introduced to the pleasure of her smile. Tracey and Kristin then went to sit on the deck, talking and giggling. I thought back to my own teenage years and the importance of having a good friend. I immediately thought of Paula and the good times we used to have. It was when they came in the house later that I realized another reason I had thought of Paula. There was nothing I could put my finger on at first. Kristin just made me think of Paula. She even looked similar to what Paula had looked like at that age, especially the unique color of her eyes. I wondered if they changed color like Paula's. I had also thought of Paula because I could see the instant connection Kristin had with Tracey. I could tell they would be friends for a very long time. I had that same connection with Paula. When I had first met her in the summer of 1967, it was like I had always known her.

As the summer went on, seeing Tracey and Kristin together kept reminding me of Paula and the special relationship we had shared. At times as the girls laughed their way through the living room, I would comment to them, "You two make me think of my best friend Paula. We used to carry on the same way."

"Who's Paula?" Kristin asked.

"My best friend. She lives in Iowa. Actually you remind me of her, especially your eyes."

"Cool," Kristin replied, and off she went with Tracey.

The phone rang more at our house since Tracey and Kristin had become friends. They spent hours on the phone. Tracey would prop herself up on the barstool by the counter with her back against the wall, or, if it were really private talk, she would sit under the counter with her long legs sprawled out in the doorway. This created a hazard for Anthony, who was legally blind. Tracey's legs were definitely not in his field of vision, and more than once when she was too intent on her conversation with Kristin she would fail to notice him and he would step on her. "Tracey, I'm so sorry, I didn't see you there. You must be on the phone with Kristin again," and he would go on with what he was doing.

I am not sure how or when Kristin started calling me Mom. Maybe it was from the beginning. I never remember her calling me anything else. It felt very right and natural for her to call me Mom. Kristin and I could communicate quite easily. Before long, she found a place in my heart right next to my own two daughters.

The more time Kristin spent at our house, the more I thought about Paula. From the way Kristin sat to how she flipped her hair with her hand, she often reminded me of Paula. Her pauses before words were often the same too.

Kristin's mother Mary and I would often call each other to compare notes on what the girls were up to, or to get each other's opinions on whether we should let them go to certain events, how late to set curfews, and so on. It was the first time either of us had parented a teenager so we felt like we were in this together. Eventually we struck up a friendship of our own. Although we didn't socialize together, a call to Mary or from her was almost always guaranteed to be thirty minutes or longer, as we chatted about our families and shared some personal things. I found out Mary had lost her mother to breast cancer when Kristin was nine. When my mother was diagnosed with lung cancer, Mary became an encouragement to me. She knew the fear I was feeling. She knew the frustration I felt at seeing my mother suffer and not being able to stop the pain and sickness.

Meanwhile life for Tracey and Kristin marched on. It was the summer of 1988 and Kristin went on a vacation to Arizona with her family. Neither Tracey nor Kristin were sure how they would survive two weeks without each other, but Kristin promised to write. Tracey was thrilled when she received Kristin's letters. It seemed they came every other day for the whole two weeks. "Look Mom, a letter from Kristin, I wonder where she wrote this one from." She ripped the letter open and sat down on the couch in one motion. "Hmmm she was in Iowa when she wrote this," she paused to continue reading, "she says her birth mother is from Iowa."

I felt like a rock dropped through the ceiling, "What?"

Tracey rolled her eyes. "Her birth mother is from Iowa," she repeated loudly in slow syllables as only a teenager does to a parent. She continued, "Wouldn't it be cool if her mother was Paula?" I sat there speechless. My mind was spinning. What if Paula was her mother?

Tracey paid no attention to my reaction as she read the rest of her letter. She then went up to her room to write a response.

I just sat there. I was awed at what I had learned. What if . . . what if . . . ? A lot of pieces were staring me in the face. I hadn't known that Kristin was adopted. The significance of her father being a dentist and her mother a former schoolteacher suddenly took on new meaning: Paula's little girl had been placed in the home of a dentist and his schoolteacher wife. I remembered how important it was to Paula and her mother that the baby be placed in a Christian home. I knew Kristin, like Tracey, had Jesus at the center of her life.

Kristin was about the same age Paula's child would have been now. In fact she and Tracey had just made plans for Kristin to spend her sixteenth birthday at our house overnight. For the first time, the significance of her July birthday became real to me. I knew Paula's baby had been born during the hottest week of the year in July of 1972.

I started to wonder. Could it be true? It was all too bizarre to believe, to even think of believing. This just can't be. It had to be coincidence. I was probably just trying to put these pieces together because that was how I wanted it to be. I cared for Kristin and wanted her to be the daughter of Paula's heart. I also wanted Paula to have the happy ending she deserved. I told myself it was only my overactive imagination wanting it to be true. I resolved to put the matter behind me.

Later that same night after some initial packing for our upcoming trip to Iowa to visit my mom, I mentioned the coincidence to Anthony, "You know what I found out?"

"No, what?"

"Kristin's birthday is in July."

"July?"

"Absolutely, it's in July. It's in three weeks."

"Is that a Tuesday?"

"The eighteenth of July, I think. Do you remember the date Paula's baby was born?"

He scratched his head, "No, do you?"

"I can't remember, it's been so long."

The next week I dug out all my journals, but I could find none for the time Paula was with us. Once again I pushed the matter to the back of my mind. My heart, however, had other ideas and the possibilities kept floating to the surface often when I least expected them. By now, I was eighty percent sure Kristin was Paula's daughter, but I had to be more certain. I had to have the exact birth date.

How to get it was another matter. Paula and I lost touch when she remarried. I didn't know where she was living now. My letters and Christmas cards came back, stamped: *Moved: Forwarding Address Expired*. I didn't want to contact Paula about this anyway. What if Kristin wasn't her daughter? Why get her hopes up and reopen old hurts for her?

I thought of contacting Paula's mother Pearl. I had even tried to call Paula's mom a few times to get Paula's address but got no answer. During our Iowa visit, I mentioned calling Pearl to my mother. Mom said she had heard Paula's mother had cancer and was not doing very well. I was afraid Pearl was dead and it was too late. The realization that my last possible link to Paula could be gone, along with my need to know for sure, gave all this a new urgency. It was as if the Lord was saying to me, go ahead and call, I have been in control of this all along, and I still am. Was my faith strong enough to know this last missing piece of the puzzle I hadn't asked for? I wasn't sure why I was the one who knew all this or what in the world I was supposed to do with it. I thought of how the mother of Jesus watched her son grow and observed the things he did. I thought of how she saved them all up in her heart, and I knew then that regardless of why God had chosen to give me all this information, He had indeed chosen me. I thought about the pieces God had already given, I prayed and knew what I had to do. I would call Pearl. I decided I would do it when we were in Iowa next week visiting my mom. Once again, my mother didn't think I should call.

"You don't know what you could stir up, Pam. That was a long time ago. Why take the risk of bringing pain into all these people's lives?"

I replied, "I'm not going to run to Paula or Kristin or Mary with what I find out, Mom. I have kept these secrets this long and I'm not about to hurt anyone with them now. It's just that I have to know for sure. I'm scared to know and scared not to know."

Mom understood. She knew I had to call and knew I would. She resignedly said, "Well, I still don't think you should call but when you do, be careful about what you say."

My hand was shaking as I dialed Pearl's number. What would I say? I couldn't just come out and ask for this information. I prayed for strength as I listened to the phone ring. Maybe no one would be there. Maybe I would have to call back.

"Hello."

"Uh, yes, is this Pearl?"

"Yes it is."

"Um, hi Pearl. This is Paula's friend, Pam Teunissen."

"Well hi, Pam, how are you?"

At least she sounded glad to hear from me, "I'm fine, how about you? My mom said you had been sick."

"Oh yes, I had cancer you know. I had a rough time of it. I had some of those treatments and it was hard. I got so sick. Pauly, bless her heart, came and took care of me, but I'm fine, doing better now. Guess I'm too tough to give up."

"Well, I'm glad to hear that." (What should I say now?) "How is Paula? I haven't had much luck getting in touch with her."

"Oh she's doing good. Her and her husband are in Texas, they keep busy working. How are Anthony and the girls doing?"

"Fine. They are growing up fast. We are all fine." (Now what?) "Um, actually I was calling to get Paula's address and to see if you remember the date her baby was born. All I can remember is that it was July. I thought I had written it down somewhere but I didn't."

"Well, yes, I do remember, Pam, it was July 18. Why do you ask?"

"Well, uh, actually I just wondered. I know some people who adopted a baby girl with a July birthday. She would be about the same age. It just made me wonder about the birth date of Paula's baby. There is probably no connection at all, but you know me, I was curious."

"Who are these people?"

"Uh . . . " (I didn't expect her to ask that.) "Their name is Roedema, and they live in Grandville," I blurted out. The minute the words were out of my mouth, I knew I shouldn't have said them. As we ended our conversation my mind was going a hundred miles an hour. Why had I shared that name with Pearl? Maybe it would be all right but somehow I felt I had betrayed everyone. I finished my conversation and wrote down Paula's address and phone number in Texas. My mother's eyes were on me as I hung up the phone.

"Pam," she said quietly, "why did you give Pearl the name?"

"I don't know. I just felt someone besides my family should know. Pearl would never say or do anything to hurt Paula. She knows how

Paula has suffered.   Besides, she probably won't remember." Little did I know that after Pearl and I ended our conversation, Pearl wrote the name down and put the piece of paper under her hankies in her top drawer—where she kept all precious things.

I really wasn't surprised that the birth date matched. I knew it would. I just knew. At that moment, I was completely convinced that Kristin was Paula's child. Oh Lord, what am I supposed to do with this secret that you have entrusted to me? Once more, I thought back to Mary in the Bible and how she must've felt watching Jesus' life unfold. There was a reason for all of this but I didn't know what it was. God would reveal it in his own time. I just needed to trust Him to show me why I was the keeper of this secret—a secret that would forever change the lives of people I loved. I decided to let the information remain mine alone for now. If God wanted me to tell Paula or Mary or Kristin, I trusted Him to let me know when the time was right.

Later that night, I thought of the joy of having a best friend. I realized that God had known long before I did how Paula and I and Tracey and Kristin were connected. I was amazed at how He began, even before the beginning of time, to weave a tapestry that only He could see. My need to express my feelings, my wonder, culminated with this poem in my journal:

Before the Beginning

Before the beginning
of time
God cupped
two little girls
yet unborn
in His hands
and began to weave
a tapestry.

Before the beginning
of time
God carefully examined
each thread
looking for just
the right colors
and consistency
to make
His tapestry
all that He wanted
it to be.
As time passed
God slowly
examined each wrinkle
and fold
reinforcing each weakness
with His love
and understanding.
He made sure to
put plenty of
patience into the
fine colors before him.
As time passed
God sat back
and waited
and when the day arrived
He unveiled His tapestry
of friendship to reveal
the names of
Tracey and Kristin.

Now that I had the matching birth date and knew Kristin was
Paula's daughter, my dilemma deepened. I still debated about what to

do and who to tell. I didn't want to just barge in and disrupt all the lives involved, yet I felt I had this information to share. I prayed that the Lord would let me know *if* and *when* beyond a shadow of a doubt. After all He had spent all these years planning and putting the pieces in place. I was sure He could pull the rest off with no problem. I just wanted to make sure I was in His will. I spent time in prayer and rested in the sure knowledge that God would tell me the proper time to share what I knew. Little did I know that a whole year would pass before God would prompt me to speak.

CHAPTER 18

Mary: An Ordinary Call

Trust in the Lord with all your heart
and lean not on your own
understanding;
In all your ways acknowledge him,
and he will make your paths straight.

Proverbs 3:5, 6 (NIV)

September 1989 had come and gone. The month had come with all of its fresh starts and new beginnings. It had ended with the Saturday celebration of my forty-fourth birthday, including wishes and hopes for a wonderful year ahead.

The next morning, our pastor continued his sermon series on the book of Exodus. His sermon entitled "God Himself is With Us" was centered on Moses and the burning bush from Exodus 3. He pointed out that God got Moses's attention with an ordinary bush. He said, "God stepped into history and Moses's life and called his name. He told Moses He was about to do something that Moses would be a part of. God reminded Moses to focus on Him because God would be with him."

That same Sunday evening, October 1, God got my attention. It was an ordinary phone call, but it changed my life. It was as if God called my name so I would realize He was at work in our family and I would have a part in it.

Soon after our evening church service, our daughter Susie answered a phone call for Kris from Tracey's mother, Pam. Since Kris was out with Lee, Susie took the message and said Kris would return the call when she got home.

Later, while I was reading with Susie before tucking her in for the night, I thought I probably should return the call to Pam to let her know Kris wouldn't be home until 11:00 p.m.—would that be too late?

Because Tracey and Kris had been best friends for a couple of years already, Pam and I had often talked together on the phone. We usually talked about parenting and mutual concerns we had about the girls.

When I returned the call, Pam first told me about her reason for calling. They were planning to drive to Indiana the next weekend to visit Tracey at college. She asked, "Would Kris like to ride along to spend some time with Tracey?" I told her I would ask Kris, and then we began to chat about Pam's mother in Iowa who had cancer. Pam told me she had just returned from Iowa after spending a few days there to encourage and cheer up her mom.

Since Pam had called me a few weeks earlier to ask me to pray for Tracey regarding a recurring dating relationship, I asked about that: "How are things going now?"

It was during that conversation that Pam mentioned some concern she had about her own roots involving health issues and what genetic traits might have been passed on to her children. I said, "I wonder about that for my kids too, because I really don't know."

Silence.

Thinking she might not realize the fact, I said, "You know that all my kids are adopted don't you, Pam?"

She hesitated and then answered cautiously, "Maybe I shouldn't say this, Mary. But I think I know who Kristin's birth mother is."

It was a good thing I was sitting down on a kitchen chair because that simple statement sent a wave of shock through my whole body.

But, instantly the Lord gave me a heaping helping of grace, enabling me to respond calmly: "What makes you think that, Pam?"

She began, "I had a high school friend named Paula. She went to the Christian high school; I went to the regular one. She met a young man from up north after high school. He moved to upper Michigan. Later, she did too. She got pregnant and lived with us until she had her baby. She gave the baby up for adoption. I've often thought that Kris looks so much like her. They both have the same unique eye color."

Thinking and screaming inwardly, "This can't be happening!!!" Aloud I asked, "What agency did she work with?"

"Bethany."

"What about the birth date?"

"It's the same."

With my mind shouting, "No!!!" I quietly asked, "What did you know about the adoptive family?"

Pam answered with details I didn't want to hear. "Paula had a baby girl who was given to a dentist and his wife. They had no children. They were Christian Reformed."

Forced out of denial, I asked a question I always wondered about: "Was she a Christian?"

"Oh, yes!"

I asked a few more questions without telling her that every detail she told me matched the non-identifying information we had received from Bethany a year ago about Kristin's birth parents.

Then she told me Paula now lived in Texas, that she never had another baby, and that she was married and had some stepchildren.

Pam went on to say that some time before when she had visited her mom in Iowa, she had talked to Paula's mother, Pearl, to confirm the birth date. Pam explained how she and Paula were not in regular contact anymore, and she hadn't remembered the exact date. She had told Pearl that she thought she knew where Paula's baby was. Pam told me Pearl had said, "Don't tell Pauly until you are sure. She's never really gotten over it."

Pam said that after her conversation with Pearl, she had prayed for an opening with me.

Still in shock, I said, "Well, I guess it's possible that Bethany might have two similar cases, but it's not too likely. I have to hang up now and tell Bill."

After I hung up, I ran to ask Bill, who was coming down the stairs, "Do you know who I was just talking to?"

"Yeah, Pam."

"You're not going to believe this, Kid. I think you better sit down."

As soon as I finished telling Bill the shocking facts that Pam had just told me, he immediately responded, "We have to tell Kris. She has to know everything we do."

When Kris came home from her date at 11:00, she came in saying she was very tired. Bill asked, "Do you want to hear something that will wake you up?"

She didn't seem real interested until I told her Pam had called. First I told her the reason why Pam had called. Then I said, "Also, she thinks she knows who your birth mother is!"

Kris just grinned and said, "Who is it? Paula?" She laughed and told us that Pam had talked to her in the past, had asked her some questions, and had commented more than once on the fact that Kris reminded her so much of her high school friend named Paula.

Then she ran upstairs and reappeared in a few minutes holding a small white graduation card bearing the first name, middle initial, and last name of Pam's high school friend, Paula. Bill and I just stared at the card asking, "How long have you known this?" and, "Where did you get that card?" She said, "Tracey found it in her grandma's basement with some of her mom's old things. She gave it to me as a joke."

Some joke! The reality of this news was dawning on me. Kris and I sat down by the kitchen table for a few minutes while Bill headed up to bed. As tears began to well up in my eyes, I said, "I always thought this would happen someday. But I really never thought it would be so soon. I thought it might happen sometime after you got married, when you had some kids of your own." I sighed, "I do know though, Kris, that God's timing is always perfect."

Kris really didn't expect it either even though there had been some kidding about it at Tracey's house. She had never mentioned it to us because she didn't think it could be true.

When she saw my tears, she just put her arms around me and said, "You will always be my mom."

I wanted to believe her, but fear was gripping my heart, and it was so hard. I hugged her and thought, "I hope so."

It was very hard to sleep that night. The next morning I felt grief clutch my heart, the same way as when my mother was dying. I cried most of the morning. I found it hard to carry out my ordinary Monday morning routine. So I took time to write in Kristin's little red journal:

Dear Kris,

Today is one of those days which is packed with emotions. I'm so thankful God doesn't give us too many of these days in our lifetime. But today is one of them. I would like to express all that I feel on paper, but today, right now, it's too hard.

What I can say, however, is that God is calling us to begin a new chapter in our lives—a chapter that He has obviously planned. I'm going to pray that this will be a chapter of growing together, a chapter of trust in God's faithfulness, a chapter of love.

Mom

In the afternoon, I was happy a friend and I had previously made plans to pick decorative weeds along the highway that day for an upcoming school bazaar. It was a good distraction. I didn't tell her my heart was bleeding. I was able to keep my composure, but the moment I was back in the privacy of my house, I again started to cry.

I called Bill. "Kid, I can't stop crying."

In response, he wisely asked me questions. "Do you know why you are crying? Do you know if you are happy or sad?" They were good questions.

I thought for a moment and then answered slowly. "I think it's shock and grief—grief over the potential loss of a relationship with Kris."

I went on to say that Kris and I were just becoming good friends again, and now this! I said, "I keep picturing Pam and Tracey, Kris and her birth mother as a cozy little foursome. Where does that leave me? I'll be the fifth wheel, literally!"

Bill let me talk but then he reminded me that we still didn't even know this was true, so why borrow trouble ahead of time. He suggested that I contact Bethany to see if they would confirm or deny our information. Then we would know how to proceed. He said, "If Pam is right, we'll need some professional help with this. If she's not, we can put this out of our minds as a mere coincidence. We also owe it to Kris so she'll know the truth on this." We felt it was wise to move quickly in case Paula's mother might leak the news to Paula. We really didn't want Kris to have a surprise phone call before we had professional help.

When I hung up the phone, I thought about the questions Bill had asked me and my response about grief over the potential loss of relationship. Kris and I had been good friends, and I guess my mother-mind was expecting this to continue, to grow as Kris entered adulthood. This shocking news seemed to be a threat to that expectation, a call to share a child I loved deeply. I wasn't ready to share. I didn't want to. Not yet!

Over the last few weeks I had been meditating on Psalm 91 (NIV), "He who dwells in the shelter of the Most High will rest in the shadow of the Almighty . . . ." When I looked at it again, I noticed part of verse 4 in particular: "His faithfulness will be your shield and rampart." I realized the Lord had shown His love and faithfulness again and again throughout our lives. He never changes. I decided He certainly wouldn't let us down now.

On Tuesday much of my crying had stopped. At least it was under control. I prepared to call Bethany by writing in my journal:

> Lord, will You prepare me, Bill, Kris, this whole family for what's ahead? We're going to call Bethany today to get some counsel, perhaps some confirmation. Lord, You know how my mind is running ahead of You. I'm becoming afraid of what this new situation will do in our lives—the changes that will come to Kris, to the other kids. Help me, Lord, to do what I have to do. Help me to keep my focus on You, on Your faithfulness, and not be afraid. I've been thinking about letting go for a while now, but I always thought I still had a year to prepare. This is early, Lord—a surprise. It reminds me of the premature death of my mother. It was premature for me, Lord, but Your timing is always right. Help me to live in that knowledge, Lord. Help me!

When I called, I was glad I could speak to our former case worker right away. We hadn't been in contact with him for many years, but he quickly remembered who I was. I told him about Sunday's phone call and asked if he would confirm the name we had.

His first response was, "Wow, Mary, you have a best-seller on your hands!" Then he said he would check the files and would return a call as soon as possible. It was less than an hour later when he called back and said, "Yes, Mary, it's a match."

When I asked what we should do next, he set up an appointment for me and Kris to meet with another case worker the following week. At the end of the week, however, she called me to hear our story herself, in brief. She told me that this was such an interesting, amazing story that she wished she could be involved with us, but due to an upcoming vacation, she would have to reassign us to her substitute, a new woman just hired in September for post-adoption counseling. The new person's name was Mary Sue.

The days until the appointment moved slowly. My emotions seemed to roll and coast from high and gracious thoughts down to ugly, sinful thoughts of selfishness and self-pity. I wondered about Paula. Would she experience a wide range of emotions too when she found out? On October 10, a few days before our appointment, I wrote in my journal:

> Lord, help me and Paula to become friends. Let neither
> of us suffer from envy or selfishness. Enable us to see the
> big picture that we all belong to You.

Then the day before we were to meet with Mary Sue, our former caseworker called with some concerns. Since Kris was still legally a minor, and consent was not usually given until an adopted person was eighteen, he advised us to keep this situation confidential for the time being. I didn't know how hard this would be. But, I agreed and called Bill at work. I also told Kris when she got home from school.

"Lee already knows," she said, "but I'll ask him to keep it to himself."

Our first meeting with Mary Sue was very encouraging. She was a short, bright-eyed, soft-spoken woman, about my age. Having just moved from the south, her accent was delightful as she asked us some questions and told us a little bit about herself as well. She had not only had experience with adoption professionally, but she had been adopted as an infant herself. She and her husband had one daughter, who was also adopted. Her calm, confident manner gave both Kris and me the feeling that we were really cared for. God had provided a wonderful helper for us.

Mary Sue asked me if I would call Pam and ask if she would be willing to call the agency to talk. I said I would call the following Monday. When Monday came, it was hard for me to call Pam. I knew that as long as I didn't call, nothing would begin to move. I also knew I had to do it, even if I didn't want to.

When I talked to Pam, I cried. I hoped I wouldn't, but I did. I told her, "I always knew this would happen sooner or later with one of my kids. But now that it has, it's an emotional blow. It feels like an impending death in our family."

Pam was sympathetic, "I can only imagine how you feel, Mary. I'm sorry."

Mary Sue called me Friday morning to tell me she had met with Pam. She said, "I'll go ahead and try to make contact with Paula using the address information I got from Pam." She told me she would make a request for correspondence with Kristin as we had all talked about at the appointment. If Paula agreed, all letters would be funneled through the agency. No last names or addresses would be used to maintain confidentiality until Kris could file for consent at age eighteen.

Pam called Friday night. She said it was harder for her to go to the agency than she thought it would be. "I feel responsible for creating disruption in your family and in Paula's life." Pam understood that there would be no turning back.

For days after Pam's initial disclosure my mind had searched for someone to blame, but I always came to a dead-end with God. I told her, "Pam, this really isn't your responsibility. It's ultimately God's. Let Him handle it. I believe this is in His will and timetable. Only He knows the reasons why." I sounded brave with Pam.

I also reminded her that Kristin does not belong to us, but neither does she belong to Paula. I said, "Kristin belongs to God. We gave her over to Him a long time ago. If we keep our focus on Him and act in obedience, this real-life drama will be played well with the praise and credit going to Him."

Pam agreed and we both hung up. For the moment, we both felt peaceful about the situation.

I had been doing some reading and thinking about forgiveness in preparation for a seminar I was to teach at a Stephen's Ministry retreat the following week. When Kris came home from her date that night, we talked together about the "what ifs" of forgiveness regarding Paula. I asked her, "Kris, have you ever forgiven Paula?" We both thought she had because we had talked about that before.

A bigger question, however, was what if Paula had never been able to forgive herself. I said, "Sometimes people are in bondage to guilt. You could be the key person to be used to set Paula free by accepting her and offering her forgiveness and assuring her of God's forgiveness. We don't know which direction this will take, Kristi, but if we keep our focus on God, and play our parts well, as difficult as that may be, there will be those watching who will see God's love and faithfulness through us."

Mary Sue called me now and then with brief progress reports regarding her preparation to contact Paula. Things were progressing slower that I expected, but that was okay. Kris didn't seem to be in a hurry, and God knew me. He knew I needed time.

Early in November, I had an idea to write a brief letter to Paula for Mary Sue to read to her when she contacted her. Bill thought it was a good idea, and Mary Sue agreed. But, Kris didn't. Kris said, "I don't want to have Mary Sue read a letter from you on the first contact." She did allow that it might be okay if we told Mary Sue a few things we hoped she might relay to Paula from us. That was the first hint we had of the adopted person's need to be in control of the situation.

My emotions were still flip-flopping. One moment I would feel strong and confident. The next I would be overcome with worry and fear about the changes we might all face. I was concerned that Kris's personality and values might change. I expressed my fears to Bill, but also to Mary Sue and to God.

On Sunday, November 12, God gave me the help I needed through our pastor's morning sermon, called "Songs of Deliverance."

He said, "Evil robs us of life and freedom. The enemy, Satan, does not want us to be free. He pursues us and raises doubts, fears, and other sins in our minds."

Then he taught us a way to gain victory. He reminded us that songs are a tremendous resource for believers. He said, "Name your enemy." I thought, "My enemy is fear."

Then he said, "Choose a song of deliverance that addresses your enemy and sing it. The enemy cannot stand in the presence of praise." He went on to say that a song of deliverance needs to honestly face the future, but it is sung *before* the crisis is over, to express trust in our God and to resist the enemy and his paralyzing schemes.

At the close of the message, our pastor asked us to sit quietly and read the words of a new song printed on the order of worship while the organ played the melody. The new song taken from Psalm 32 was "You Are My Hiding Place." It became my song of deliverance.

You are my hiding place;
you will protect me from trouble
and surround me with songs
of deliverance.

Psalm 32:7 (NIV)

CHAPTER 19

Kristin: Stepping Through

I walked into the house at 11:05 pm. I was returning from a date with my boyfriend, Lee. It was just like any other date, any other night, and I was totally unprepared for what came next.

My mom was sitting on the couch, my dad in his old worn leather recliner. "Have a seat, Kris," Dad said in his ever-calm voice. "There's something we need to tell you."

My first thought was panic. I was five minutes late and they were overreacting. Soon I realized my tardiness had nothing to do with it. My mom's face was grave as she told me she had received some shocking news. "You're pregnant?" I tried to lighten the moment. It didn't work.

Mom folded her hands in her lap and twisted her wedding ring around her finger. "I talked with Pam Teunissen this evening. She told me she thinks she knows who your birth mother is." As her eyes lifted from her hands to meet mine, I gave my poor mom her second shock of the evening.

"Who, Paula?"

Her eyes widened. "You knew about Paula?"

"Hold on a second." I ran upstairs to my room and dug out the graduation card with Paula's name on it that Tracey had given me over a year earlier. I returned with it momentarily and gave it to my mom. Then I sat down as it began to sink in. They were serious.

My mom stared at the card in her hand. Then she stared at me, "What? . . . is this?"

"A long time ago, Pam mentioned to me that her best friend had given a baby up for adoption, and that her baby had been born the same time I was. She even had the same adoption agency. She told me I reminded her of this friend, Paula, and Tracey gave me that card sort of as a joke. Mostly. I guess . . ."

I had to assure my parents that I had not known anything beyond unbelievable speculation. "I wasn't keeping anything secret on purpose. I just never believed it could possibly be real . . . . Do you really think it could be true? Could this really happen?"

"I don't know, but if it is, it's an amazing thing." Dad shook his head slowly back and forth and leaned back in his chair.

Mom said she felt pretty sure it was for real. "Kris, Pam told me things she couldn't have known unless she knew your birth mother personally. I didn't tell her that every detail she told me matched up with what we knew from before. She had your birth date, and Bethany Christian Services, and everything else right."

The three of us sat quietly for a moment, each in our own thoughts. I was wondering how we could find out for sure, and how soon. Now that the idea had warmed in my head, I wanted to know right now.

Right now, however, there was nothing I could do. Mom and I talked briefly, and I tried to reassure her that nothing would change between us. We hugged and said "Good Night." Still in shock, I went slowly upstairs to bed.

It was a shaky night. One moment, lying awake in the darkness, I would still doubt that it was possible, shake my head, and laugh at myself for being tempted to believe. The next, I was hoping it was true, hoping we would find out that Paula really was my birth mother. Now, I *wanted* it to be her.

The next morning, Monday, I got up and got ready for school. It wasn't just a normal day, however. Something inside was different. A whole new life chapter was in front of me. New chances, possibilities of questions answered, and new relationships. I could hardly wait to be sure—I didn't want to believe prematurely, but having gotten my hopes up, it would be hard if it wasn't true. If Pam believed, it must be right, and now I could hardly imagine my birth mother as someone other than Pam's best friend. The shock was wearing off, and I was ready for answers the next day.

My mother was the one to make the first move in confirming this new information. She called Bethany on Tuesday, spoke to a caseworker, and gave him our names and Paula's maiden name (read off her graduation card). When I got home from school, she showed me the notes she took from that conversation. "It's a match." she said. "Pam was right. This is your birth mother! Can you believe it?"

I shook my head and tried to think of something to say. "We have an appointment with a caseworker next week," Mom continued. Next week was good. I needed some time to get used to this.

Dad got home from work soon after that. "Well, Kris," he said slowly in his calm, flatline voice, with a hint of something like a twinkle in his eye, "It's true. It's really, really true."

Confirmation! Excitement was coursing through me, followed by trepidation. My knees felt weak. "Believe it," half my mind said. The other half said, "How? How can I believe it? How am I supposed to feel? How am I supposed to deal with this?"

I smiled, and then stopped. Now what? I was standing in a figurative doorway. Behind me was the past, the innocence of not knowing. A whole childhood, a whole me used to not knowing anything about her, of being completely on my own. Not knowing her, or how, or any of the story. I could imagine my birth mother in whatever circumstances I chose. Soon I would not be able to imagine, wonder, or say, "Someday," with no fear and no risk. This was happening now, no more putting it off in my mind; no more telling myself I had plenty of time to prepare, to deal with any feelings I may have hidden. It was looming in front of me before I even knew it was coming or started looking for it. Since I didn't have to go through the whole search process, I had very little time to think about what to expect, or even to know what I wanted. Suddenly I felt my childish innocence standing beside me and, once I stepped through the door leaving it behind, there would be no returning. I didn't know why this mattered, but in a way I was afraid to step through because I knew there was no going back to "not knowing". Suddenly I needed to be alone, and went up the stairs to my room to curl up in a ball on my bed and think.

Before me were all of the answers to every question I had wondered over seventeen years, and a good measure of fear. Fear for her—what if she didn't want to be found? If my *birth* had been a secret, would I ruin her life by my actual *appearance*? Would I be a bad reminder of a time she would rather forget? Would I only hurt her? I had learned from talking to Pam about Paula that she had a husband and step children. Would I ruin something for her marriage or family? And fear for myself, too. How could I compete with her other (step) children, and how would I feel knowing they had lived with her all their lives and I had not? What would she expect of me? Less or more than I was willing to give? What if she rejected me, could I handle facing that as a conscious adult? In my journal on October 2, 1989, I wrote:

> They've found my birth mother. Paula. I'm excited, happy, concerned, apprehensive, maybe even a little scared. What will she be thinking? Feeling? I think it's neat how I have some of Paula's traits. The things I like, and how I look…. But, what will happen now? Will she come and find me? I hope so, yet I'm nervous. And isn't it strange—it must be God—how Tracey's mother and Paula were best friends in high school, and how Tracey and I are as close as sisters . . . ? Of all the people in the whole world! Pam figured it out. I didn't know.
>
> Paula!?!!

A few days after the initial shock, Mom and I went to Bethany Christian Services. She stayed in the waiting room while I spoke one on one to a caseworker named Mary Sue. She was a cute, short woman with an adorable Georgian accent. She made me feel comfortable immediately, offering me a Pepsi and refilling her coffee before we started talking in her tiny office. Cross-stitched scripture verses and pictures of her family hung on the walls above her desk and around my chair. She explained that she was adopted herself, and that she and her husband had adopted a daughter. Hearing that, I felt like she could know and understand firsthand some of the things I was feeling.

Mary Sue pulled her chair from behind her desk and faced me. "This is a frightening time for you," she began. "Let's spend some time dealing with any fears you might have. What scares you most about this time?"

"Well, for one thing, I'm afraid of ruining her life!" I answered. "What if she hasn't told her family about me? I don't want to hurt anyone, especially Paula."

"That's a realistic fear. It's a chance we are going to take if we call her. It will be an interruption of her life—hopefully a positive one. Are you afraid of rejection by Paula?"

I thought about my answer. Everything in my mind and heart was telling me I had nothing to worry about, but how did I explain it? "I really don't believe that she would turn me away. I feel close to her already. I suppose I should think about it, though."

"What are your expectations? What do you hope for the future? What relationship do you want with Paula?" She leaned forward. "You need to decide ahead of time how involved you want her to be— whether you would like to just meet her once and end it there, or if you would like a continuing relationship with her."

"I expect to go slow," I answered. I realized I was sitting with my arms and legs crossed defensively, and tried to relax. "I want to know her and everything about her. I want to see how alike we are, because that means a lot to me, having someone just like me. I would like to write her, see pictures of her now and growing up. It would be neat to compare our looks—after all, that's how Pam knew me! I can't wait to see that. I would like to talk to her over the phone, and eventually meet her in person. I would love to spend some time with her and meet my extended family."

Mary Sue nodded. Because she was adopted and in the midst of a search for her birth family, I knew she truly understood that point. "What kind of relationship are you looking for? What do you need from Paula?" She sipped her coffee, never taking her eyes from mine.

I had thought about this. "I don't need another 'mother', my own is wonderful. I would like her for a friend. I would like to share ideas and thoughts, and hear the story behind my birth and adoption. I think I have a right to know how everything happened." Mary Sue agreed that Paula would help to complete my internal puzzle, and validate a lot of things about me. I felt that by knowing Paula, and knowing how she felt, reacted to, and thought about things would explain why I was different and thought differently in some ways from my parents. "I figure I will be able to answer the psychologist's "Nature vs. Nurture" questions. Because if I compare my views with my parents—and I differ on a lot of things!—I bet they came from Paula, from my blood somehow. I would like to see that!" I was very interested in this "Nature/Nurture" concept. I was looking forward to finding out if some of my more laid-back, relaxed views came from Paula, because they were not from my upbringing. I didn't know how "blood" worked and was eager to see how (or if) perspectives were passed down biologically, like blue eyes.

Mary Sue brought up a new subject. "Have you thought about how you will deal with her husband and your new stepsiblings?"

"I really don't want to hurt anyone. I'm a little afraid that if she hasn't told them about me, I may cause problems for them. I'm pretty sure her own family knows about me, because my information sheet mentioned her mother and siblings, and said that they were a very close-knit family. I don't know about my new siblings. Wow. In a way, that would be really exciting too." I didn't tell Mary Sue that I was secretly glad Paula had had no other children of her own. Now that I would be back in her picture, I wanted her for myself, and wanted her to love me as her only daughter. I wasn't ready to share. If there were other children, our bond wouldn't be as special, as unique, and maybe she wouldn't need me at all. I thought that putting those feelings into words would sound selfish, so I didn't.

I hoped her husband wouldn't be upset, but I guessed it was worth the risk, and figured if I would be too much trouble, she could say so the first time she was contacted. Mary Sue tried to prepare me, "There are several ways Paula could react. We hope she will be happy and excited, but she may not be. Some birth mothers are embarrassed, or afraid others will find out about their past. Some birth mothers do not want to revisit their grief or the pain of the past. She may not want to be found, and may not want any relationship with you at all. I don't want to discourage you, but you need to be ready for any possible reaction. Would you be okay if she said she didn't want to know you?"

I tried to imagine that response from my birth mother and couldn't. "I think I could deal with that. It would hurt, but I really don't expect that from her. She said that she loved me then, and I really believe she will be happy now."

Mary Sue grinned at me over her coffee. "So do I."

She told me I would grieve, and I didn't really understand why at first. "You don't really miss what you don't know," she said. "Once you get to know her, you will see everything she gave up, and you will experience your separation in a new way." Again it had to do with that door of not knowing. "You will look back on all the years that have been lost to you. Those years and experiences are irretrievable, Kristin, and no matter what happens now, seventeen years and millions of moments will never happen for you and Paula together. It's painful to realize that loss, and it is important for you to feel that pain and deal with it when it comes." I heard and acknowledged Mary Sue's words, but at that time, grieving was far from my mind. I was filled with nervous anticipation and simultaneously felt my ever-cautious conscience tell me to be wary, to be careful, and not to hope too much. That warning sure was hard to listen to!

Mary Sue would be the one to make the first contact with Paula. When we talked about that moment, my stomach told me I was nervous by knotting up and doing summersaults, but my mind said, "Relax. In your heart you know this woman. She is just like you. Don't you believe she will be glad to hear from you?" and in my heart I was sure she would be. Beside the excitement there was peace. I was confident I understood the "person" of Paula, and I was sure of her love. I did feel nervous for her, though. I knew she would be even more surprised than I had been, and I wished there was some way I could prepare her. My journal:

> November 13, 1989. Mary Sue has been in touch almost every day. She said she needed a list of questions for when she called Paula. I said, "Forget it. I don't have a list of questions and I'm not going to come up with one. When Paula is called, it's up to her to tell me what she wants. I want to be friends."

Of course I wanted to know the story behind my birth, I wanted to know about my birth father and the failure of their relationship, and the reason she gave me up for adoption. I knew she loved me and that had been enough. But now, if I had the chance, I would like to know the whole story. I wanted to know if she was happy with her decision or if she had ever regretted it. I wondered how her family had reacted in the long run, and if she was still in touch with my birth father. However, I didn't want to pester or pressure her or make demands on her to talk about anything that might be painful for her. I didn't want to make her uncomfortable at all, but to be completely accepting. I knew eventually she would tell me the story, and I was content to wait until the time was right. The most important thing was to know her, and begin establishing a relationship with her based on the present and the future. Questions about the past could come later.

At Mary Sue's request, Pam also met her at Bethany Christian Services. Pam told me she felt torn. She knew me and loved me so much, and she also loved Paula. She didn't want to hurt either of us. Even though she had initiated the whole thing, and knew she had God's timing and blessing, it was with some reluctance that she had handed the note with Paula's latest known address, phone number, and married name to Mary Sue. I think she also knew we could never go back and that each of us had a rough time ahead. She gave the information she had to Mary Sue and then did her best to step out of the picture. She didn't want to cause any pain or be any more responsible for the coming changes in our lives than she already was. Nor did she want to "steal the spotlight" or come between Paula and me. Building the relationship by direct communication would be ours to do. I loved her for telling, and I loved her for letting us do the rest on our own.

Mary Sue made contact with Paula on November 27, 1989.

CHAPTER 20

Paula: Baby Girl

It was late afternoon when the phone rang. My husband Kenny answered and handed the phone to me.

"Is this Paula Huston?" a female voice asked.

"Yes," I replied.

"I have to find out if you are the right person," she said. "Were you Paula Roskamp?"

"Yes." I answered slowly.

"Did you have a baby girl in 1972 and give her up for adoption?" she asked.

"Yes, is she all right?!" I was absolutely shocked. The thought racing through my mind was that something terrible had happened to her. I thought the records were sealed forever. It had to be something very bad if someone was calling me about her.

"Yes. She's fine, she's fine! She is a beautiful young lady," she answered, "This is Mary Sue Kendrick from Bethany Christian Services. Your daughter would like to know you."

At these words I totally lost it! I started crying and shaking and almost fell onto a kitchen chair. When Kenny heard me ask if she was all right he got up and came toward me. I shook my head and motioned for him to pick up the phone in the bedroom. I knew he was going to have to help me with this.

I normally stay in control of situations and my emotions. After seventeen years I was pretty good at it. This was the only thing that could cause this reaction in me.

I was speechless. A thousand questions and I was speechless!

"Do you want some time to think about it?" Mary Sue knew what a shock it must be to me, "I can call back later or tomorrow to talk."

I was terrified that she would hang up and never call back. Seventeen long years were within my grasp and all I could do was cry?! Come on, I thought, get a grip. I took a couple of deep breaths and tried to get myself under control. I wasn't totally successful, but I said, "No, now. Let's talk now." I honestly don't remember most of that first conversation, but I did know my daughter was all right, her name was Kristin, and she wanted to know me. Praise God! I told Mary Sue that I most assuredly wanted to get to know her too. I'd been thinking and praying about it for seventeen years.

Mary Sue's voice was calm, "I'll get back with Kristin and call you again in a couple of days about writing letters. That will be our first step." After we hung up Kenny came out to the kitchen.

"My daughter . . . ," my voice was trembling. He nodded and held me in his arms, and we both cried.

As usual, when something overwhelming happens, I said, "I have to call my mom." Then I said, "I have to call Pam." I hadn't talked to Pam in years, yet I knew she was close to my heart. She had been my support at the hardest time in my life and I couldn't wait to share my excitement with her.

Kenny wanted to call everybody. He could hardly contain himself. I'm sure he would have handed out cigars saying, "It's a girl," if there had been anyone around. As it was, for all the years many people close to me never knew. They were about to find out.

First I called Mom. I expected her to be as excited and surprised as I was. While she was excited and very happy, she didn't seem all that surprised.

"Pauly, do you remember last May when you were here and we talked?" She took me back to a time six months ago when I was home visiting and she and I were sitting by the kitchen table talking. My mother had asked me a very hard question.

"What would you do if someday there was a knock on your door, and when you went to open it there she stood?"

I had thought about it a minute and then said, "I don't know."

"I wouldn't be a bit surprised if that happened." I thought it a bit strange she would say that, but we let the subject drop.

After reminding me of that time, she told me she had talked to Pam over a year ago, in the summer of 1988. My mother then said something that took me completely by surprise, "Pam told me that she might know who your daughter is."

I had no response to this. I sat in silence as I tried to absorb the fact that my mother had known this for over a year and had never told me! Mom continued, "Pam told me about a girl she knew that reminded her of you. Pam said there were so many things she did that reminded her of you. Even the way she brushed her hair back away from her face with her hand. I wanted to tell you many times, but I couldn't. I wouldn't put you through that pain if it turned out not to be her. Of course at that time Pam didn't know if the girl was your daughter, but now that you have heard from that adoption agency, I'll bet Pam had something to do with it. How else would they find out your married name and phone number in Texas?"

At first I felt betrayed. Of all the people in the world, I would never have dreamed that my mother and Pam would keep something so important from me. I can't say I was angry, but I was very hurt. After talking to Mom, I sat down and tried to think this through rationally. I came to realize that of all the people in the world my mother and Pam are two of the people who would never hurt me, and they knew how disappointed I would be if it wasn't her. This was being kept from me because they loved me. They had no idea if this information was the truth. Even if they would have told me, there was no way for me to confirm anything. I knew my daughter wasn't eighteen yet and adoption agencies won't give out information on minors. I knew that having such information and not being able to confirm it would have driven me crazy.

When I called Pam a short time later I had myself under control, at least for a little while. I told her about my life-changing call from Mary Sue. As I expected, she didn't sound surprised.

I wanted to hear everything Pam knew about my daughter. I was so excited, and I knew Pam was excited too. "Pam, I know you have something to do with this. I talked to my mom. She told me how you told her about the girl you knew. Kristin is that girl, isn't she?"

"Yes," Pam answered slowly.

"Tell me how you know her, Pam, tell me everything."

"I can't," she said softly.

"What does she look like?" I asked.

"Oh, Paula, she's beautiful," Pam replied.

"How well do you know her?" I asked.

"Pretty well."

"How far away does she live from you?"

"Not too far."

"Do you know her parents? What are they like?"

"I really don't know them very well," Pam said.

By this time we were both in tears. I was so frustrated with her evasive answers! Why wouldn't she tell me anything? She knew how much this meant to me. She went through it with me—she helped me through it day by day, and now she wouldn't tell me? This is the closest I'd ever come to being really angry with her.

"Pam," I said, "Why did you tell my mom?"

"Oh, Paula, please understand. I had to tell her," Pam said. "What if something happened to me, and I was the only one who knew about this? I had to tell her. Did Mary Sue tell you how this whole thing came about?"

"No," I replied, "Please tell me Pam."

All she would say was that my daughter was a beautiful girl inside and out, and she thought Kristin should be the one to tell me everything else. She cried as she said, "I love you. But I can't tell you anything else, I just can't."

Like I said before, she's little but very tenacious. I could feel how much she wanted to tell me everything. I could hear it in her voice. I knew she wanted to talk to me about it for hours, and I also knew she wouldn't. I would have to be content with what I knew, for now. Soon all my questions would be answered. I could wait. I would hear the rest from my daughter!

We talked instead of how we knew God would take care of her, and how very much we had wanted and prayed for this over the years. How exciting it was to think about getting letters from her, and pictures, and maybe sometime soon even talking to her!

I wouldn't let my mind think about seeing her. I was apprehensive about how she felt. What if she resented me or didn't understand my long ago decision? What if she didn't want to see me? How could I handle losing her all over again? I just couldn't let that happen! I took comfort in knowing God had led us all to this moment. In my heart I had known for seventeen years that this day would come. I was certain she knew how much I loved her and how much I needed her love in return. I knew that over the years she could feel my heart and my love reaching out for her, just as I could feel hers reaching out for me. That one phone call from Mary Sue took me back through seventeen years, only this time she was there, waiting to know me.

The hardest thing about that first phone call was not being able to talk to her right then. I wanted it all right then. I didn't want to wait for her letters, and I wasn't sure what to write in mine. I knew I was a terrible letter writer. I could express myself and my feelings talking, but I couldn't find the right words to put down on paper. Somehow everything always looked so cold and emotionless. However, I realized this was the way it had to be. After waiting all those years for word of her, I could now look forward to words from her. Amazing, but already I could feel the empty part of me filling with the knowledge that she had been looking for me, she had found me, and she wanted to know me. I was so excited and so happy. God is good!

He had watched over each of us and kept us safe for seventeen years, guiding us ever forward to this wonderful time in our lives.

After waiting for me to get off the phone with Pam, poor Kenny was almost beside himself. He wanted to call everyone we knew, right now. I, on the other hand, didn't know how to go about doing that. After so many years of keeping her all to myself it was very hard to talk about her with anyone else. I was barely able to grasp it myself yet. I was also concerned about how our other three kids would take the news. Would they be upset that we hadn't shared this with them? I told Kenny I didn't know what to say, and he, never at a loss for words, said he would tell them. I said, "Okay, let's call," while he smiled at me.

He just came out and said, "You have a sister." Of course they had no idea what he was talking about. After explaining it to them they were happy for me and excited and wanted to know when they could meet her. Shawn lived in Nebraska, Teresa in Iowa, and Michael in California. Getting all four of them in the same place would be quite a maneuver.

Two people who seemed to immediately grasp this extraordinary news were my stepdaughter Teresa and my good friend Candy. While talking to Teresa on the phone she said, "Now it makes sense."

"What do you mean?" I asked.

"I remember how I heard you crying and talking to Dad about wanting a baby some years ago. Now I know why." Being older and hearing my news, she now understood the significance of my tears.

When I told Candy, she was both surprised and happy for me. I had been there with her through her entire pregnancy day by day. There were so many times I wanted to tell her, to share with her the thoughts and feelings I had experienced as she was going through her first pregnancy. At that time I wasn't yet ready to share my child or anything about her. All the thoughts and emotions of my pregnancy and the birth of my baby girl were cradled deep inside me. I felt that if I shared anything with anybody, a tiny part of her would be gone, and I could never get it back. I couldn't lose even a tiny part of her. What little I had was mine alone to hold and cherish.

A couple of days later I received a card from Candy expressing her feelings. It read:

> You've had a rough time of it, and no one can know how hard it's been for you, but now it's time to move on, to look to tomorrow again instead of yesterday, so, as you make a start on your new life, remember that you can count on our friendship for support and as long as you're in need of help or a shoulder to lean on and a reassuring word—as long as I'm here, you're never alone.

Inside she wrote "I'm so happy for you! I always felt bad that you were never going to enjoy being a mother to a child of your own. I can remember when I was trying so hard to get pregnant and the doctors told me I probably would never be able to. It was a very hard time in my life. Then two miracles were given to me. The first was a friend, you, who I would have for life and the second was my daughter Melissa. I wouldn't have made it through those times if it weren't for you and your love and support. I know now why you were so strong for me, and I love you dearly for it. Kristin is your reward for the strength you gave me. I only wish I could have been there for you. I love you, Paula, and like the card says: "As long as I am here, you're never alone."

Her card made me feel so close to her. I knew she meant every word. It brought tears to my eyes. How richly God has blessed me with my family and friends. There was nothing, nothing more important.

My baby girl had always been the daughter of my heart and soul. It seemed strange at first to call her "Kristin", but not for long. I thought Kristin was a beautiful name, given to her by loving parents. It seemed to "fit" her even before our letters and phone calls. After years of silence, talking about her with people suddenly came very easily. In fact it was hard not to talk about her all the time. At last I didn't have to worry about losing that tiny little part of her, I could now have all of her! It was a just matter of finally being able to put my thoughts into words.

Mary Sue was the link to my daughter, and I clung to her for dear life. She was wonderful. From that first phone call we seemed "connected". I felt comfortable calling her with any question I had, no matter how small. "Can I send her a Christmas gift? What would be appropriate to send? What should I include in my first letter? How long do you think it will take to get a letter back from her? What is she like, Mary Sue? What does she look like? Can we send pictures? What is her personality like? When can we talk on the phone? What are her parents like? Are they okay with all of this? I will never ask her to, Mary Sue, but do you think she will ever call me Mom?"

When I was feeling overwhelmed Mary Sue was always there with encouragement. She gave me her home phone number in case I needed to talk to her in the evening or weekends. She sent articles and book titles she thought I might be interested in. Mary Sue always let me know when she was going on vacation or wouldn't be in the office, and she always returned my phone calls, if not from her office, from her home in the evening. She truly cared for me as an individual, not just a "case". I felt very close to her not only as a counselor but as a friend as well.

According to the adoption agency procedures, there were limitations we had to follow because of Kristin's age. We were not allowed to actually talk to each other or meet until she was eighteen. For now I would have to be content with written correspondence, and for now I was content. I didn't know what to write, and I didn't know what she would write to me. Still, she was my daughter and I loved her so much. I could hardly wait for her first letter. Mary Sue told me I would be the one to take the first step by writing to my daughter and sending the letter to Mary Sue. Then she would give it to my baby girl.

Mary Sue wrote, "I pray your pain and loss of the past will now be replaced with love and peace." And now, even before our first letters, both love and peace were beginning to replace the pain and loss.

After anticipating for so long, when the time finally came to write my daughter I sat with pen in hand looking at a blank piece of paper. Where do I start? What do I say? How do I say it? The questions ran through my mind. There was no way to put my thoughts and feelings on paper. "How do you introduce yourself to a part of yourself?" I wondered. I sat alone in my recliner in the bedroom. Kenny always respected my need for privacy, so he stayed in the living room watching television. He knew how very much this meant to me, and he was concerned for my anxiety. He came in often to see how I was doing and if there was anything he could do to help me.

There was so much to say to her and yet nothing at all. As it turned out once I finally got started, it was surprisingly easy. The only thing I could do was be totally honest with her, always. I told her how I felt and how very much I loved her.

When I put that letter in the mailbox it was still very hard for me to grasp it was actually going to her. I was actually writing to my daughter, and it was a wonderful thing! She was like someone I'd always known, because she *was* someone I'd always known. She was the missing part of me. I never once thought that her reaction to my letter would be anything other than love and acceptance. Somehow I knew her return letter would not be full of cold questions, but of warmth and joy and love. My first letter to my daughter held some facts about myself and my family, but more importantly, it held a whole lot of love.

CHAPTER 21

Mary: This is Scary

When I am afraid, I will trust in You.
Psalm 56:3 (NIV)

About a week after Thanksgiving, Mary Sue called to tell me she had made contact with Paula the previous day. She said, "The call couldn't have gone any better. Paula was quiet at first, but when I told her why I was calling, she was concerned. She asked, 'Is she okay? Do her parents support her in this?' Then she was overwhelmed saying, 'Of course I will write her! What do I say?'"

Mary Sue told Paula to take a week to let the news sink in and then she would call again. In the meantime, she set up an appointment for Kris and me to come the day after her next call. At that time she would report on the conversation and describe the Michigan adoption laws regarding guidelines for correspondence.

When Kris came home from school, I told her everything Mary Sue had said. Then I said, "I know this is right, Kris. It's so exciting, but it's so scary for me. I just don't want to lose you!"

She assured me, "Don't worry, Mom. You won't."

I called Pam to let her know contact had been made with Paula. She was glad to hear that, and said, "I've been praying." She also said, "I don't intend to tell Paula the story of how this all came about even if she calls me. I think Krisin should tell her that." I agreed.

A week later Kris and I kept our appointment with Mary Sue at Bethany. She had called Paula, who had asked for permission to send Kristin a Christmas gift. Also, Paula's first words to us through Mary Sue were very gracious and encouraging: "Tell her parents I don't want to intrude. I just want permission to love her."

Mary Sue described what we could expect during the initial stages of the relationship. She said, "There will be much urgency in both Kristin and Paula in trying to make up for lost time. Try to step back and consider all the positions of everyone involved. For adoptive parents, letting go at adulthood is hard anyway. This complicates it. To the child, it's no big deal. The early months will seem out of balance. Perhaps by July, when Kris turns eighteen, the roles of everyone involved will be more set."

"Does Paula intend to write me soon?" Kris asked.

Mary Sue smiled. "I have a letter and some pictures here already."

Kris grinned and said, "I knew she would."

When we arrived home, no one else was in the house. Kris raced up to her room to open the manila envelope from Paula. She stayed upstairs a long time. When I checked on her, I knocked gently on her door and asked, "Are you okay?"

"Yes," she answered. But I could hear by her voice that she'd been crying. I decided she needed time alone to let all this sink in. So I whispered a prayer, "Lord, will You help her, please?"

A week passed. Kris did not share the contents of the letter nor did she show us the pictures. She was withdrawn and kept all her thoughts and feelings to herself. My fears of loss were being confirmed. Each night when I went to bed, I softly said, "You are my hiding place. Whenever I am afraid, I will trust in You."

Finally one day the following week, in frustration, I stopped her briefly as she was hurrying out of the house after school. "Kris, we need some time to talk. We need to tell each other how we feel so we can understand each other. I'm hurting and it seems like you're running."

"I am," she said.

We agreed to talk that night after Lee brought her home.

I also cornered Lee and spoke to him about my resentment of his "omnipresence". "You are over here or on the phone so much that we have no time as a family, nor does Kris have any time alone. I'm hurting. I need some time to talk with Kris." He said he understood and would bring Kris home a little earlier that night.

A few minutes after they left, Mary Sue called me. "I felt compelled to call you," she said.

With a lump in my throat, realizing God's care for me, I answered, "I'm not doing so hot."

Since she was calling from work and sensing my need, she asked, "Can I call you back later this evening? Then we can talk." I thanked her for her care for me and we agreed on a time.

Mary Sue kept her word and called back later that evening. I was able to experience great release by sharing my thoughts and feelings with her.

Later, when Kris came in that night, we sat down at the kitchen table and shared some of our feelings. She went upstairs and got the pictures she had received from Paula to show to Bill and me. We were eager to see them.

Paula was a slim person whose facial features resembled Kris's, but they were not exact look-alikes. I had pictured someone with long, lustrous brown hair with a tint of auburn like Kris had, but Paula's hair was short, lighter, and it didn't look nearly as thick. In my mind's eye, Paula was still the twenty year old woman who gave birth to Kristin. In reality, she was closer to my age than to Kristin's.

The next morning Susie took a little time before school to encourage me. She knew I was having a hard time with my emotions. "Mom, the other kids seem ungrateful, but you try to be a good mother. Can I pray for you before I go?"

She held my hand and prayed, "Lord, will You fill Mom with Your strength and get rid of her weakness. Lord, will You chase Satan away from Mom?" I thanked her and praised God for the strong faith of a child.

Christmas came that year with all the usual family get-togethers at our house. None of the relatives knew about the life-drama God was directing in our family. We were being silent and confidential, as Bethany had instructed. The conversation focused instead on the short term mission trip that Bill, Kristin, and Uncle Ken were planning to go on in January.

Right in the midst of exam week at the end of Kristin's semester, she had gotten permission from her school to leave for Honduras as a general helper on a two-week medical-dental trip. Brian, Susie, Lee and I went to the airport to see them off. Kris was excited to be able to participate in such a project. I was happy for a break.

While they were gone, I got an ugly insight into myself. The confidentiality of this all was getting to me. I thought, "I'm sure I could tell someone what's happening in our family, maybe Mary, my mentor in Ann Arbor." I asked God about it. I said, "What do You think, Lord? Would it be okay if I told someone?"

Within a day or two, God's answer came clearly three different times. "My grace is sufficient for you." I thought about my motive and realized it was self-pity. I wanted a friend to know what I was feeling and say, "Poor Mare."

The Lord gave me something else to think about that weekend through a woman at church. She didn't know anything about our family, but she was telling me about a difficulty she had with her son. She said, "God showed me that I needed to focus on Him instead of on my son. I had invested so much energy and time into him that my focus was on him. God wanted me to change that."

About a month after the mission trip, we went up north to go down-hill skiing with Bill's sister, Joyce, and her family. Kris couldn't ski because of a previous skiing injury to her knee. I quit early so she and I could take a walk together in the snow. We had a delightful time walking and talking together. Then she asked me a question. "What would you think about my going to Texas to meet Paula?"

Scary thought! I gave her a few negatives and suggested she talk to Mary Sue about it. I thought that if she went she would need a place of retreat which might not be available to her. And I really didn't like the thought of being left out completely. I noticed that as soon as Kris brought up Paula, no matter how gently, I would feel a lump in my throat and tears in my eyes. I was not doing well at trusting.

When we walked back to our van, Susie and Brian were in their cousins' van, so just Kris, Bill, and I rode together to the pizza place. It was already dark, so neither Bill nor Kris could see the tears running down my cheeks. God could. Just when I was reviewing in my mind what He had told me about trusting Him when I am afraid, Bill, who isn't even a singer, began to sing softly. He only sang one line. "Fear not, I am with you."[11]

Amazed, my spirit whispered, "Oh God, was that You speaking to me?"

Just then a second and final line from the same song came from Bill's lips, "To you who for refuge to Jesus have fled." Wow! I knew it was the Lord speaking to me! He was surrounding me with His presence. Through the words of Bill's song God was showing me His love and care for me as He promises those who run to Him.

Kristin: Completely Mine

For me, the week after Mary Sue's call to Paula was filled with nervous anticipation. I thought about Paula almost constantly. I went to school, worked at the bookstore, did homework, and sat in my room—all the time wondering what that first phone call had been like for her. She had no warning, no idea who would be on the other end of the line when she answered the phone. How would that feel? I couldn't imagine.

Mary Sue called soon after she spoke with Paula. When I returned from school, I learned Paula was accepting, even excited, and her husband was supportive. This was the best I could have hoped for! In my heart I thanked Mary Sue, took a deep breath, and began to prepare myself for the next step.

I didn't have any idea what to do next. I was glad Paula would be making the next move. First, she would write me a letter. I would wait.

We had to go through Bethany for a while yet, because I was still seventeen. Paula would write to me and send the letter to Mary Sue. She would read it and be sure no last names or addresses were given, for legal purposes I didn't understand but had to agree to. It was okay. Things were moving along, and going fast enough. Where she lived didn't matter. The fact that she wanted to write, wanted to start again, wanted to know me, these things mattered!

The week after Mary Sue made phone contact with Paula, Mom and I drove to Bethany to meet with her again. After we talked about what to expect next, Mary Sue handed me an envelope. "Here's your first letter! This is just the beginning. You guys have such an exciting time ahead. I'm excited for you!" I thanked her and we said goodbye.

I could hardly wait to get home and up to my room. I wanted to be alone for my first glimpse into her current life.

I carried that letter like it was gold. I sat on the edge of my green bedspread and studied the neat cursive handwriting on the envelope. I didn't want to rush the moment, yet I was eager to read what she had written me. I was aware that yet another figurative door loomed before me, and once the reading was done, there would be no going back.

The envelope was already ripped open, and when I pulled the letter out several pictures fell into my hand. I wanted to save them for last, but the eyes of the woman in the top picture grabbed onto my heart and as they blurred through my tears, I couldn't look away. It was a picture of Paula and her husband, framed in a doorway. They were dressed up and smiling, and her eyes shone with laughter. She was looking into the camera like it was a friend. I stared at her face, studying it carefully, memorizing each line. I couldn't even move on for several moments, feeling that a huge, momentous thing was happening. I was seeing her. My birth mother. For the first time, seeing what she looked like. Finally, I set the photo aside, wiped my eyes, and settled back against the wall to read her letter.

I cried through that as well. I felt a wrenching in my heart when I read the words she had written. I felt the huge gap that was between us, but also felt the connecting thread grow tighter. I was distressed by the hurt she had endured, and felt the first tug of black bitterness for the years of togetherness we had lost. They were gone, irreplaceable, and I began to understand what Mary Sue had told me about grieving. We could never go back. Still, we could go on! It was the best we could do—and it would be okay. We would make up in the future for those years lost to the past. It would be better than okay. It would be wonderful!

She wrote:

December 4, 1989
Dear Kristin,

Seventeen years ago on July 18 at 4:52 p.m. I gave birth to a beautiful baby girl. I loved her so very much that I almost couldn't do what I knew in my heart was best for her. I remember walking down the halls and talking to the other girls at the hospital. Some of them told me they planned to keep their babies. I remember wondering how they would be able to give them what they needed and wanted. I knew they would love their babies just as I loved you Kristin. But I also knew that you needed two parents, a mother and a father, who would both love you together and would be able to give you the things and the home I knew I couldn't. It broke my heart to walk out of that hospital without you in my arms but I knew in my heart I had done the right thing for you no matter how much it hurt me. And I knew that you would always be a part of me, in my thoughts and prayers.

For seventeen years I have cried on your birthday. Not for you, because I knew you were loved and well taken care of. I guess I cried for me, wondering what you were doing, what you looked like, how much you had grown, all kinds of things. That was always the hardest day for me. Please know Kristin, I have always loved you and I always will.

I thank God for your parents. That He sent them at just the right time for us. He couldn't have picked any better. I am so grateful to them for keeping their promise to me. I knew they would tell you why I gave you up for adoption, because I loved you too much to keep you. And please tell them both thank-you for understanding and helping us get to know each other.

Kristin, it is so hard for me to think of you as seventeen years old. I guess my mind pictures you as the beautiful baby girl you were when I saw you last. But a lot of time has gone by and you will soon be eighteen. I want so much to know everything about you and I'm so happy you want to know me. I know we can't get it all done in one letter, but we can get a start, right?

I was born on March 5, 1952, in Forest City, Iowa. I weighed 5 lbs. 4 ozs. I have one older sister and three younger brothers. When I was very young, we moved to the country. We lived on the farm until I was eleven years old. That was when my father had a heart attack and passed away. He was thirty-nine years old.

We moved back to town and after about two years my mom remarried. My stepfather had four children, one girl and three boys. Again we lived in the country for about ten years until my stepfather passed away. My mother has since remarried, about four years ago to another wonderful man. He had three children. One boy and two girls. So our house was always full of children. And we always had lots of dogs and cats and horses.

I am now thirty-seven years old. I'm five foot, six inches tall and I've always been rather thin, I only weigh 105. I guess that runs in my family because none of us have ever been heavy. I have worn glasses since I was in the fifth grade. I tried contacts but one of my eyes just couldn't seem to adjust to them. My hair is kind of a light brown which turns blond in the summer, and I have blue eyes. I have always loved to read. I can sit for hours at a time and read a good book. I also like to knit and crochet. I've made many afghans for people. If you would tell me what colors you like I would love to make one for you.

I have been a secretary for ten years and I work for the Air Force. I am married to a great guy. We have been married for twelve years. He is 47 years old. I have three stepchildren. Shawn is 26, Teresa is 25, and Michael is 22. They are all married, living in different parts of the country. Michael and his wife are expecting a baby any day.

Kristin, for over seventeen years now I have been waiting for that phone call, because I knew deep down that I would hear from you someday. When the phone rang and Mary Sue told me who she was and where she was calling from, my heart stopped. The first thing I said was, "Is she okay?" I thought something had happened to you. When she told me everything was all right and that you wanted to get to know me, I cried. I am so happy and excited about this, words just can't begin to say it. I am going to find some pictures to send you. Please send me some too. I want to know how you looked as you were growing up (I bet you were a beautiful child) and what you look like now, as a young woman of seventeen. I can't wait to see them!

I just don't know where to start with all the questions I have to ask you. Please tell me about your family, do you have any brothers or sisters? Are they younger or older than you? Tell me about your childhood. Just anything that comes to your mind. Tell me about your friends, do you have any boyfriends? What are your hobbies? What church do you go to? Do you get good grades in school? What subject do you like best? I just want to know anything and everything about you Kristin. And I want so very much to know what you look like. For seventeen years I've wondered and now I can finally find out. This is the most wonderful thing, the most precious Christmas gift I have ever had and ever will.

I love you.
Paula

I read the letter again, smiling this time in places. I recognized my own fears, feelings, and sense of humor in the unfamiliar script. She thought and wrote like me, and I was grateful for such a complete and obvious connection. I turned to the pictures and examined her face in each one, drinking in details. I searched the faces of her family with wonder. She had marked the back of each photo with little notes, so I could place and identify each person. This was not only Paula's family. These faces belonged to my family! These were my aunts, uncles, and cousins! This was my stepfather?

Paula herself was the most intriguing. Her eyes almost mirrored mine. One of the pictures, taken when she was seventeen, showed that her cheekbones, lips and smile almost exactly matched my own. I got out my school picture and held them together, comparing them closely. A chill of recognition went through me—a good chill. I had never this closely resembled someone before. It was another confirmation. Another piece clicked into my puzzle.

I hugged the letter to my chest and let myself feel and cry for a few minutes before getting out a pen and paper and beginning my return letter. The tide of emotion was high, and I wanted to write while I still remembered each feeling. I just let it flow, trying to make my pen keep up with it:

December 12, 1989
Dear Paula,

Can you believe this has finally happened? I've waited for this all my life!

I hardly know where to start. There's so much I want to tell you! Paula, I'm so happy this has happened. I always knew it would. I knew you loved me and wanted the best for me. I always understood that, and loved you for it. I remember my friends and people who knew I was adopted would ask me, do you think you'll ever find (or look for) your mother? It was so neat to see in your letter that you "knew deep down" that you'd meet me someday, because that's exactly how I felt! I've been waiting for you forever, because I knew there was a part of me out there somewhere. I always hoped you'd still love me and want to be close friends when we met.

These pictures are incredible. You look just like me! Or should I say I look like you! I'll find some to send to you.

I really do want to get to know you. I'm so glad you do too! That means a lot to me.

You said you still thought of me as a baby. Well, I still thought of you as twenty! Since then seventeen years have gone by. We have a lot of catching up to do!

I guess you know when I was born so I'll skip that much. Your family sounds neat. I love to think about all these aunts and uncles, stepbrothers and sisters I never knew I had! I hope I can meet them someday too.

It's so strange, Paula, in describing yourself, you could have been describing me! I am 5 feet, 5 inches, have medium brown hair that turns lighter in the summer. I weigh about 110 pounds. (It must run in the family, like you said! This is so wonderful, Paula!) My eyes are blue/green/gray, they sort of change. I love to read, write and especially sing. I'm singing a solo for church next Wednesday, on the 13th. I'm singing "Because of Who You Are" by Sandi Patti. I love all kinds of music. I'm thinking about going into it as a career. Or youth counseling. I love to listen and I feel a real burden for teens. Anyway, my room is a mess. I love the color green, and I collect camels. Yes (strange, aren't I?). I would love an afghan. It would be really special from you.

I started writing a journal as soon as I found out about you, to remember how I was feeling. I'd like you to read it someday.

Most people think I am older than I am. They always have, maybe because most of my friends are older.

I have a part time job, besides being in high school, a senior. I work twenty to twenty-five hours a week in a Christian bookstore. I love it there. It's the first real job I've had (I started a year and a half ago). Before that I volunteered in a nursing home for two years. That was an awesome experience.

I love this picture of you. I love all of them! Kenny seems great. He must be. Somehow the pictures make it so real, don't they? It's so hard to believe, to really grasp it. I know you! You're not just someone out there anymore. I always loved you and wanted to know you. But now suddenly, you're here! Real! It's almost overwhelming! But I'm so happy. I wanted you to want to know me too . . .

Anyway, I got glasses in the third grade, and then switched to contacts in ninth. They seem to work okay for me.

I have always loved animals and wanted a dog or cat. I love to ride horseback. I'm a pro (actually I try!). I feel free on horseback. But all I got were gerbils, gold fish, and finally a parakeet. He caught cold and died three years later.

I was so excited when Mary Sue handed me the envelope with your letter in it. When we got home I opened it and just stared at the pictures and read the letter and cried. It's all true, Paula! I'm so happy.

Well, I have a younger brother and sister. Brian is thirteen, Susan is eleven. They pal around together, which suits me fine. I like being alone, my own person. Not everyone can get close to me. I don't think. But you—you will.

My childhood? That could take forever. I had a happy childhood. I always lived in a city, but not very busy. I've been to Iowa. There's a difference. I have always been a "country girl", I loved to be outside, climb trees, catch turtles, pet horses, pick flowers, build castles . . . . I had a sandbox, and monkey bars. I loved to climb them. I love heights. I wasn't scared of big dogs, just spiders. I can't stand spiders. When I was little, there was a collie who lived in the house behind us. They had a field for a back yard. Nikki (the dog) and I would run in it.

We moved here when I was nine. In fourth grade. My grandma died the same year, it was traumatic. But I survived.

Even then I knew I'd know you someday. Now I can hardly believe the someday is here!

I do have a boyfriend. Lee and I have been going out almost a year. It will be a year Jan.1. What a date, huh? He's a really neat guy, you'll like him. I hope you don't mind, I've told him a little about you too. I trust him and he really cares about me and us.

I have a lot of close friends, but Lee takes up a lot of my time. That and school, work, a Bible study we're helping to start with some married friends . . . . I'm always busy! Or cleaning my room or standing still in the dark with the door of my room closed, singing to my favorite tapes. I still have a field behind my house—I think I'd get claustrophobic if I didn't! Sometimes at night I go out there alone to a secret place no one except Tracey and Lee know about. There I can just look at stars, pray, think—I always leave there peaceful.

School is okay, I'd rather not be there most of the time, but that's normal. I'm taking English Literature, Spanish 2, and Reformed Doctrine, as well as concert choir and physiology. I'm an office aide, too. Last year I had creative writing (I love to write, especially poetry!) and psychology. I hate all math and science. I guess I'm more dreamer than mathematician.

Officially I belong to a CRC church, but I've been going to an Assemblies of God church. I really love that. I'm part of their youth group. I'm pretty active in that, too. I love the people there, the excitement in God's word, the sincerity. I've grown so much spiritually since I've gone there (about a year ago, maybe more). On Wednesday we have youth services, which is where I have to sing next week. I've sung duets there, and in churches around the area (once in a church that played on the radio, how about that!) but never a solo. I'm a little nervous.

I get semi-decent grades in school. I should study more, but I hate to.

I play the guitar, a little. I used to a lot more.

You are beautiful like I thought, Paula. This picture of you in the living room looks like me in the morning!

Is your hair still long like this one of you and Kenny? Well, longer than when you got married? How are Shawn, Teresa, and Michael? My stepbrothers and stepsister! Is that okay, that I claim them? I want to be close to you, Paula, a part of you. I want you to stay part of me, too. Do they (Shawn and them) know about me? Has Michael's wife had her baby? I want to know all about you, too. I don't know where to start asking questions, just talk to me!

I'm so glad . . . This is the best thing in the world! I want you to know I thank you for what you did for me seventeen years ago. I would like to have been part of your life but you did the right thing. I don't resent or blame you for anything. I'm just glad everything worked out so well for both of us!

I will look for more pictures. The ones with my name are my senior pictures. Do you think I look like you?

I'm so happy, Paula! I'm so glad to finally know you! I've always known you loved me and I've always loved you.

I love you.

Kristin

P.S. I'm getting some prints made of earlier pictures, I'll send those later.

Dinner that night was quiet—I was in my own world, a new one that didn't (at first) include my parents. I told them I had read the letter and gave them an outline with a few details, but I didn't show it to them. It was very important to me that this feeling—this proof, this new aspect—be completely mine for a while. Not only did I need time to sort out these emotions, I needed to revel in the fact that Paula was mine, I was hers, and we were together again. There was no room for my mom and dad at that point—I needed to distance myself from them in order to form a new bond with Paula. In the back of my mind, I wondered—knew—that it would hurt my parents if I pulled away, but I needed to do this for myself. I had to be alone, separate, to meet her.

She was mine. She was a page in my life that was new. She was different, she was my blood (which I had never known or understood before), and she belonged to me and me alone. She was a piece of me I had always waited and longed for, and I intended to go through this new phase alone.

I mailed my letter off to Mary Sue and waited for Paula's reply. It was near Christmas, and when her next letter arrived, it was with a card and a small white box. She had sent me a beautiful gold nugget bracelet. I was thrilled, and put it on immediately, wearing it proudly.

The gift meant even more to me when I read in the letter that she had purchased two identical bracelets. She would wear one also, and every time she wore it, she would be thinking of me. It established yet another link in the chain quickly forming between us.

CHAPTER 23

Paula: For Me Alone

It was very hard waiting for her letter. Every day I waited for the mail to come, and when there was no letter Kenny would say, "Nothing today? Well, probably tomorrow."

Then the day finally came when her letter was there. I was thrilled—a letter from my daughter! I sat alone at the kitchen table to read it. There were tears in my eyes before I even got the envelope open. Her letter was exactly what I'd been waiting to hear for seventeen years! Just as I knew it would be, it was full of warmth and joy and love.

The most important thing in the world for a birth mother to hear is exactly what Kristin wrote in that first letter:

> You did the right thing. I don't resent or blame you for anything . . . I've always known you love me and I've always loved you . . . You needed me as much as I needed you . . . You are like me, you love me the way I love you. You're not just someone out there anymore . . . I don't know where to start asking questions, just talk to me.

Reading these words made me feel as if a giant weight had been lifted from my shoulders. For years I had prayed she wouldn't hate me or resent me for that difficult decision I had made so long ago. To know she had wondered about me and had loved me and needed me seemed to seal the bond and closeness I had always felt for her. Knowing at last that she had always felt the same made me cry.

I read her letter over and over again. She sent several of her senior pictures with her letter. Looking at her pictures brought a feeling of peace and love I had never felt before. The pictures made it all seem real. Year after year of wondering what she looked like, holding onto the only image I had of her, my tiny beautiful baby girl. For me it was like longing for something for what seemed to be forever. When I finally got what I had longed and prayed for, it was even better than I could have ever hoped or imagined. This was my daughter and she looked just like me! It seemed I couldn't look at the pictures long enough. One was taken in an outdoor setting. She had one hand on her hip and was looking straight into the camera. She was wearing slacks and a pretty plaid blouse. The shape of Kristin's face, her eyes, her hair color, her smile, even her posture were mine. I could have been looking at a picture of myself at her age. Also from her first letter I learned we not only looked alike but *were* alike. The similarities were uncanny. We were both the same height, the same weight. We had the same hair color and the same changing eye color (blue, green, gray). We liked the same things, reading, singing, and animals. We even had our own special place where we could be alone to think and wonder, to watch the sunset and dream. It was like reading a letter about myself. I knew every word she wrote came straight from her heart.

I shared her pictures and parts of her letter with Kenny shortly after reading it myself. He didn't pressure me at all, but I knew how much this meant to him also. He sat with tears in his eyes as I read portions of her letter to him. Kenny was the only person who really knew the depth of my feelings and emotions. Even so, I could not share all of her, or all of her letters, even with him. I wanted, I needed her for me alone. I had created inside myself a space just for her and me. Finally she was in there with me. There was no room for anyone else. She will be in that space with me forever.

My mother wrote to me shortly after hearing about her first letter. She said "We think about things that have happened long ago, and we are so grateful to God for His loving care of us all, and for taking care of our little daughter and granddaughter all these years." Her words made me think how faithful God had been in watching over this baby I had committed to His care so long ago. He shared our love for her. He made sure she was brought up in a good Christian home with a mother and father who loved her very much, and she loved them too. When the time was right He led her to me. He knew the only thing in the world that could give me the inner peace I craved was her. He gave us to each other. God is good! I already had a home and family that I loved very much. He had blessed me with a wonderful husband who was kind and faithful and loved me unconditionally. He had also blessed me with three wonderful children to help raise. I was happy and proud to be their "mom". I always would be. Michael at age twenty-one stepped aside as the youngest in our family, and Kristin took that honored position. The two of them had that in common though: Michael would always be my baby boy, and Kristin would always be my baby girl.

Mary Sue was our "go-between" and became a very special friend and confidant to me. We talked many times in those first months, both by letters and by telephone. She understood me right from the start and always knew just what to say when I was feeling overwhelmed or inadequate. I felt completely comfortable with her. I could ask her or tell her anything. At one of my inadequate times she wrote, "I sense when I talked to you that there is such a strong desire on your part to do and be *everything right*, so to speak. Is that true? Let me say to you—you're doing great—you'll be fine. I urge you to take a deep breath and know what a special person you are in all this. I've gotten to know a very wise, very loving woman who has handled life well and who many people have come to love and admire, Kristin included." Mary Sue could always bring me back down to earth and reality.

After Kristin and I had been writing and talking for about six months Mary Sue mentioned in one of her letters that she wanted to get some correspondence started between Kristin's adoptive mother and me. I was rather anxious about this but I knew it was very important that we get to know each other. After all, we had something priceless in common. I soon found out there was nothing to be nervous about. Kristin's mother Mary was just as anxious as I was. She wrote, "I have thought of you and prayed for you often over the years—always suspecting, almost hoping that we would meet one day. Now that the thought is almost reality, it seems more scary." I felt the same way. I think it helped both of us to write to each other a few times before we met. It let us get to know each other as real people, sharing some of our thoughts and feelings. Learning that we had more in common than our daughter helped alleviate my anxiety about meeting her. We both loved to read and enjoyed music. We shared some of our background with each other and wrote about our families. I felt comfortable about our eventual face to face meeting.

CHAPTER 24

Kristin: Voices

Even though I knew this time was hard for them, my mom and dad were very supportive and understanding. They never pushed or pried, and let me take a few steps back without trying to guilt or crowd me. I know my mother hurt, and sometimes I found her crying. It hurt me to see her in pain, and I hugged and tried to reassure her, but I knew we had to do this separately. I knew she had to deal with her fears and loss on her own. I also knew that my love for them would never change. I would be back. They were my parents 100% and I loved them 100%. My mind was full. I couldn't deal with myself and their emotions at the same time. I also wanted their trust—that I would "come back" to them. They were the only parents I knew. They had raised me correctly and given me everything. Why would I ever turn away? They were always interested any time I talked about Paula or got a new letter or pictures (which I did show them), and they never tried to avoid the reality of our forming relationship.

In one of our early correspondences, I asked Paula a question I had always wondered about. Had she chosen a name for me? I wondered how I would feel to know the answer. What would it do to me? She answered in her return letter:

"Yes, I did have a name picked out for you. I was going to name you Kendra Dawn. Do you like it? How would you have liked a nickname like Kenny? I think Kendra is a beautiful name. But I knew your parents would want to give you a name from them, and they picked a beautiful name too."

I read that part of her letter over and over. Kendra Dawn. Who was Kendra Dawn? Was I supposed to be Kendra Dawn? Was I? Was she a different person than me?

This was my mother, the person who gave birth to me. She chose this name for me long before my parents chose the name Kristin. I had always liked my name and thought it fit me well. But now, Kendra? Should I be Kendra? Would it change me?

I wondered if she should have told me—if it would put my identity in crisis. Would I have been better not knowing? It was another "might have been". What was I supposed to do?

I wrote back:

I like the name you picked for me. I wonder how to react to it. It's like I legally have two names—which one am I, since you called me Kendra and they called me Kristin? I know you don't expect me to change my name or anything, but . . . which one am I, really?"

I'm not sure what kind of response I was looking for. In a way I wanted her to say I was Kendra—her daughter. But no, I was Kristin. I was who I had become. I wanted her to claim me as her own, yet accept me for who I was. Could I have it both ways?

Her answer was perfect.

"Kristin or Kendra—which one are you really? You are one and both. You are you! I would have named you Kendra; they named you Kristin. That does not change how you are or who you are. You are one very special person who is loved by a great number of people."

Paula gave me the permission to just be me—Kristin and Kendra, product of both her and my parents. It was a confirmation and a relief. I was her—I was me! The pieces of Paula that I carried within me bore the name Kendra.

Soon after this, Paula and my mother began to communicate by letter. They were very cautious and careful, not wanting to hurt each other or me. At first, I felt wary, almost jealous. Paula was mine. However, before long I began to understand the necessity of their relationship, and realized I felt secure enough in my relationship with each of them to encourage them in building their own. Mom often expressed to me how thankful she was for Paula and her decision to give me life, and I knew she had much to offer Paula in the way of facts and memories. I loved, and could trust, each of them.

Paula and I communicated only by letter for several months. It was slow going, but that was okay. We both needed time to get our thoughts in order. The few questions I had about my birth father and their relationship, I saved for a later date. Our first few letters talked mostly about the present, and our likenesses and differences. We were feeling each other out, and every time we agreed on something, I felt more elated. She was the piece I had been waiting for.

I could tell from her letters the depth of her love for me. She explained a little about how she gave me up, how hard it was, and that she did it because she believed it was best for me. When I was being completely honest with myself, I didn't know how to feel about that. Did I agree with her decision? I didn't know. I certainly couldn't say for sure, not knowing all the circumstances, and never having been in that situation myself. While dealing with these questions I experienced many conflicting emotions that took me months to work through. I did believe that she loved me then and now. That was really all that was important. The past couldn't be changed anyway. I felt sorry for her anguish at my birth, but I couldn't put myself in that place. It was her pain, her decision. It was almost like feeling sorry for a stranger, because it was so long ago, and there was nothing I could do to ease it. Initially, I felt some resentment because such a momentous decision had been made for me, and I wasn't given a choice. Of course, I was an infant, and that only makes sense, but it left me with a vague feeling of helplessness. On the other hand, she truly believed she had done the right thing, and I wanted to accept it and move on. Everything had worked out well for me.

I wrote in my journal a lot, although most of the things I was feeling were new to me and extremely hard to put into words. How do you describe ten emotions at once? I spent quiet hours in my room, contemplating alone what Paula meant to me, and how knowing her would change my life. I talked many things out with Lee as a listening ear. He was a wonderful support, and many evenings when I was mourning the loss of years, feeling frustrated, or trying to get a handle on some new, unexplainable emotion, he let me cry or talk, and took time to comfort me.

Shortly before my eighteenth birthday, Mary Sue gave me Paula's phone number. In our letters we had begun discussing plans for a reunion. Paula would be coming to Michigan in July, and we would get to meet, hug, and talk in person for the first time. It was a wonderful thing to look forward to, but hard to plan through the mail. Mary Sue knew that it would be easier for planning if we were able to speak together.

On that Sunday afternoon, I took the kitchen phone with its long winding cord down the steps of the basement and shut the door. I sat in the darkness on the floor with my back to the paneled wall. My stomach was spinning somewhere by my feet on the cold carpeted cement as I read the number from a scrap of paper and placed my first call to Paula. She knew I would be calling that afternoon, so when she answered, she expected it to be me.

"Hello?" Her voice was hesitant.

"Hi," I said. "It's Kris."

"Well, Hi!"

"Hi...," Silence. "This is kind of strange, isn't it?' I said. "I can't believe I'm finally, actually talking to you," I heard a sniff on the other end. "Are you crying already? I haven't said anything yet!"

"I know," Paula laughed through her tears. "It's just so wonderful to hear the voice of my baby girl after almost eighteen years!"

I knew what she meant. A lump was in my throat as well, and we just sat silently for a moment. I was saddened by the years that divided us and made this first conversation so difficult.

"Where are you?" Paula finally asked, and I responded by describing the basement where I had spent so many hours playing while I grew up. After that the words flowed more smoothly, both of us often interjecting many times with "Wow! I can't believe it!" Those words made us both laugh. And laughing lightened things up considerably. Once the initial awkwardness was over, we talked like old friends for an hour. I gave her more details about my family, school classes, friends, and my boyfriend Lee.

"Do you know how we found you?" I asked, because I wasn't sure how much of the story she had heard.

"Not exactly," she said slowly. "I know Pam had a part in it somehow, but Mary Sue didn't give me any details. Pam wouldn't tell me either, she said it was yours to tell. It didn't matter, though. All that matters to me is that I have you back!"

"Tracey is my best friend," I told her.

"Tracey...?" she sounded confused. Then she understood. "Tracey?!"

I told her the whole story. "Tracey and I met in Kentucky at a music conference four years ago. We clicked right away, and have been best friends ever since. I began to spend a lot of time with her at her house, and got to know Pam really well too. Pam told me right away that I reminded her of her best friend. She always watched me, and asked questions. Especially once she found out I was adopted. Then she started asking questions about my birth mother and what I knew. Some time later she mentioned to me that this friend, who she thought I looked like, had given her baby up for adoption."

Paula made an incredulous sound. I could appreciate her astonishment.

"Yes, I know." I said. "Just by looking at me and watching me, Pam recognized how much like you I am, and put two and two together. Can you believe that? She finally called your mom to confirm the dates, but she already knew. I guess she knew for sure a while ago, but was waiting for the right time to tell us."

"Wow. That is truly amazing. That Pam! That figures, it would be like her to figure this out. Well, she knows me, all right, and she would know if you were acting like me. What an incredible story!"

"Never heard anything like it."

"I just can't believe that you . . . . So you—chose my best friend's daughter for your best friend . . . and Pam recognized you to be my daughter even though seventeen years had passed . . .?" I could tell she was still trying to sort it all out. I understood. It was incredible.

"Everyone I talk to says we should write a book." I laughed.

"Maybe we should, at that, baby girl. Maybe we should."

In the next half hour she told me my birth father's name, how they had met, and that they had lived together for four months. After that, she had moved in with Pam until I was born. I did have questions about the past, but I didn't ask for any more details. That would come later. I wanted her to know I accepted her for her and wanted to build a new relationship based on the future. I wasn't calling her only for answers. I told her I forgave her, and as we cried together for the first time, I assured her I never blamed or felt angry with her, and never doubted her love for me.

It was a wonderful talk, but exhausting, and afterward I felt satisfied and drained. It took a lot of energy to feel that many emotions and to try to face and explain them. We had promised to talk again the following Sunday, and exchanged "I love yous" as we said goodbye. I went upstairs, and felt that unexplainable grief and emptiness. On the one hand our conversation and reassurances fulfilled me, but on the other I grieved again for lost time and lost chances.

CHAPTER 25

Paula: The Most Beautiful Things

Kristin and I wrote letters and sent pictures back and forth sharing our lives and our hopes for the future. The time finally came when we could talk on the phone. Mary Sue said, "I think you are both ready." We were ready and very eager. Mary Sue set up that first call. It was decided Kristin would call me first. I was very excited. I could hardly wait for this next giant step toward my daughter! I had always known one day we would be face to face, a time when I could do something I'd been waiting seventeen years to do, hold her in my arms and tell her I love her. Still I knew we had to go through the steps, and we could do that. We both knew the time would come. We knew about each other. In our letters we had shared our lives, our hearts, and our innermost feelings with each other. Now, finally, I would actually hear her voice and talk to her. It was a very exciting time for me and also very emotional.

The day of our first phone call finally came. I was a very happy, very excited, nervous wreck! What on earth would I say to her? I knew it didn't really matter what I said or what she said. What did matter is that we would be actually talking to each other. I just could not wait to tell her—really tell her—I loved her, and to hear her say she loved me! I finally knew what she looked like through her pictures, and this very day I would hear the sound of her voice for the first time.

I put on an old comfortable shirt of Kenny's, and as the hours and then minutes went by I sat at the kitchen table and worked on the afghan I was making for her. Finally the phone rang, and as I heard my daughter's voice for the first time, Kenny took my picture. I was upset with him at first, but after the pictures were developed and I saw the look on my face I was happy to have it. I could see in my eyes what I was feeling in my heart. I could hear the trepidation in her voice, but I could also hear the emotion and the love. This was the beautiful baby girl I had given birth to! I was overwhelmed. After the initial hello and a few tears, I wasn't nervous any more. The most important part was simply talking to her. In those moments on the phone that day, I took out the piece of my heart that belonged only to her and gave it to her with love. In return, she took out the piece of her heart that belonged only to me and trustingly held it out for me to take. We both knew the pieces would slip gently into place and fit perfectly. The most beautiful things in the world are not seen or touched, they are felt with the heart. It truly was the missing piece. She said, "I love you," in her soft quiet voice and I could hear tears behind those treasured words.

There was no hesitation in my answer, "I love you too." My voice was steady, but there were tears in my eyes. As we said goodbye we both knew and understood we were whole at last. Finally I knew exactly where my daughter was, and we were just a phone call away. I had actually talked to her and heard her tell me she loved me. My heart was full, and I had never been happier!

I spoke with Mary briefly that day after talking to Kristin. I didn't know what to say to her. Quite frankly, I don't have any recollection of what I did say. My mind and emotions were completely filled with the sound of my daughter's voice and her first words to me. Still, I felt a connection with Mary and a sense of peace about her. I was emotionally overwhelmed when I hung up the phone. I sat still for a long time and just enjoyed the happiness I felt.

Mary wrote that every year on Kristin's birthday she prayed for me, thinking what I must be going through. It's strange to think that all those years she was thinking and wondering about me while I was thinking and wondering about her, and we were both loving "our" daughter with all our hearts! She also wrote, "I have been praying since October that we could become friends, and that neither of us would be tempted to selfishness or jealousy." My first thought, *that is so true*. It became absolutely imperative that we didn't let that happen. We had to realize Kristin loved us both and, of course, we both loved her.

The first time I read the poem, "Legacy of an Adopted Child," I couldn't help but think how it so accurately described the deep love both Mary and I had for Kristin:

Once there were two women who never knew each other,
One you do not remember—the other you call Mother.
Two different lives shaped to make yours one.
One became your guiding star—the other became your sun.

The first gave you life and the second
Taught you to live in it.
The first gave you a need for love
And the second was there to give it.

One gave you a nationality; the other gave you a name.
One gave you the seed of talent; the other gave you an aim.
One gave you emotions; the other calmed your fears.
One saw your first sweet smile; the other dried your tears.

One gave you up,
It was all that she could do.
The other prayed for a child
And God led her straight to you.

And now you ask me through your tears
The age old question through the years:

Heredity or Environment—
Which are you the product of?

Neither, my darling, neither—
Just two different kinds of love. [12]

I had given birth to Kristin. She was physically, emotionally, and mentally a living part of me, and I loved her with all my heart. I was her mother. Mary took those parts and nurtured them. She guided her with love and compassion and complete devotion. She was her mother. Mary and I both understood this and respected each other. We had become friends, and I was very thankful for that.

I was one very happy person. I finally had my daughter. We were connected at last. Never would we be separated again.

The whole thing seemed like a dream. It had to be a dream, my mind reasoned as I thought of Mary Sue's first phone call, then writing to my daughter and getting letters from her—letters full of love and promise for all the years ahead. I looked at the pictures, my first glimpse of her since the day she was born. It was hard to believe I was seeing my daughter.

We talked for hours on the phone, pretty much about everything. I learned her emotions, her humor, her personality, her likes and dislikes. We were so very much alike, and now every birth mother's dream was about to come true for me. I was going to see my child. I was going to look into her eyes, and I knew I would see myself there. I was going to hold her tight and tell her face to face just how much she had always meant to me. I couldn't wait to tell her how much I loved her and how much I wanted her in my life forever. Of course, she had always been in my life, but the years of not knowing where she was or if she was all right were over. We would be as close as the nearest phone. It was almost impossible to believe this was really happening!

Kristin and I decided I would fly to Michigan and we would meet at Bethany. I would be able to meet and speak with Mary Sue for a few minutes before seeing Kristin. I was looking forward to meeting this sweet counselor who had been such a help to us. We had been very close for the past months through our letters and phone calls. I already felt like I knew her.

Kenny and I would drive from Texas to Des Moines a couple of days early. All of his family lived there, so I would spend a few days with him visiting family and friends. He would stay in Des Moines while I flew on alone to Michigan. Pam would meet me at the airport and I would stay with her and Anthony. She would drive me to Bethany, just like that day so long ago. She wouldn't have it any other way and neither would I. Kristin and I talked at least every Sunday afternoon and our bond grew stronger as we shared our thoughts and feelings with each other. I knew the time would come for my prayers to be answered. I would meet my daughter and hold her in my arms at last. My thoughts took me back to the day she was born, when she was ready and I wasn't. This time she was ready, and so was I.

CHAPTER 26

Mary: Okay, I'll Do It

"He is no fool who gives what he cannot keep to gain what he cannot lose."[13]

Jim Elliot

In the spring I watched the relationship between Kris and myself change even more. She became more distant; I became more sad. Bill said, "Let go, Mare!" When I talked to Mary Sue, she said, "Let go. She'll come around." I didn't know how to let go.

I kept thinking, if I could just communicate with Paula, I might feel better. Both Paula and I had expressed a desire to write each other through Mary Sue, but followed Kristin's wishes and didn't. Finally after Kris had some time to get to know Paula, she gave her permission for us to write. Paula asked Mary Sue if I would write first since she didn't know what to say.

Toward the end of April, I wrote the first letter to the mother of my oldest child. It was a step in building the bridge of friendship I had prayed for. I wrote:

Dear Paula,

Thank you for choosing life for Kristin and for giving her to us to enjoy through her growing up years. She has been a delightful child and seems to be quickly growing into a woman. I thought of you and prayed for you often over the years—always suspecting, almost hoping that we would meet someday. Now that the thought is almost reality, it seems more scary. I hope writing a few times will help us to get to know each other a bit before we meet.

Whenever Kristin celebrated a birthday, my prayer for you was that you would experience God's peace and the assurance that you made a right choice considering the circumstances. I hope you found that to be true. I am eager to hear from you when you have the time to write back. I'm looking forward to this correspondence.

Sincerely,

Mary

May arrived marking another month closer on the countdown to Kristin's eighteenth birthday in July. Time seemed to accelerate with a big conglomeration of year-end school events.

Bill had a mission board meeting scheduled in Mississippi. He invited me to go along. When we returned home, we were greeted with rough edges around our relationship with Kris and a request from Paula through Mary Sue for permission to begin phone calls to Kris and us.

Frustrated, I answered Mary Sue, "I'm sorry. I can't do it yet. She's still a stranger to me. Kris has shared nothing but the pictures. I really wouldn't know what to say."

Mother's Day came as an "upper" a few days later. Susie gave me a rose; Brian, a bouquet of spring flowers. Kris gave me a very meaningful card and a small plaque inscribed with the words, "Mom—thanks for being there." Kris and I shared an encouraging moment alone, hugging and telling each other that we did love each other even though some of the times were rough right now. Even Tracey sent a special card to "Mom" expressing her love for me during a difficult time.

Soon after Mother's Day, Paula responded to my letter with some very personal, touching thoughts which encouraged me. She wrote:

Dear Mary,

I am so glad to get your letter. After all these years I'm sure you and I have a lot to share. It does my heart and mind good to get your letter. I feel as if I know you, like we have been close all these years, which I guess we have been.

You say, "Thank You for choosing life for Kristin." Mary, there was never any other choice for me. I knew I had to have my baby. I couldn't have an abortion—I've never believed in that!

As for "giving her to us," Mary, I believe in my heart that it was God's plan, it was meant to be. I'm glad He chose you for her, you have done a wonderful job of raising her into the beautiful young woman she is today.

I know what you mean about scary. It's as if our whole world has changed, isn't it? All I can say, Mary, is thank you for making my world scary.

I just know that when we two meet it won't be scary for us anymore. I think we will be more like friends meeting for the first time.

Sincerely,
Paula

After Paula's letter came, Mary Sue suggested phone calls begin, and we decided it was time for a break in confidentiality. Each time I told the story to a relative or one of our close friends, those listening were amazed at God's hand in it, and I found God was changing me. I was no longer looking for pity, but instead I was eager to tell of God's leading in all of our lives.

As pious as I sounded, however, I was still not where God wanted me to be. Toward the end of May, on a Saturday, I recorded in my journal:

I'm having a difficult time today. The joy is gone. The song is missing from my spirit. I feel like Kris and I are in a power struggle, a tug of war. I want to put down my side and quit. If I could run away today, I would. My whole body is tense with stress.

This whole week has been hard. Much of the conflict is centered on the word *control*. Kris wants it, and I want it. Lord, teach me how to lay it down, to let go and let You.

The following day, early in the afternoon, Kris made her first phone call to Paula in Texas. We had agreed that I would not talk to Paula unless she asked to speak with me. While Kris was talking on a phone on the basement stairs, I was reading a book by Elisabeth Elliot, *Shadow of the Almighty*. I read something that was perfect for me at the moment. Elisabeth said that God's will is always bigger than we think it might be, but we must trust that it is good.

When Kris and Paula finished their conversation, Kris came up the stairs to ask me to get on the kitchen phone. Seemingly to protect Paula, Kris had warned me not to intimidate Paula by talking too much, so I carefully greeted her.

She said, "I don't really know what to say. I just feel overwhelmed! I've been nervous all morning waiting for this call." She was friendly, open, but shy. She expressed herself slowly. She sounded just like Kris!

I responded by assuring her, "We're just ordinary people. You don't have to be afraid of us. I'm hoping the letters and phone calls will help the reunion to be easier." I also told her, "Kris is being very private about all this. We are trying to stand back and not be controlling, but at the same time we're trying to give her the love and support she needs."

Having had teenagers, Paula was sympathetic. Then I said, "Mary Sue reminded us that adoption is a triangle, so we cannot and must not get out of the picture entirely." With that in mind, Paula and I agreed to exchange some information about ourselves through letters.

The phone calls between Paula and Kristin continued twice a week as Kristin's graduation approached. Jealousy raised its ugly head in me as I could hear talking and laughter coming from the phone conversations. There seemed never to be time for Kris to talk with me.

It was during this difficult season that I began to pray two very specific prayers to resist temptation and to overcome my self-centered thoughts. As I sat on the floor behind an easy chair, in front of a heat vent, in our family room for my early morning quiet times, I prayed, "This is too unusual, God. Don't let this go to waste."

While thinking about all that God and Paula had shared with me, I prayed, "Lord, give me a love big enough to share."

The end of the school year came with all its roller coaster moments of grace and grind. All three kids were graduating from a different school: Susie, from grade school; Brian, from middle school; and Kris, from high school. Kris was one of several students given special recognition in "honors convocation" for those achieving a grade point average greater than 3.0. She also received a small trophy to recognize her as the recipient of the National School Choral Award. We were proud of her and thankful.

On Monday, after the graduation weekend, Bill, Brian, Susie and I left for a two week vacation with our pop-up tent trailer to the Rocky Mountains in Colorado. It provided a much needed break after the whirlwind of activity and emotions that the graduations brought. There was also the stress of watching some red flags go up in the relationship between Kris and Lee. Both Bill and I thought the relationship was slipping into one that was less than healthy.

About a week into our vacation, Bill made a pointed comment to me: "Mare, you're having too much trouble letting go of Kris." He observed that I was having stressful dreams every night and no peace during the days. I didn't want to admit it, but I knew he was right.

Every day I would think about Kris and Paula, Kris and Lee, Kris and Mary Sue, Kris and Pam, Kris and me. Every time I thought about Kris and me, I felt sad, wondering if it would ever be Kris and me again. I prayed, "I feel very left out and lonely, Lord. Is this what letting go is all about? Teach me to let go of my children and cling to You, Lord. You are my strength and my best friend. Psalm 108:1-4 (NIV) says, 'My heart is steadfast, O God; I will sing and make music with all my soul. I will praise You and I will sing to You . . . for great is Your love, higher than the heavens; Your faithfulness reaches to the skies.' O God, help me to be an encourager to Kris and not be paralyzed by self-pity."

The next day, while I was reading *Shadow of the Almighty*, the Lord spoke to me. I was reading the epilogue which contained a letter Jim Elliot wrote to his mother when his brother, Bert, sailed to Peru. One paragraph really got my attention. Apparently, Jim's mom was having a hard time with Bert's departure. Jim reminded her that we, as believers, are to identify with Jesus, who actually suffered death on a cross. In His work with His followers, Jesus emphasized the need to be willing to sacrifice, not so much worldly stuff, but family relationships. Jim went on to say that's how we grow strong— through releasing those we love. Nothing else would do.

Oh, wow! When I read that, I knew God had spoken to me. He was asking me to love Him more than Kristin. He was telling me to trust Him and let go.

That evening, in our trailer, as Bill was reading one of C.S. Lewis's Narnia series to the kids and me, I sat with tears running down my cheeks thinking about what God had said. Bill and the kids ignored my tears. By now tears were a familiar sight to them.

The next morning, when I woke up, I knew what I had to do. On my way to the outhouse, walking alone in the brilliant morning sun among towering mountain peaks, I looked up and raised my voice to the Lord. I said, "Okay, God. I'll do it. I'll let her go even if it means she never comes back!"

That was the decisive moment when I finally let go. It took words of surrender spoken out loud to Almighty God, and in exchange He poured peace into my soul, incredible peace.

On the way home from Colorado, as we drove across the Midwestern states, I wrote Paula a letter describing our family history as well as a brief description of each of us individually. It was fun writing to someone who was truly interested. She responded with a similar letter about herself.

The reunion between Paula and Kris had been set for the last weekend in July. Paula had plans to fly to Grand Rapids and would stay with Pam. Before she came, she wanted another opportunity for conversation with me. She asked Mary Sue if I would call her one more time.

On July 17, Kris called Paula first and told her I would call later that evening. When I did call, we ended up talking for an hour! We had a ball!

Among other things, Paula assured me by saying, "You will never lose your children, Mary. You raised them. They're yours. I just want permission to love Kris too."

I told her, "Sometimes I think adoptive parents try too hard. It's almost as if we're trying to prove something. This may sound funny, but have you ever gone to a 4-H fair? I feel like I'm at one. We raised our kids first of all to present them to the Lord. When you came into the picture, I was reminded of 4-H fairs. We did our best. Now it's time to present her to the judge. I wonder if the judge will like the finished product. Will we get a blue ribbon?"

Paula laughed softly, and said, "It's blue ribbon time for you, Mary."

Later that evening when Kris came in, she and I sat at the kitchen table so I could tell her as much of the phone conversation as I could remember. Kris seemed pleased. Then she asked me the question I had been waiting for.

She spoke slowly and hesitantly, "I don't know quite how to say this, Mom. How would you feel if I called Paula 'Mom'? I don't want to hurt you. It would have a different meaning than the word 'Mom' means for you."

I was honored to be asked. It allowed me an opportunity to be gracious, to practice letting go. I answered, "I think you should. It would make her feel good and it would be less awkward with Pam whom you already call 'Mom'." Then I added, "Do what your heart feels, honey. You'll know what's right."

A couple of days later, I called Mary Sue. I thought she deserved to hear good news for a change. "Kristin's attitude is changing. She's more positive and inclusive." I also told her about my hour-long phone call with Paula.

She was happy to hear things were going well at our house, but she said, "I'm especially happy to hear Kris seems to be thinking about the needs and feelings of others now, not just her own."

A few days before the reunion, I wrote in Kristin's little red encouragement journal:

> The day we've been waiting for is almost here—the day you will meet your birth mother, Paula. I don't know what this reunion will be like, but I want you to remember two things. Remember Whose you are. You're a child of the King. And remember that Dad and I love you more than you can imagine, and we always will.

CHAPTER 27

Pam: Let Go and Let God

Paula and Kristin continued to write letters and eventually began talking on the phone. Kristin did not offer to share what they talked about. Although I wanted to know every word, I had to continue to let go and let God be in control. When Kristin had questions for me, I answered honestly and tried not to pry. One day she asked, "Mom, how am I like Paula?"

I thought of all the ways Kristin reminded me of Paula and tried to pick a general answer, "Paula looked about like you do now when I met her, except for her hair of course. She already had it colored quite blond. I think it was naturally about the color of yours. Of course she probably looks older now."

"When did you last see Paula?"

"Boy, let me think about that a minute. I think Tracey was about eight or nine years old. Paula was never much of a letter writer, and once she remarried and moved, we just lost touch. Now of course, we talk to each other on the phone." This seemed to satisfy Kristin for the time being. Most of our conversations about Paula were rather brief. Kristin wanted information just a little at a time. She would process it for a week or so, and when she had more questions, she would ask. I could sense her wonder over Paula and her need to find similarities. Yet at the same time, Paula was precious to Kristin and not something she wanted to share. I tried to be sensitive and not overwhelm her with details or answers she needed to hear from Paula.

Of course that wasn't what I wanted to do. I wanted to sit and tell her about Paula for hours. I wanted to tell her that she got her love of reading and poetry from Paula, to tell her that she sat the way Paula sat, and even laughed like her. Although I wanted to share these things with Kristin, I held back. The bond that already existed between them needed to be strengthened without me in the middle.

I also ached for Paula. As much as I wanted to fill the empty places in her heart with Kristin's laughter, words, and love of the outdoors, I wouldn't. Paula and Kristin needed to share these precious details between them to strengthen the bond God had put in place so long ago. As hard as it was, the Lord reminded me I needed to step back.

The day of Paula's arrival finally came. It was a hot, hazy day, the kind we get in Michigan in July, and the kind it had been so many years ago when Kristin had been born. I couldn't help but think how far God had brought this all since that time.

I was feeling both nervous and excited. I wanted things to go right for Paula and for Kristin. I was nervous that Paula would begin to question me again about Kristin and ask questions whose answers she needed to hear from Kristin. I had no idea how much of the whole story Kristin had shared with Paula so I felt a little on shaky ground, not something I was used to feeling when I was around Paula.

My concerns immediately disappeared when Paula came walking off the plane. She looked like the same Paula I had held in my heart for so many years. She had on blue jeans and a shirt and still carried herself with the same calm assurance she always had. We flew into each other's arms, both laughing and crying at the same time. We would hug, hold each other at arm's length, laugh and then hug again. As we walked through the airport, we kept looking at each other and smiling like a couple of grade school girls. I think neither of us could actually believe we were seeing each other again, much less believe the story that the Lord was unfolding before our very eyes.

"So, how was your flight?"

"Nerve-wracking, actually. I don't know why I am so nervous about all this, Pam, but I am. Plus I am not crazy about flying."

"Anybody would be nervous. I mean you are going to be reunited with your daughter today. I can hardly believe it."

"Me neither. I thought I would probably never see her again and now, I get to. It seems like a precious gift. I'm afraid this is only a dream and I'm going to wake up."

"Well, it's not. It's as real as can be." With both of us still grinning, we got in the car and began the ride to my house. As we rode, we continued to sort out our feelings.

"I can't even begin to imagine what all of this is like for you, Paula. After all these years and all the pain you had over giving Kristin up, and yet feeling you did the right thing. Do you still feel that way?"

"Like I did the right thing? You bet I do. It was hard, you above all people know that, Pam. You were there with me through the whole thing. I know she has a good home, with two Christian parents, the kind of home I wanted her to have, but knew I couldn't give her."

"I still feel like you did the right thing too, Paula. And you know, God did have a plan, just like we both knew He did."

Paula and I talked of other things then. I reviewed happenings in our family and how Anthony and the girls were doing, until we got home.

Tracey had offered to let Paula stay in her room while Paula was here. I took Paula upstairs, showed her where everything was, and went down to the kitchen. What I really wanted to do was to plop down on Tracey's bed next to Paula and talk a blue streak. But more than that, I wanted Paula to feel like this room was a place of her own while she was with us, a place where she could go to sort out her feelings or to just be alone if she wanted to be. It was only the first of many conflicting feelings I would experience over the next few days.

After about twenty minutes, Paula came downstairs.

"Well, did you get any sleep?"

"No, I think I am too wound up to sleep, but I did get a little rest. Thanks for giving me the time alone. I guess I needed it more than I realized."

We had some iced tea and spent a short while visiting. Tracey and Holli came in, and Paula got reacquainted with them. They had both been little girls when she had last seen them, and now they were teenagers. We marveled at how quickly the years had passed. Yet my heart reminded me that while I had experienced the joy of watching my girls grow up, Paula had missed out on Kristin's childhood. As I looked at Paula's face across the room, I knew the same hurt was in her heart. Yet I also knew that beside that hurt hope was now budding. I sent up a prayer that all would go well at the reunion that afternoon.

The day continued to be hot and muggy. My whole family and Paula were filled with awe, anticipation, and nervousness over the events ahead.

I was struggling to sort out and make sense of the feelings that were floating around me like dandelion fluff on a summer's day.

I was both envious and angry with Mary Sue, the caseworker at Bethany. I felt like an outsider. What right did she have to be so involved while I felt so shut out of what Paula and Kristin had shared with each other? After all, Mary Sue did not know, couldn't even begin to fathom, the pain Paula had experienced through all of this. I knew Paula's pain. It had become a part of me. And just as she did, I wore the scar of it on my own heart too. Yet I knew Paula's scar was much deeper and wider than mine was, and I knew that each July, for eighteen years, it once again broke open and bled.

I prayed for God to strengthen everyone involved in this. There were so many people and so many feelings involved that it scared me, but in my heart I knew that Paula and Kristin's reunion belonged only to the two of them and to God. It was a special gift the Lord was giving them in giving them back to each other. I had only been one of the instruments He used to bring this all about. Mary Sue was another. God was the conductor here, not me.

Paula and I were both fairly quiet on our ride to Bethany. We were both thinking back to the other rides we had made there. When we started down Lydia hill, I spoke, "I didn't think this would be so hard, did you?"

"No, but it's not as hard as the last trip we made here, is it?"

"It sure isn't." We rode in silence until we pulled into the parking lot, "Well, here we are, Paula, here we are again," and I began to cry.

Paula reached over and hugged me, "This is hard for you, isn't it, Pam?"

"Yeah, harder than I thought it would be. I feel like I should go in there with you, yet I know it is your moment to share with Kristin, not mine. I've just been looking out for you for so long through all of this that part of me just wants to be there, to make sure everything goes okay, even though I know it will."

"You will be with me, Pam. You'll be where you have been all along, in my heart. I love you Pam, you are the best friend anyone could ask for."

"I love you too, Paula, and I will be praying for you all afternoon." With that, we hugged one last time, and Paula got out of the car, walked up the sidewalk and through the doors of Bethany.

Although I knew Kristin would be along soon, I sat in the parking lot, crying and praying for about five minutes before I was able to begin the drive home. I asked God to protect Kristin's and Paula's hearts from pain, to bless this reunion, and to give them only joy at finally having each other to touch and talk to. I had no idea it was going to be this hard to step away from Paula and Kristin at this time. I loved them both so much. But I knew I had to. I knew it was what the Lord wanted me to do.

I passed the time at home doing laundry and straightening the already clean house. The afternoon seemed to drag.

At last, I heard the familiar sound of Kristin's car pull into the driveway. The sound of Paula's and Kristin's laughter drifted in through the window and I began to cry again. Only this time, they were tears of joy at how richly God had blessed all of us. God had taken brokenness and put it back together. And he had turned pain into happiness. I stood in awe of it all. Only God could have brought them back together again, and He had planned it from the very beginning.

CHAPTER 28

Paula: Paula, Meet Your Daughter

The day finally came. July 27, the day I had first thought would never happen, and then the day I so looked forward to, was finally reality. In a few hours, not years or months or days, in just a few hours, I would be with my daughter after eighteen long years. I arrived in Grand Rapids at 2:15 p.m., and Pam was there to greet me. She had not aged a bit! She looked exactly as I had last seen her. Our hugs and tears, of course, started there. It was so good to see her. Of course she looked into my eyes and read my heart. She knew how eager and excited I was, and how nervous. As always, being with her and talking to her was just what I needed to gain some control over my emotions.

We went back to her house first so I could freshen up and change clothes. I would be staying in Tracey's room. That alone was hard to believe. It was a sunny, pleasant room with light yellow walls surrounding a big double bed covered with stuffed animals. There was a bookshelf full of books and horse posters on the door, a teenager's room. Here I was, getting ready in my daughter's best friend's room. A room Kristin had stood in, laughed in, slept in, and shared secrets in. It was all so hard to believe. A short time later I took a deep breath, and left Tracey's room. I went downstairs to talk to Pam and see her two daughters again.

Tracey was all grown up. She was a beautiful young lady. She looked very much like her mother and was just as thoughtful and sincere. She wanted me to stay in her room, and that meant a lot to me. Tracey wasn't a year old anymore, and, as hard as it was to imagine, my baby girl wasn't a baby. Kristin and Tracey were best friends.

God's plan for us all was falling into place and had been for all these many years. When they met, Tracey and Kristin were the same age Pam and I had been when we had met. Their friendship and their special closeness continued to be as strong as ours had been right from the start. It was incredible how God worked his plan for us step by step, day by day.

It was soon time to leave. Pam gave me an encouraging smile as we got into the car and began the drive. I was ready for this moment. I could feel her concern for me was just as strong as it had been when she drove me there eighteen years ago. When we arrived at Bethany and parked, there was time for just one more close-hug and a heartfelt prayer. We both knew if we sat there for even one minute more and looked at each other we would totally break down. As it was, we were very close to it! In her last correspondence Mary Sue wrote, "You have been patient and have done a beautiful job of preparing yourself and allowing Kristin and her parents time to prepare. I want you to feel confident and empowered in your goal for a reunion. I pray for you the same joy you have provided." At that moment I didn't feel very prepared or empowered, yet I wouldn't have traded this moment for anything else on earth. One last whispered prayer and I opened the door that would lead me to my daughter.

Mary Sue was ready and waiting. She must have heard me come in the front door because as I walked toward the receptionist area she was walking down the hall toward me with a big smile on her face. I'm sure she knew what I looked like by my pictures, and she looked exactly like I thought she would. She was short with dark hair and eyes. She had been very open, honest, and sincere. I could tell she really cared about me, and was happy and eager for Kristin and me to finally reunite. We talked for a few minutes as she led me down a short hall to a room at the end. "I don't know if Kristin is here yet,"

Mary Sue said. "If not, she should be here shortly. Why don't you have a seat and relax, and I'll go check." I sat down and looked around. The room was pleasant and comfortable. A large window let in plenty of afternoon sunlight. There was a tan colored couch in front of the window with a coffee table. A few chairs of a green color were placed against the cream colored walls. A lamp stood in the corner near the couch.

After I waited for what seemed a lifetime, Mary Sue came back and said, "Kristin is here. I'll bring her in." When she closed that door I knew the next time it opened my daughter would be there. I sat on the couch and stared directly across the room at the clock, just as I had done so long ago in the labor room. Incredibly, at 4:52 (the exact moment of her birth) the door opened. Mary Sue leaned into the room and said, "Paula, meet your daughter." The feeling of being in a dream returned. For that one moment everything seemed to move in slow motion. Mary Sue disappeared and the door slowly opened as I came to my feet and held out my arms. My daughter walked through the door and with no hesitation what-so-ever came straight into my waiting arms. I heard the door close softly and we were alone at last.

We held tight to each other for a long time. She said, "You're finally here. You're finally here." I looked into her tear filled eyes and I did see myself there, just as I'm sure she saw herself in mine. Everything seemed to be said and understood in that first long look. All her emotions were there in her eyes, and I could see her love for me.

"I'm here, I love you," I said.

"I love you too," she said. This was the tiny baby girl I gave birth to. Somehow holding her close in my arms at last seemed like a release for me. The longing and pain I'd carried inside for so long started to ease. I was complete now, I could actually feel the aching empty place in my heart being replaced with such a peace and love I can't begin to describe it. I was so happy! We were finally able to let go of each other long enough to sit side by side on the couch. We were content then just to look at each other. We looked very much alike. The shape of her face, the color and texture of her hair, the shape and unusual color of her eyes, even the little dimples at the corners of her mouth were mine. When I was her age I had looked exactly as she did. I could only sit there and look at her. I could find no words for the emotions that had completely taken over. Kristin finally said, "Those are my eyes! You have my eyes! I mean, I have your eyes!"

We laughed and I said, "I think you have my eyes."

I had a photo album with me. We looked at it for just a minute and then put it aside. We wanted to look at each other, not pictures. She asked no questions about the past. Although if she had, I was not at all anxious about it. Anything she wanted to know I would tell her with complete honesty. There would be no lies about the past between us. She most certainly deserved to know everything, and if she asked, I would tell her. Mainly we just sat close, happy and content to be with each other at last. There would be plenty of time for anything she wanted to know later. We both knew we would never be parted again.

When Mary Sue came back, she could see by our faces how happy we were. She was so happy for us, she was practically beaming! She was a wonderful person. Having a third person in the room of course meant it was time to take pictures. Mary Sue took some with both of our cameras. We wanted pictures with her, too. So another gal came in and took some for us. Then it was time for us to leave. This time when I left Bethany my daughter was at my side. I would never have to leave her behind again.

CHAPTER 29

Kristin: The Comfort of Her

I parked my old and slightly battered, flame-orange Chevette and walked up the steps into Bethany Christian Services. The day was beautiful, bright and sunny, a fitting day for such a momentous occasion. All the way there I had thought about what I was about to do—meet in person the woman who gave me life. Paula.

My mind spun with images and questions. I had seen pictures, but what would she really look like? Was this such a good idea? Maybe I couldn't do it. I tried to organize my thoughts and took what was supposed to be a calming breath. Well, this was it. My hand was on the figurative doorknob. I had reached the "point of no return".

Mary Sue met me at the door with the usual grin of hers, "Well, your mother is here, Kristin. She's wonderful! She's waiting for you in the 'reunion room', so you have a minute to collect yourself." Paula had arrived ahead of me as was the plan, and now she sat waiting in the special room Bethany had set up for just this purpose. Mary Sue had suggested that we each bring a photo album to diffuse the initial tension, and give us a conversation starter. I had brought one my mother had filled with pictures of my childhood memories and vacations, carefully put together as I was growing up. Now I clutched it to my chest and sat for a moment in Mary Sue's office trying to calm my mind and my heartbeat.

I turned down a Pepsi—I was too nervous!—and we began the short walk down the wood-paneled corridor to the room where Paula waited. It was at the end of the hall, and the door was closed. I walked slowly, Mary Sue ahead of me, and wondered if I was wearing the right thing. Questions peppered my mind. Is she really in there? Is this some elaborate game? What if she doesn't like me? What if I've been completely wrong in all of my imaginings? What if there's nothing to say and we just stand there looking at each other and feeling stupid? Maybe Mary Sue should stay with us so I'll know somebody. Wait. I do know somebody. This is Paula we're talking about. Hey, I don't think I saw that painting last time I was here. Maybe it's new. Oh, God, here's the door.

I turned to Mary Sue whose eyes were bright with excitement. "I don't think I can do this," I said in a voice that sounded small even to myself.

"Now, just relax. Of course you can. She's a very nice person, don't worry. You both have waited a long time for this moment."

I took her advice and another deep breath as she turned the doorknob and stepped into the room. "Paula, meet your daughter."

Directly in front of me, sitting on the low couch in a short turquoise jumpsuit, was a very thin, sandy-haired woman with my eyes. She slowly stood to her feet and came around the table. Suddenly I was in her arms, feeling the embrace and the arms I had been waiting for for eighteen years, and all of my life. From that first touch, I knew everything would be all right. The piece that was me and the piece that was her locked into place securely and I felt the bond that was there from the beginning growing to fuse us together forever. I hugged her tight, and rested my cheek on her shoulder. For a moment, I let my mind go and thought of nothing at all, just feeling the comfort of her. After several minutes we stepped back, and Mary Sue was gone. We wiped our eyes in unison, smiled and then laughed in unison. "Wow," I said, "You're finally here!" and she nodded.

My hands were shaking as we sat on the edge of the couch. She had brought a photo album as well, but neither of us wanted to look away from each other, so we saved them for later. I asked about her flight because I could hardly think of anything else that made sense to say. Suddenly I wanted to be out of there, that strange half-way place, and bring her into my world, somewhere I was at home. I needed to be on familiar ground, somewhere I was at ease and in control of the situation. Mary Sue returned and we took pictures. The interruption was good, and gave each of us time to get control of our thoughts and emotions.

We weren't there very long. Paula and I said a heartfelt thank-you and goodbye to Mary Sue. Paula bravely climbed into my car, and I drove to Palmer Park, a beautiful and quiet wooded place where I knew we could walk in peace and be alone. I wanted to talk, but only about what she wanted to talk about. I was determined not to push her for any details that would make her uncomfortable.

There was a lot of catching up to do, but we had the rest of the week and the rest of our lives. As we walked on the paved trail through the rich green woods we talked about day-to-day things like work and our special friendships with Pam and Tracey, and for the time being avoided the heavier, more emotional issues. It was enough just to be together comfortably. "I want to see where you work, and went to school, and everything." Paula said.

"Yes, I'll show you. You can see my house and my room when you meet my folks tomorrow."

"Do you think Brian and Sue will be there?" she asked, and I was sure she was trying to picture what that meeting would be like.

"As far as I know, they're planning on it. They're very excited. You don't have to worry, they're a great family."

"I'm sure." Paula sighed and I was quiet, thinking maybe I had hurt her feelings. She went on, "I'm so glad you had a good place to grow up, and I really am looking forward to meeting Bill and Mary in person and getting to say thanks."

It was strange and wonderful, being able to see the face and the expressions behind the voice I had come to know so well from the phone. When for a moment I felt disoriented, I only had to listen to her laugh and her slight Texas accent to remember. I wondered as we talked if some part of my subconscious remembered her voice from before I was even born. I mentioned this to Paula.

"Yes, I talked to you all the time, and when you would move around inside, I would rub my stomach like this." She showed me. "You would settle down right away."

I had never had this experience before, someone talking about what it had been like to be pregnant with *me*. It was odd, but soon became more comfortable.

"I wonder if maybe somehow I recognized Pam's voice too?"

"Or Tracey's. She was just a little baby, but I spent a lot of time with her before you were born."

"That is just so amazing."

"Isn't it? I know. And I'm so glad! So glad." She put her arm around me as we continued to walk slowly through the green, shady patches and out into the sun.

We didn't need to go through everything all at once. We even walked quietly part of the time, our steps matching in line exactly. Talking too much would have destroyed the time of just soaking each other up, getting re-acquainted, making up for so much lost time. It was just a getting-to-know-you, side by side sort of walk. We were learning each other, learning to trust, feeling the comfortable edges around the bond that would keep the two of us together forever, no matter what. We didn't need words to explain it. It was something we felt working and building with every moment we spent together. It was enough just to be there, in reality, with this woman who was my mother.

We stopped for dinner, and then went back to Pam's house where Paula was staying. All four of us, united again in the same room, cried as we looked at the photo albums. Paula exclaimed and laughed over a picture of Tracey and me posing in the matching outfits we had worn, unplanned, one summer day. Tracey's sister Holli and her dad joined us after a while, and Paula, Pam, and Anthony told stories of when they all lived together eighteen years ago.

Half of my mind listened to the stories, while the other half went its own way. I imagined Paula holding baby Tracey on her lap and talking to her and was amazed that I had been literally only inches away from my best friend. I imagined Paula sleeping on the couch in their trailer, and heard Pam's voice speaking in friendship and comfort. So much had happened between then and now, including the beginning of my friendship with Tracey, and its growth. Now, I sat inches away from Tracey again. We were once again all together. This time for good. I could hardly grasp the enormity of it all.

The discussion shifted from the past to the future as we began to make final plans for the next morning. I would pick Paula up and show her a few significant spots around town, beginning at my parents' house. Then the two of us would return, pick up Pam and Tracey, and head west toward another of my favorite places, one of Lake Michigan's beaches.

It was late that night when we stood up and hugged all around. For once there were no tears. It was wonderful to say, "I'll see you in the morning!"

CHAPTER 30

Paula: This Perfect Day

O nce I was in bed, I was too wound up to sleep. I thought of how excited Pam had been to finally see us together. She couldn't believe how much we looked alike. I was so happy to be there. Anthony had a big hug for me. He hadn't changed a bit either. He looked just the same as the last time I saw him. It was good to see Pam's younger daughter, Holli. At just fifteen she was a cute little thing bubbling over with energy and mischief. I could see it in her eyes. I'll bet she kept Pam on her toes!

To finally see Tracey and Kristin together felt so good. It was incredible. As I sat and watched the two of them together it was obvious they needed no words to communicate. They read each other's thoughts and feelings through their eyes, just as Pam and I had always done. I could actually feel the bond between the four of us, and as I looked at Pam and her eyes met mine, I knew she felt it too. Pam and I were as close as we had ever been, and seeing how close our daughters were, was so heartwarming. It made us both very happy. If ever I could have chosen Kristin's best friend, it would have been Tracey. My wish for her would have been to have a friendship as close as Pam and I had.

They had all sat on the couch and looked through my photo album while Kristin sat on the floor and I sat on a chair nearby. We couldn't stop looking at each other and smiling. Every time I looked at her she was looking at me. I still couldn't believe this whole thing was actually happening. I was there with Pam and Anthony, and that was my daughter sitting there on the floor looking at me with eyes exactly like mine! If this had been a dream, I sure didn't want to wake up! It seemed but a short time later, after one last hug and kiss, Kristin left for the night. It sure felt good to say, "I'll see you in the morning, I love you."

My body started to relax and I realized I was completely exhausted. I lay there, in my daughter's best friend's room, thinking about my daughter, and about tomorrow. I prayed about meeting her parents the next day.

"Lord," I prayed, "tomorrow I meet the parents You chose for my daughter. Please keep me focused and give me the right words to answer any questions they may have. Let them see me as the person I truly am on the inside, and help me to see them that way as well. Thank You for the many blessings I have received on this perfect day, Lord, and thank You for the miracle of my daughter."

I was very eager to meet Mary and Bill. I didn't feel nervous about it. I looked forward to it. Mary and I had had the chance to get to know a little about each other through our written correspondence. One letter in particular gave me much insight into the happiness Mary felt when Kristin joined their family. It was a long wonderful letter filled with her personal thoughts and feelings. In part it read:

When we saw Kristin for the first time at Bethany, I remember thinking she looked like a small pink rosebud. Her complexion was so rosy and beautiful. The fact that she was just a little over six pounds when we took her home was very special to me because I had been a 6 pound baby and had always hoped for a small baby girl. With adoption as our way, I thought a small baby was out of the question since the child would be five weeks or older. To my delight, Kristin's small size filled that desire of my heart.

I could picture Mary holding out her arms to receive this tiny beautiful baby girl. I could also picture the joy and love in her eyes as she had held her close. Even though I felt a moment of intense jealousy over that precious moment that was never mine to have, my heart was truly thankful the Lord had given Kristin such a wonderful family. In closing Mary's letter read:

> And now, in July, she's come full circle to meet you—the person who gave her life. What a year, a lifetime God has blessed Kris with! I never have had an experience to share like this before about one of the children God gave me, so I thank you for this wonderful opportunity. It gave me reason for much praise and thanksgiving to God who created her and planned her life before either of us knew her.
>
> Love in Christ,
> Mary

That letter made me feel very close to Mary. We were, in fact, very much alike, and I knew we would get along just fine.

My first day in my daughter's life had come to an end. As I lay in bed and closed my eyes all I could see was Kristin. Over and over again came the image of her walking through the door at Bethany and into my arms. The weight seemed to be lifted from my shoulders. The longing and emptiness had been replaced with contentment and happiness. This was not a dream, and I thanked God once again for the miracle of my daughter.

CHAPTER 31

Mary: The Part God Wrote for Me

It was hard to let you go:
To watch womanhood reach out and snatch you
Long before the mothering was done.
But if God listened to mothers and gave in,
Would the time for turning loose of daughters
ever come?

It was hard when you went away—
For how was I to know
The serendipity of letting go
Would be seeing you come home again
And meeting in a new way
Woman to woman—
Friend to friend.[14]

Marilee Zdenek

Letting go in real life begins with a decision but is followed by practice, a lot of practice. Opportunities to practice popped up again and again as plans were made for the reunion weekend. I had to be caring, but not controlling. I tried to listen, but not to meddle. I practiced saying *yes* more and *no* less. I took a "hands-off" approach to the plans, allowing Kris to make her own decisions. I asked God to help me fear less and love more. I tried to play only the part that was mine. And now that the reunion was soon approaching, we could tell our relatives and close friends what was about to happen. We were no longer bound to secrecy required by Kristi's age. Nevertheless, I purposed to ask Kris's permission each time I would tell her story.

Kris took the lead and planned the weekend with Paula, Pam, and Mary Sue. On Friday, the week after Kris's eighteenth birthday, Kris and Paula would meet each other at Bethany, facilitated by Mary Sue. Some time on Saturday, Kris would bring Paula to our house to meet the family. Sunday was unplanned. On Monday, Kris would fly out of Grand Rapids with Paula to Des Moines, Iowa, where they would meet with a variety of relatives and friends of Paula and her husband Kenny.

I wondered aloud over lunch with Marianne, a close friend, just what role I would play in the reunion drama: "What I thought might be a leading role is dwindling down to what seems more like a minor one."

She laughed and said, "Minor? You'll probably be more like an understudy."

"What's an understudy?"

She grinned and answered, "It's an actress who prepares as a substitute, but usually never gets on stage."

It looked as if she was right. Later I asked Kris, "How much time will we have with Paula when she comes to the house? Maybe we could look at the family photo albums or the slides."

She didn't seem to like the suggestion. Instead she got defensive and answered with her own questions: "How long will it take her to see my room? Are you planning to sit her down and ask twenty questions?"

I chose not to respond.

I had thought of inviting Paula for Sunday dinner. Perhaps she and I could take a leisurely walk to talk more. When I brought that idea up to Bill, he said, "Forget it, Mare. Let Kris plan her own weekend."

I chose to let the idea go.

I prepared for the weekend in ways that were mine to do. I sent Paula pictures, at her request, of Bill and myself, as well as of Brian and Susie. She wanted a peek preview of us. I hung pictures in the house which I had never gotten around to hanging before. I also hung new bedroom curtains that I had ordered. I wanted the house to look as attractive as possible.

Bill commented, "Paula ought to come more often! The house looks great! And Kris's room is amazingly clean!"

Susie remarked, "Isn't Kris's room pretty with her floor showing?"

Susie was eager to meet Paula; Brian seemed threatened. They were both identifying with Kris in their own ways, with their own expectations. Bill and I were both at peace in our minds, but my body felt tense.

The night before Paula's plane was to arrive, I asked Kris, "Are you ready for this, honey?"

"I'm ready," she answered, "but I'm just a little nervous."

"I think I know what you mean. I would be too. I know you'll do just fine."

She had gotten a note of encouragement in the mail from Mary, my mentor, in Ann Arbor. Also, Pam had written and given Kris a beautiful poem about two little girls and the plan God had for them. It was titled, "Before the Beginning." I was thankful that Pam and Tracey were involved with Kris in all of this.

On Friday, July 27, the day Kris was to meet Paula, morning dawned warm and humid. I felt fragile and weepy before I left home for my job as receptionist at Bill's office. This was the day we had anticipated for months. This was the day, the weekend, to really walk my talk of letting go. I didn't feel very confident, but then I thought of all the people who cared about us and were praying for all of us through the weekend. God would help me.

Before leaving, I quickly wrote in my journal, "This is the day the Lord has made." I knew that was true. "Let us rejoice and be glad in it." Psalm 118:24 (NIV) I determined to try to do that, to rejoice, but as I walked out the door, I whispered, "Please help me, God!"

My thoughtful friend, Jane, took Brian to the beach for the day. She said, "I'll be praying that all of you will see how much God loves you through all of this."

Kris and Susie called me at the office mid-morning to tell me pink roses had arrived from the florist for Bill and me. They were from Mary Sue who sent an attached note which read, "I will be praying for you on this special day." I cried tears of gratitude in Bill's back-room lab thinking about God's detailed provision for us. He knew how much I needed encouragement. He knew I needed flowers.

At 4:20 p.m. Kris called again, "I'm leaving for Bethany now, Mom." We had confidence in her ability to present herself well. I told her bravely, "Dad and I will be praying for you all. We love you, Kristi."

"Thanks, Mom." She sounded nervous, yet confident. She knew prayer worked. Still, I burst into tears when I hung up the phone. While Kristin needed to do this alone, my mothering instincts wanted to somehow be there with her as she faced this new situation. It was like watching my daughter climb aboard the school bus for the first time. I knew she would never be the same.

While Kris was acting out one of the most important scenes of her life, we went through the motions of dismissing our last patient, then picking up the other kids at home to go out for supper at a local restaurant with Grandpa and Grandma, and constantly wondering, "What's happening now? How is it going?"

After our meal, we all had things to do. I took Susie to the beach to go swimming and then out for ice cream. We got home quite late for Susie, but much to my surprise, Bill said, "Kris is already home. She's upstairs, in bed."

When she heard us coming up the stairs, she got up to tell us about the reunion and what they did afterward. Mary Sue had facilitated the reunion beautifully, letting them work through the initial awkward moments as they met face to face, embraced, and wept. Mary Sue also took pictures as they simply held the photo albums each had taken along.

Susie and I listened eagerly. I laughed when Kris added, "It seemed like Mary Sue was the most excited!"

After Paula and Kris had left Bethany, they had taken a walk in a park, had gone to a restaurant for a bite to eat, and then on to Tracey's house to spend some time with Pam and Tracey.

"Paula needs seven or eight hours of sleep, so I left Tracey's house early and came home." Then she added, "I'm going to pick her up there tomorrow morning and bring her here to meet you all around 9:30, before the four of us leave for the beach."

I thought 9:30 sounded like a good time and said, "That will work, and the beach sounds like a good idea." Still my heart struggled to agree with my words. My mind flashed back to the day after Pam's phone call. I pictured the cozy four-some going to the beach together. Tonight, right now, it was okay because I had said so to God. I had said I would let go.

The next morning Kris left to get Paula while Bill and I quickly straightened up the house and positioned ourselves on the back screened-in porch off the family room. We sat and waited while Kris drove the short distance over to Tracey's and back. Brian and Susie were in and out, also waiting.

We heard Kris's Chevette pull into our front driveway and heard car doors slamming. "That's them," Bill said. When we heard the squeak of the side screen door opening, we stood up. I said, "This is it, Kid," as we walked into our family room to greet them coming in the opposite doorway.

There stood Kris beside a taller, very thin woman. Paula had light brown hair, cut short, and she was wearing glasses. Even before Kris could introduce us, Paula smiled and walked toward me. She stretched out her arms and we hugged each other tightly like old friends. No words were needed for that moment. We noticed tears in each other's eyes as we pulled away and looked at each other smiling. Paula then hugged Bill and I introduced Brian and Susie. Kris stood by smiling amidst her own gentle tears.

Bill said, "Welcome to our home!" and invited Paula to sit on the back porch with all of us. Kris sat beside Paula. The rest of us formed a circle around them. We asked about her trip and the reunion at Bethany. She laughed when I told her Kris had said it seemed like Mary Sue was having the most fun, taking pictures and all. Paula commented on Bill's garden and the fruit trees he grows for a hobby. We mentioned that one of our favorite apple trees was our Paula Red, of all names! I could barely concentrate on the conversation because I found myself just wanting to stare at her, to look at her face, her hands, her figure, her legs and feet to compare with the younger body I knew so well.

Since staring and being polite don't mix well, I had to control myself. I did manage to notice the long thin legs and longer narrow feet were not familiar. Kris and I had similar feet, short and wide. I wondered about the birth father's side, still unknown.

Time moved quickly during Paula's brief visit. After our polite conversation on the porch, we went into the back yard to take some pictures among the apple trees. For the first time in my life, I felt fat in comparison to her slender figure.

The air was getting warmer, and Kris and Paula had plans for a picnic at Lake Michigan with Pam and Tracey. Kris invited Paula back into the house to quickly go upstairs to see her room and the rest of the house before they had to leave.

While they were upstairs, some friends from church called to ask, "What are you doing?"

I lied and said, "Not much."

They invited Bill, me, and the kids to go boating on Lake Michigan. I accepted the invitation and said in my spirit, "Thank You, Lord! We needed that."

We all walked Kris and Paula out to Kris's little orange Chevette, hugged them both and waved, "Goodbye!" as they sped away and around the corner. Mimicking what my Grandma used to say, Bill said, "Well, that's done now!"

Back in the house, I phoned Bill's mom, my wonderful mother-in-law. "Well Mom, it's over already. Kris came with Paula. She's a very gracious person, easy to have here. She's a lot like Kris, rather quiet."

Mom said, "Well, I'm glad Mare. Now you can relax and have some fun today. What are you going to do?"

I told her our plans and then added, "Thanks for your prayers. I prayed for a love big enough to share, and I think I got it. I didn't have all those old feelings of selfishness or jealousy."

The rest of the weekend went according to plan. None of us saw Paula again except me for a few minutes on Monday. I had to take Brian and a friend to begin a week at summer camp. When I came back home around noon, I found Kris and Paula standing in the kitchen, looking at family photo albums and Kris's baby book. I felt awkward, like an intruder in my own kitchen. I quickly greeted them and went to the basement to continue the laundry I had started before I left.

When I came back up to the kitchen, Kris asked, "Could Paula take my baby book?" I misunderstood and thought, "Oh no! I don't want her to keep that! Not yet!" Instead, I said, "I'm not quite finished writing in it yet. Could I send it to you later?"

Paula, realizing I misunderstood, said, "I just want to take it to Iowa to show my Mom. I'll send it back with Kris."

Relieved, I said, "Oh, sure! That's fine," as I put some rubber bands around the album to keep any loose items from falling out.

In just a few minutes Pam arrived to take them to the airport, and they were gone. It turned out that while my role for the weekend did resemble that of an understudy, it was really the part God wrote for me.

While Kris was gone, I wrote another note in her little red journal. I wrote it to her, but I wrote it also for my own benefit:

Dear Kris,

This morning I'm wondering who you will be when you come back. I had to reread that poem, "If you love something, set it free . . . ." That's what I tried to do, but today it's hard. I did it because I love you and I want you to be and become the woman God intended you to be.

It's been a difficult assignment for a young woman balancing between childhood and adulthood, but I believe in you. I trust God Who began a good work in you to bring it to completion.

Dad and I are praying for you today. Our prayer is that it will be a good day, that God will give you strength for your departure alone, and that you will ultimately be filled with God's joy and peace.

Love,
Mom

CHAPTER 32

Paula: Sharing Treasures

It was my second day in Michigan and I was going to meet Kristin's parents, Bill and Mary. I was eager for this meeting. Kristin picked me up at Pam's. On the drive to her house she kept saying, "Are you nervous?"

I kept saying, "No." At that time I really wasn't, but as we got closer I began to doubt my words. As we pulled into their drive I said, "OK, now I'm nervous!"

I wasn't concerned about meeting them, nor was I afraid of what they would think of me. Mary Sue had paved the way well for us by having us write letters to each other, and that correspondence between Mary and me helped very much. Mary had sent me a picture so I even knew what they looked like. It was a picture of Mary and Bill standing in an outdoor setting. I thought of how Mary and I somewhat resembled each other, and how well God had placed Kristin in this family. Mary was just a little taller than me. We had the same color hair and build. By reading her letters I discovered she was an open and honest person, willing to share anything I wanted to know. Another thing that helped a little was the certain knowledge that Mary had to be just as anxious as I was! But all that didn't help much in those first moments. I was still nervous. This was another one of those once in a lifetime things. I was about to meet my daughter's parents!

Kristin and I walked into the house. There was a deck right off the family room where they were sitting as they waited for us to arrive.

When they heard us come in Mary came into the family room with Bill right behind her. It just felt natural and right for Mary and me to share a heartfelt hug—which we did before we even spoke. When we were through, Bill and I hugged also. My nervous feelings didn't last long. Even though I hadn't known them, these two people had been a part of my life for eighteen years. It was a beautiful day so we went back out on the deck to sit. Kristin sat next to me.

As we began to visit, Mary said, "I can see where she got her smile." We talked mostly about my family history, and theirs, getting to know each other. They asked what it was like for me being so young when my father passed on, and how I felt about Mom getting married again. I talked about how all us kids got along and what it was like moving and adjusting to a totally new family life. It was really easy for me to talk about that. With six brothers there was always something going on.

We had a nice visit. We were all open with each other and happy to answer any questions that were asked. We talked a little about Kristin's childhood, but not much. That seemed to be a subject that belonged to Mary, Kristin and me. This was more of a family thing. Kristin had told me that Bill was a man of few words. My dad was like that, content to sit back and listen, but when he had something to say, it was usually worth listening to. That day no one seemed to have a problem, and there wasn't a silent moment. I was living in Texas and, of course, they were in Michigan, so this was probably one of very few opportunities we would have to visit face to face. To have this chance to meet them and see where Kristin had grown up was very good for me. It gave everything a background, made everything more "solid" and "stable". They were very nice people, two parents raising a family just like everybody else. I was put at ease and felt very welcome.

They had a beautiful back yard. Landscaping was a hobby Bill enjoyed and he was very good at it. We walked back and looked at the flowers and fruit trees. We took pictures of each other there in the back yard against the green backdrop of summer apple trees. Sue and Brian were there also, so I was able to meet the whole family. Everyone got pictures of everyone. It was a good feeling, standing next to my daughter's mom, our arms around each other's waists, smiling for a picture. God had surely blessed us all. He had given Kristin wonderful Christian parents. He had given me the opportunity to know them. He also had given me my baby girl, all grown up, but still my baby girl.

After all the pictures were taken, I happened to glance at Brian. He was an energetic fourteen-year-old who only stood still for pictures. The look on his teenage face clearly stated "You made me promise to stay so we could take pictures. Can I please go now?" My sudden appearance, and the importance of it to the rest of us, obviously didn't impress him all that much. He had better things to do. I smiled as I watched him walk back into the house, thinking of my own brothers at that age.

Sue was a beautiful child with dark hair and sparkling eyes. I was sure her charming smile had won many hearts already, and would continue to do so for many years to come. She watched and listened with curiosity and interest to everything that was happening around her.

Bill said something to me that took me completely by surprise. We were walking in from the back yard, he was right behind me. "Thank you, Paula," he said, "for giving Kristin to us to raise."

I was taken totally off guard. I had no words to reply. I knew exactly what he meant and why he said it, but what is the reply to a comment like that? "You're welcome" certainly didn't cover it. I blurted out something stupid like "Abortion was never an option for me." Anybody who remotely knows me or anything about me already knows that. I knew Bill was well aware of that, and that was not what he was implying. He was grateful for all the joy and pleasure Kristin had given him through the years, and he was very thankful for the opportunity God had given him to be her father. He wanted to express that to me, and I understood. God had made a very good choice in making Bill Kristin's dad.

After we came inside, Kristin, Mary, and I looked through her baby book and talked a little about Kristin's younger years, but my visit wasn't very long so Mary and I didn't have a chance to talk alone. Mary told me she would send me a letter with some pictures of Kristin's growing up years, and I was grateful for her thoughtfulness. God in his wisdom had chosen Mary as Kristin's mom. We had become friends, and I was so thankful for that.

Just as we were about to leave, Mary asked Kristin, "Aren't you going to show Paula the rest of house? I worked hard to get it clean, so you better show her!"

Mary and I laughed as I said, "That sounds just like something I would say. I would love to see the rest of your house." I was very happy to have met them. I knew Mary and I were comfortable with our places in Kristin's life. Kristin loved us both, and we both loved her. Mary and I hugged again as Kristin and I were leaving. We didn't know exactly what our schedule would be for the rest of my short visit, so Mary and I didn't make plans to meet again. However, we did assure each other we would keep in touch.

Kristin showed me where she went to school. She also wanted the people she worked with to meet me and I wanted to see where she worked so we stopped at the book store. I was happy to see anyplace or meet anyone who was involved in Kristin's life. Later when she wrote or spoke about them, I would be able to picture the person or place in my mind.

Pam, Tracey, Kristin, and I wanted to do something special together, just the four of us. After meeting Kristin's parents and co-workers, we headed to Pam's where we packed up and went to the beach. Pam and I were in the front seat and Kristin and Tracey were in the back. It was a beautiful ride, and we had so much fun laughing and teasing and talking. At the beach we picked our spot and settled in. Tracey and Kristin left to get in the water. Pam and I were alone, just like we had been so very many times before, but this time was so different. This time was an answer to prayer. We didn't talk much. As usual, we didn't need to speak our thoughts and emotions. We knew what they were. All those years ago when I left her home to go back to Iowa, only God knew it was the first step that would lead us through the years to this very moment. It felt so natural to be with Pam. The two of us sitting together watching our daughters play in the water and build a sandcastle was an experience we never dreamed we would have to share. My best friend's daughter was my daughter's best friend! I never thought in a million years that something this wonderful would ever happen. I knew this was a perfect example that through God all things are possible. Pam and I took a walk on the beach, then came back to watch our girls work on their castle. All in all it was a perfect day, full of companionship and love.

After the beach, we headed back to Pam's. They had rented a couple of movies, so after dinner we settled in to watch them. I sat on the couch with Kristin close beside me. I put my arm around her, and she laid her head on my shoulder. Oh, how long I had wanted to sit like that with my daughter! It felt so "right". We didn't watch very much of the movies. We were content just being together, looking at each other and talking softly. Pam had tears in her eyes as she watched us. The day ended far too soon. After a hug and a mutual, "I love you," Kristin left for home.

The phone rang a few minutes later. Pam said it was for me. "Hello," I answered.

Kristin's voice was on the other end, "Hi, Mom."

All the excitement of this emotion-filled day combined did not have the impact on me that those two little words from my daughter did. I totally broke down. To finally hear her call me Mom took my breath away. I cried as I said, "You don't know how happy it makes me to hear you call me Mom."

"Well, you are!"

"Yes, I am," but I never in my wildest dreams thought I would ever hear my daughter call me Mom! When we first started corresponding I was hoping someday she would, but I would never ask her to. When she did, I knew it was because she wanted to. It was a very, very happy moment for me. One I'll never forget!

There was one dark cloud hanging over us. Time was getting short. I would have to leave soon. Neither of us was ready for that to happen. Kristin and I had talked about the possibility of her flying back to Des Moines with me, but finances had seemed too tight for either of us. After more thought, we decided to go for it, to split the cost of her ticket. The trip would give us a few more days with each other, and she would be able to meet a lot of her "other" family. They were all so excited to meet her! Since our tickets had been purchased separately, we were on separate flights. We turned to our problem solver, Pam. God knew this was going to happen, that's why He gave Pam a job at a travel agency. In no time she had Kristin booked on the same flight I was taking, sitting in the seat next to me! I was still sad at the thought of saying goodbye to Pam and Tracey, but I was very happy my daughter and I would have a little more time together.

I knew my mother and sister would make the trip to Des Moines (about a five hour drive) to meet Kristin. I thought it would be great to borrow her baby book to show them. The morning we left, when I said goodbye to Mary, I asked "Would it be all right with you if I take Kristin's baby book with me?"

I will never forget the stricken look on Mary's face as she said, "I'm sorry, Paula, I'm just not ready to give that up yet." To think this very special woman would actually give me something so filled with her own precious moments made me feel very humble.

"Oh no, Mary, not to keep!" I explained. "I just want to take it with me to Des Moines so I can show it to my family. They would all love to look at it. Then Kristin can bring it back with her. I could never ask you to give it to me, Mary! It's yours, not mine."

"Of course, take it with you," she said. Mary and I hugged one last time as we said goodbye. We both knew we would keep in touch.

Pam and Tracey came to pick us up, and we hurried through our goodbyes to Mary. It was getting late. We should have already left for the airport. When we finally got under way, I was pretty sure we would miss our plane. Apparently I had forgotten how Pam drives! I'm not sure how, but she got us there just in time. They held the plane for us as we ran through the airport. It was for the best, though, because we didn't have any time for long goodbyes. With a quick hug and I love you, Kris and I were on our way to Des Moines.

I was very happy to have her sitting beside me on that plane. I was so eager for everyone to meet her, especially Kenny. He had been at my side for many years waiting for her entrance into our lives. My wait was over, and within hours, his would be too. All the times I had cried for her, he had held me in his arms and comforted me. He had grown to love her because of how much she meant to me. I was excited to be bringing Kristin with me to meet him.

CHAPTER 33

Kristin: My Two Moms

Seeing both of my moms together completed something for me. It made the internal puzzle of who I was into a whole picture. There was extraordinary significance in the fact that I would be picking up and presenting Paula to my parents. I was the bridge between them, and this act on my part showed not only how I fit between them, but also that I was willing for each of them to see pieces of me in each other.

For a while, I had felt the need to keep Paula for myself, and away from my parents. I was protective of our new relationship, and unwilling to risk anything or anyone getting in the way of this new bond. By the time we all got together at my house I was ready to take that risk. I had spent time alone with Paula and trusted her.

As I knew they would, my moms got along fine. I watched as they communicated, each hugging and thanking the other, reaching out to bridge the gap between them and giving more of themselves. We sat together on the back porch, and I mostly watched as they chatted about Paula's life, my dad's fruit tree hobby, Paula's trip to Michigan, and our recent reunion. I felt a satisfied smile crossing my face as my moms stood in the backyard, arms around each other, posing for a picture near my dad's apple trees. Seeing them together was like looking into a mirror at the reflection of a whole me. The final link in my puzzle was in place, the circle finished. I was like each of my moms in a unique way, and having the three of us together made me feel connected and completed. The two sides of me had met and matched beautifully.

There were so many ways that morning could have gone, and I thanked God for the wonderful way it did, and the wonderful people in my life.

By the time we left, a real friendship had begun between my two moms, and that was truly wonderful with me. I knew nothing would jeopardize our new relationship and had grown enough to be glad my mom could be friends with Paula as well.

Paula's time in Michigan would be short, and so the next few hours were busy. I took her to visit my favorite places, my old school, my new school, and the bookstore where I was working. After this tour, we teamed back up with Pam and Tracey and hit the beach.

It was a wonderful, relaxing afternoon. Pam and Paula sat back in beach chairs and watched as Tracey and I reverted to childhood and built a huge sandcastle at the edge of the water. In a way, I was a child, my mother watching me play for the first time. It couldn't make up for eighteen years, but it was a start, and that day was wonderful. The sand was hot and white, the sun shone brightly and reflected off the water into our eyes. Tracey and I laughed and talked, leaving our mothers alone to chat. For an hour, it was like it might have been.

That evening, tired and sunburnt, we watched movies at Pam's. While watching, we discussed the exciting plans we had made for our next few days. Paula had invited me to fly back to Iowa with her, to meet her husband and family. Now that I was back in her life, there were about a hundred people I needed to be acquainted with.

Before we left for Iowa, I thought about whom I would be meeting. What would it be like to see the faces of people who were my actual relatives? They were my blood, my extended family. I was used to Paula now. After letters and phone conversations and a few days together, we had gotten over the initial strangeness and now were very comfortable together. Would it be very scary to meet everyone else? What would they think of me?

I was thrilled, but nervous, to be sitting on the plane next to Paula, heading for Iowa. We had nearly missed the takeoff, but, thanks to Pam's assertive driving, had squeezed through the gates at the last second. It left very little time for goodbyes to Pam and Tracey, but we agreed it was probably better that way. Once my heartbeat slowed down from the runway rush, it sped up again at the thought of what was about to happen. I would meet my blood family for the first time. I didn't know what to expect. I knew it would be wonderful, but I was nervous all the same. Paula understood, and was still squeezing my hand as we taxied to a stop in Des Moines.

Paula's husband, Kenny, met us at the gate. His brown eyes sparkled through tears as he hugged me and then held me away to look at me. "Paula, my goodness. I just can't believe it." I took in his eyes and smile, and I loved him immediately.

"This—this is my daughter," Paula's voice was choked with emotion. "Kristin, I'd like you to meet my husband Kenny."

"Hi," I smiled, already trying to hold back tears of my own. "It's so good to finally meet you in person!"

"Honey," he said earnestly, taking my bag from my hand and putting the other arm around me as the two of us started walking, "you have no idea what finding you has done for your mom. Or me! I haven't been waiting eighteen years, but I'll tell you what. As soon as I heard about you, I loved you like my own daughter."

I nodded, choked up again at how serious and kind his eyes were.

He went on. "I know what it was doing to Paula, all those years of not knowing where you were. She was torn up every day. Then the minute she found out that you wanted to get to know her, she was like a new person. She's been so happy ever since."

"He's right," Paula said, catching up with us and patting my cheek. "I can't tell you how happy."

"You don't even need to try," I said, feeling overwhelmingly thankful for each of them.

Kenny, more than anyone else besides Pam, was struck by and verbal about my likeness to Paula. Since he knew her better than anyone, that made sense. As we got to know each other and strengthen our own bond that week, I lost count of how many times Kenny said, "You sounded just like Paula right then." Or, "Look how she's sitting, Paula. You guys are like twins!" Sometimes he just looked from one of us to the other and shook his head. But he was always smiling.

We stayed at Kenny's brother, Johnny's place. In three days I met my grandmother, step grandfather, aunt, uncles, cousins, stepbrother and sister-in-law, stepsister and brother-in-law, step grandma and step uncles. We took a thousand pictures. Everyone talked at once, and at times I wanted to say, "Stop everything. Who are you and how are you related to me again?" It was a daunting and overwhelming, but very positive, weekend. I felt like a star, welcomed, watched, and treated like royalty.

The first day, as we stood hugging in a knot in Johnny's kitchen, my grandma, Paula's mom, handed me a rose. It was perfect, beautiful. Inserted in the paper was a card that said, "Welcome back to our family—our prayers have been answered. Love, Grandma and Grandpa Klay." This of course made us all cry again. It was a good cry, healing and cleansing. Grandma Pearl held me for a long time and whispered in my ear, "We have waited a long time for this moment, Paula especially. We have thought of you so many times throughout the years and wondered about you, and it is so wonderful to finally be able to give you a hug."

In the few quiet moments of that weekend, I reflected on some new emotions. In a whole new way, I was searching for my place. I thought back to my home in Michigan and the previous Christmas spent with my extended family there. With them, I could look around the room and see and know that they shared the same physical blood connection. Then I would take a step back in my mind and realize I wasn't connected with them that way. Yet they were my family and I knew each of them well, had spent hours and years with them, had laughed with them, and watched them grow. I loved them all. I "fit in." I was comfortable there. But, I wasn't connected by blood.

When I stood amongst my relatives in Iowa, I felt the opposite way. I looked around the room and knew that by my birth and blood I did belong there. I was exactly as much a part of that family as my cousins were—no more and no less. I belonged there, but I didn't know them. The comfort of shared memory was missing.

In the middle of that exhilarating, exciting weekend, a sadness touched me as I wondered—where do I belong? Am I alone? Am I an island? It seemed that I was drifting between two worlds without an anchor. Then the moment of loneliness passed and the thrill of my "new" blood relatives found me again.

"Wow, Paula, she really does look like you!" everyone said, and, to me, "You definitely have Paula's eyes." Every word was a validation of our similarities and I felt a thrill each time I heard them. It was their acknowledgement of who I was and how I "fit"—with Paula and with them. With each smile I felt more accepted into the fold.

It was a wonderful feeling. I was gaining so much—a family I never knew about—and I felt so blessed. I put my questions behind me and thought only about what would be.

CHAPTER 34

Paula: Happy Mother's Day

Together, Kristin and I had left Grand Rapids and arrived in Des Moines about 3:30 p.m. Kenny was eagerly waiting at the airport for us. There had been many down times over the years. He had seen my pain, and felt it with me. I was so glad I could share this great joy with him. He was very happy to meet my baby girl at last. Kenny and Kristin hit it off right from the start. There was an instant connection that was obvious to see. He was amazed by how much she looked like me. He watched the two of us over the next few days and kept saying, "You two do that just alike," or "Paula, your mom and you do the exact same thing your daughter does." He was right, it was amazing. I know that some of the things I do are exactly like my mother does, and Kristin does the same things exactly like I do, even to the way we sit and cross our legs, or the way we fold our arms.

When Kenny's brother, Johnny, learned Kristin was coming back with me, he insisted on staying with a friend so we could have the house to ourselves for the few days she was to stay. That was very generous and thoughtful of him but not surprising. That's the way he is. He loves Kenny and me very much. Knowing how much Kristin meant to us, he already loved her. Kristin got to meet her stepsister, Teresa, and one of her stepbrothers, Shawn, who drove from Omaha to meet her. I was very happy they were able to come and meet her. We were sorry Michael, our youngest son, couldn't be there, but he lives in California. As this trip with her to Des Moines was quickly planned, it was impossible. We all understood, but I missed him just the same.

Kristin did get to meet Kenny's oldest brother, Jimmy and his family. Of course, she also met Candy, who was such a vital and important part of my life, and Missy, my little goddaughter. Things seemed to be going by us so fast it was like a whirlwind. We just hung onto each other and enjoyed every minute.

Then the most important and special thing happened. I had the honor of introducing my daughter to my mother and my sister Pat! Pat and her husband and family got there first. After all the introductions were said and we finally got settled in to talk, Mom and Dad arrived. I couldn't wait for my mom to see her! It was a very important moment for me. Kristin and I stood side by side in the kitchen. Mom came in first and set two roses on the kitchen table. I stepped toward her, and she hugged me long and close, and then turned to Kristin. She cried as she finally held her granddaughter in her arms. "Oh, Paula, it's you, it's you!" she said. It took a little time for all of us to get control of our emotions. When we all had dried our tears, she handed Kristin and me each a rose with a small card. My card said "Happy Mother's Day." I cried and hugged her again. What a beautiful thing to say, I thought. We talked and took pictures, and we all gathered around the kitchen table to look at Kristin's baby book. Then, far too soon, it was time for them all to leave. It had been a long, emotional, wonderful day.

Kristin and I finally found ourselves alone early one evening, so we took a long walk. As we walked slowly along she said softly to me, "Are you ready to tell me about you and Dave?"

"Yes," I took a deep breath and reached out my hand, which she readily took and held tightly. I started at the very beginning, from the time I met Dave, and told her everything. I told her how very much I had always loved her, and how painful it was for me to make the decision I had to make. As we walked slowly along I talked and she asked questions which I answered with complete honesty. I knew there would be no secrets about the past between us. I assured her that if she ever had a question in the future about anything, she could come to me and I would answer as best I could. "If I don't know the answer," I told her, "I will do my very best to help you find it." At the end of our talk and our walk I stopped and turned her toward me. "Kristin, I love you. I always have, and I always will."

She looked me straight in the eye and said, "I love you too, Mom."

It seemed like we had just arrived in Des Moines and it was already time to take Kristin back to the airport. Kenny and I would be leaving the next day to head back to Texas. I had pushed this moment to the back of my mind, but it couldn't be ignored any longer. Kenny and I took her to the airport and went in with her to wait for her departure call. I tried to be strong. I tried not to cry, and so did she. But when the last call came, so did the tears. We clung to each other and cried. She said, "I don't want to say goodbye again. I don't want to say goodbye!"

"No, honey, no, not goodbye. Never goodbye again! We will always have each other." As Kenny took our picture, we were all three crying. For the rest of that day, whenever someone mentioned her name I cried. Although Kristin went back to Michigan, and I went back to Texas, we were still together—we would never be parted again!

CHAPTER 35

Kristin: Seeing the Sacrifice

T he days in Iowa flew past too quickly, as we tried to spend time with everyone in my extended family. They visited as they had the time, in little groups. We swam in Jimmy's pool, and sun bathed on the deck. Kenny, in his earnest way, told me the best way to tan was to jump in the pool, dry off in the sun, and then jump back in. Within hours, I was sunburnt all over. I felt like a lobster. Kenny assured me that I'd live. We stayed up late, and played card games. We didn't go out much. There was too much going on *in*. The adjustments in our minds and hearts were enough to deal with for a while.

One of the mornings I was in Iowa, Kenny, Paula, and I went out for a Mexican breakfast. Paula and I sat together on one side of the booth. Kenny sat opposite, grinning at us as usual. Before the waiter came to take our order, Kenny leaned back and said, "Ladies—your eyes are green today." Not surprised, we smiled at each other, and at him.

Later that evening, after Kenny and I had spent hours making his special "secret family recipe" spaghetti sauce, I suggested to Paula that we take a walk around the neighborhood. It was time for me to hear the whole story. We both knew it—our relationship was strong enough now to face the toughest thing we had gone through together. I was ready to know, and she was ready to tell.

The night was young and fresh. The sun had just set, and the streetlights were beginning to glow. The warm July night air felt good on our arms and legs as we began walking, and she started talking.

"Your birth father's name is Dave, and we were together for just over two years. He came from Rock Rapids, Iowa, and after we met and fell in love, he moved to Michigan. I was miserable without him. When he called and asked if he could come for me, I said yes."

She glanced at me, and I nodded encouragement. She didn't seem nervous. I felt a twinge of excitement that I was at last hearing the whole story, but I was also calm. Paula took a deep breath and continued. "I was flattered and happy that he wanted to be with me that much. We rented a little house together on the edge of a forest, and were very happy for several months."

We turned a corner and kept walking. I didn't ask any questions at first, I just listened to the events that preceded my birth. I knew she would share everything that was important, and I wanted to let her tell it her own way, and all at once. "Shortly after I found out I was pregnant with you, Dave seemed to change. He wanted me to move to Florida with him, and even bought me an engagement and wedding ring set. I couldn't do that though. I was reaching the point where I knew the relationship would not work out, and it was time to let it go. I had you to consider as well, and I wanted to do what was right for both of us. Dave went on to Florida alone, and on the way he dropped me off at Pam's house."

I wasn't surprised, because I knew that she had stayed with Pam while pregnant. It felt strange, though, because for the first time it was like I was there, watching it happen. I asked my first question. "Did you know you were going to give me up for adoption already then?" I wanted to get the timing straight in my mind.

Paula shook her head. It was dark now, and as we walked under a streetlight I thought I saw a tear in her eye. "No, I really didn't know what I was going to do then. I needed to get away from Dave, and I needed time to make the right decision. I can tell you now, it was the hardest decision I ever had to make."

I put my arm around her for assurance as we kept walking. "I believe it was the right decision. For both of us."

She stopped and turned toward me. "Do you? I am so glad to hear that! I was hoping you wouldn't resent me for choosing to give you up. It was the only thing I could have done at that time."

"No," I said. "I don't resent you at all. It was the right thing to do, even if it was hard. You had it worse than me. You had to think about it all these years. I had a really good life, good parents, a good place to live. I always knew I was adopted and that I would find you someday, but I never really hurt like you did." I wanted her to know that my time away from her had been happy, an innocent childhood. I wanted her to feel peace, not guilt over any pain she imagined that she had caused me, and I wanted her to understand that I understood what a painful sacrifice she had made for me.

"Oh, baby girl, it was all worth it. Every tear, every little bit."

We wiped our eyes and resumed walking. "He actually gave you a ring set?" I asked, remembering what she had said. I thought about what those rings now meant to me. It was a symbol of the love that had created me. It was another piece of tangible proof of the bond my birth parents had. The only thing that connected the two together— besides me. There was no marriage to show how they cared for each other, or even that they were together, only the rings that said he had loved her enough to want to marry her. In some way, the rings made me feel almost "legitimate". "Do you still have them?"

"Well, Pam has the set right now. When she and Anthony were married they were young and couldn't afford one. I sold those rings to Anthony to give to Pam on their second anniversary. I didn't really have any use for them, and they did. I know that those rings meant even more to Pam because I had worn them too."

The seed of something like resentment started growing in the pit of my stomach. I was suddenly desperate to have them, to own for myself the only other proof of my birth parents' love. "You know, those rings would mean something to me. They were a gift from Dave to you, the only things left. I would really like to have those rings."

"Well, now that you mention it, I guess they should belong to you. I know Anthony bought Pam a new set not too long ago. I wonder if she would consider giving them to you. Maybe you should ask her."

"Maybe I will," I said, nodding. "They're mine. They really do belong to me."

All too soon, we were on our way to the Des Moines airport, and I was leaving for home. All three of us cried, and no one wanted me to leave. Kenny took horrible pictures of us hugging and red-eyed. At last call I boarded the plane, sat in my seat and stared out the window. I felt again that loss and emptiness, but I knew it was a different kind of sadness. It was a sadness that had an end. I knew when I finished grieving over this temporary separation, she would still be there. I still knew her. I would see her again. There was comfort behind the tears this time.

CHAPTER 36

Kristin: My Healing Heart

After my trip, Paula and I corresponded through letters, cards, and weekly phone calls. In August, 1990, a week after my return from Iowa, I moved into the dorm at Grace Bible College, in town and close to my family and work. My boyfriend, Lee, also decided to attend this school and moved into the men's dorm across the grassy quad. I loved being there, my classes, and my fellow students. The only thing missing was Tracey. She was away at Indiana Wesleyan University, and I only got to see her when she came home on vacations and holidays.

I was in the choir at Grace. Each year, eight choir members were selected to be in a small group called Grace Singers. I was also chosen for this group, and enjoyed traveling around with them and singing solos in chapel. We toured in New York my first semester there.

During my first few months at Grace, I tried to talk to Pam about the ring set Dave had given Paula. She knew what I wanted immediately. "Yes, I still have the rings," she said slowly.

I tried to explain what they meant to me. Instead of giving them to me, she said, "You may not understand this, but those rings are really important to me, too. Those are the rings Anthony gave me, and they are the only wedding rings I had for fifteen years. They are a symbol of our marriage and our love. I looked at those rings on my hand every day for fifteen years. I can't just easily give them up."

Again, I told her I wanted them and why, and we both cried. She wouldn't give them to me, finally saying, "I understand where you're coming from and what the rings mean to you. I just can't give them to you now. I'm not ready. The time isn't right." It didn't make me feel much better when she said she would give them to me when the time was right. However, I had no choice but to agree with her. It was the first time I was every really hurt by Pam. I was angry with her, and I hated the feeling. She wrote me a letter that explained her reasoning and her own feelings, which helped me to better understand. I had to trust her. I couldn't stand being angry or having anything between us. Our relationship was too important—worth too much to me. I knew those rings did mean something special to her too. She was like another mother to me, and I didn't want to lose her. I would wait.

During my Thanksgiving break from school, I traveled alone to Texas for a week. I was thrilled to be heading toward my birth mother again, and excited to see what her home and life were really like. I could hardly wait to see her and Kenny again.

That trip was wonderful. We rented movies, cooked spaghetti (the "secret family recipe"), and ate pizza. Early mornings, I walked in the desert, only a block from their ranch house. I met more people— Paula's brother Preston and his wife Gail, and their two children. Together we visited a flea market and bought books. Paula and Kenny showed me proudly around their town and the air force base where they both worked. It warmed my heart and made me smile every time Paula introduced me as "my daughter."

Spending time in Paula's world opened my eyes into myself even more. I watched her move around the house, and read her mind before she even spoke. I could see in her eyes what she was thinking, and I discovered we laughed exactly the same.

Paula showed me a poem she had found called "Legacy of an Adopted Child." I reflected that week on my two moms and how I was like each of them. It seemed I was a combination of both.

My easy, laid-back attitudes were born of Paula—and then structured and polished by Mary. For a while, on vacation, I could relax and take it easy with Paula—but soon I would feel Mary's energy and active creativity break through.

I felt I had inherited my emotional stability and a simple, peaceful composure from Paula, along with her passion for loyalty. These senses lay side by side in my mind with the conscious lessons and values I had learned from Mary, who took my instincts and developed them through stories and by example.

By now I knew Paula tended to roll with life. She accepted what came, made the best of it, and maintained a cheerful mind-set while dealing with whatever life handed her. Mary felt every emotion strongly and tried to make a difference, to change things for the better. I found myself somewhere in the middle.

Kenny again spent most of the time shaking his head at us, looking from one to the other with his huge, delighted grin. He told me how he would take care of me after he hit the lottery, how I would be a singer and he would be my manager. Several times, I was pleased to hear him introduce me as *his* daughter. He was thrilled to have me there, and I knew he loved me almost as much as Paula did.

That week we absorbed each other, talking some but mostly just sitting there together, cross-stitching and watching each other. The casual time spent together seemed to help make up for lost years more than constant soul-searching would. I didn't ask any more deep questions, and she didn't volunteer much more. We did share stories about growing up, watched TV talk shows, solved all the problems of the world, and laughed a lot.

Once I was back at Grace, life continued as normal through semester finals, and Christmas arrived with two feet of snow. For about a week, the dorms were closed. I moved back home to spend the holiday time with my family.

It was the same, but different, living with my parents and sleeping in my own room again. Our relationship seemed slightly changed also. It was almost as though my parents were becoming my friends. Almost as though we were peers, or equals. They seemed more relaxed, less concerned about things. I found myself sharing more, because I wanted to. I told them about my trip to Texas, my classes, and my new friends at school. I realized it was good to be home. I felt like I had been living away much longer than a few months.

Mom and I spent time alone together that week, for the first time in a while. We talked about daily things, and sat in the dark listening to an instrumental Christmas CD. It was good to spend time quietly together, enjoying the company and the music.

A few days before Christmas, I received a large box from Texas. I ran up to my room to open it. From inside the paper wrapping, a funny furry face grinned back. It was a wide-mouthed stuffed gorilla, with wild hair going in every direction. It was so cute! For the first time, I wanted to run back downstairs and share this gift with my mother.

She was in the basement. I shook the monkey so his hair stood up further and waited at the top of the steps, out of sight. Within seconds, I heard mom's steps climbing the stairs. I smiled, thrust the animal around the corner and said, "See what I got from Paula?"

There was a high-pitched shriek. I started laughing. Mom dropped the laundry basket and clutched at her heart. "Oh, I get it!" She joked when she could speak again, "Knock me off with a heart attack so Paula can have you all to herself!"

Things were definitely loosening up around my house.

In January of 1991, Lee and I broke up. After two years, differences were too great to allow us to continue growing in our relationship. It was a little awkward because we both lived on campus, and Grace was a very small school. In the beginning, there were tense feelings from both sides, and we mostly tried to avoid each other. As we ate in the same cafeteria and attended the same classes, avoidance was difficult. Because of the small numbers of fellow classmates, our break-up became a school affair, seeming to divide everyone into "sides". After a few weeks, however, the scandal blew over, and Lee and I settled into an uncomfortable, polite, surface friendship. He began spending more time at home, and very little time on campus, which helped us get over our hurts and begin to move on to new relationships.

About that same time, I found myself falling for another young man at Grace. He was a new student, joining the school for the winter semester in January. We were also in some of the same classes, and he ran the sound board for our concerts and chapel services twice a week. His name was Dana, and from the moment our eyes met, I was hooked. I had never experienced such overwhelming feelings for someone before. My heart was completely out of my control. I was ecstatically happy, but at the same time more miserable than I had ever been before. Although our friendship blossomed into love, he was involved in a long distance relationship with someone else and unable, or afraid, to choose between us. For three months I rode a roller coaster of highs and lows, until finally I understood the truth. He would never choose. While heading to California on the bus with Grace Singers in April of 1991, I nursed the worst broken heart I ever had.

Grace let out for the year about the same time as we went on tour. When I returned, instead of moving back home with my parents, my friend Linda and I decided to rent an apartment together. We had shared a dorm room for the last half of the year at Grace, and got along famously. We scouted town for the apartment with just the right "feel," and moved in that spring. Linda not only lived with me and went to school with me, but she also worked with me at the bookstore. The rest of that summer we spent trying to convince our manager to schedule our shifts together, which for some reason she never did.

The apartment was fun. We had our share of mishaps, like locking ourselves out, and almost getting caught with our pet rabbits. Her box turtle, Sprite, lumbered his eighty-year-old body around at will, and we sat on the deck evenings and watched the ducks on the lake. It was idyllic, peaceful, fun. I wasn't over Dana, and didn't date much. Linda was from St. Louis, and aside from her sister and myself, she didn't know too many people, so we had a lot of good times together.

Once we went shopping for a Siamese fighting fish at Meijer's at four o'clock in the morning, because I couldn't sleep. We decorated our apartment with Mandalas, dream catchers, and other Indian things, because she was part Indian and I always wished I was. We went on camping trips with my family, her sister, and by ourselves to Mackinac Island, Green Lake, and Cran-Hill Ranch. I taught her the art of Turtle Hunting. Once we had mice squatting in our apartment, and she had nightmares for weeks. One mouse committed suicide by diving headfirst off of our third story balcony. We caught another with mouse poison, and as the poor thing lay dying on the floor, we felt so guilty we called a vet and tried everything we could think of to save its life.

In early June, Linda went to St. Louis to visit her family for a week. Tracey, home on vacation from school for the summer, moved in. We had a ball. She was working third shift, so our schedules weren't exactly the same, but we did manage to have fun! On one of her evenings off, her boyfriend Ryan and our mutual friend Keith came over to watch movies, and we played cards until dawn. Just like the forever bond between Pam and Paula, and despite the fact that we hadn't communicated much while she was in Indiana, our friendship remained strong, and the trust between us unbreakable.

I had decided to take a year off from school. Although I knew I wanted to go into some kind of social work, I wasn't sure exactly what type. I thought a year off to decide and to work full time might help. Linda felt the same, and life settled into a comfortable routine.

My mother, always trying to "expand my horizons," decided I was bored and that I needed to get back into music. I had to admit that I was missing it. I had more or less gone straight from my high school group MAGI into Grace Singers, and now I had no prospects for singing. However, at that point I considered myself really too busy having fun, working and playing full-time, and trying to afford my half of the rent.

Mom didn't let it go. She found the name of a group that had recently sung in her church. Several times she mentioned the name, Heaven Connection, but I had never heard of them, so I just dropped it. Finally she wrote down the name of the contact person and her phone number. "I really think you should check this out, Kris. They seemed like a nice group of people, and their music was really neat."

Okay, Mom. Why not?

On June 28, 1991, I auditioned for Heaven Connection, and met the man who would eventually become my husband.

Neither of us realized it at the time, of course, but the attraction was there. He opened the door for me while I secretly observed and admired his intense blue eyes and long dark curls. My audition was the only one he watched, and the fact that he was standing quietly in the back of the sanctuary made me more nervous than I usually was. "You sounded great," he said, walking out with me afterwards. "I'm sure you'll make it. I'm Scott."

"Kristin," I said. "Nice to meet you. And I hope so!"

"I'm sure," he said again, and smiled while my heart flipped back to life once more. As I pulled out of the parking lot of the church a few minutes later, I had a talk with God.

"Okay, God. I didn't really care if I made this group or not. If You want me to sing for You, then I'll make it. I think I really would like to make it now, though." I didn't tell God why, but I'm pretty sure He knew.

I made the group.

Practices wouldn't start until our retreat in September. I couldn't attend this retreat, however, because I had planned a trip to Texas before I joined Heaven Connection. I again ventured down to visit Paula and Kenny in Cibolo, Texas.

288-| A LOVE BIG ENOUGH TO SHARE·|

I almost knew the way to their house from the airport. Walking in the door, the dogs welcomed me back. I brought my bag to the room I now considered mine and tossed it on my bed. It was good to be there again.

Paula's back had been bothering her since early June. She didn't know what the problem was, but she was in a lot of pain so we didn't move around too much. It was a vacation to relax and chat, not run around town. I brought out the cross-stitch I hadn't touched since the last time. Kenny tried to fry my Michigan-white body with the southern sun. Again.

I thought about Scott while I was there. When I returned, and Heaven Connection began having regular Sunday afternoon practices, we became friends. Linda usually came with me when concerts began in late October, and a friendship began to grow between her and Dave, another singer in the group.

On a snowy Sunday afternoon in early November, the phone rang. It was Scott. "Do you have the map to the concert tonight?" he asked. "I know it's in Kalamazoo but I can't seem to find mine."

"Sure," I said, rifling through my music folder, "it's right here."

"Can I stop by and take a look at it on my way?" he asked. "Actually, we can ride together if you want. I have plenty of room in my car."

"Okay, sounds great." I replied, said goodbye, and hung up the phone grinning. Linda looked at me suspiciously. "It's a forty-five minute drive," I said, "No need for us to all take separate cars."

She smiled and shook her finger at me, "Very convenient!"

On November 12, 1991, I invited Scott to our apartment to watch a few movies with Linda and me. I sat on the couch as close to him as I dared, trying to keep my eyes on the movies. By the end of the second one, we were holding hands, and as we said goodbye that night, he kissed my cheek. I was thrilled! My heart was healing at last.

Our relationship progressed from one to two dates, then three or four a week. We attended all of the Heaven Connection concerts, practices, and parties together, sometimes accompanied by Linda and Dave. We grew more comfortable together. From the very beginning, I promised myself that this time I would just be myself. If he loved me, it would be for who I was, not for who I was pretending to be—trying to impress a very good-looking guy. We did have a lot in common, and always had a good time together.

After a few months he confessed that he had had the map to the Kalamazoo concert in his back pocket the whole time. He just wanted an excuse to pick me up so we could be together. As the days grew warmer, we went on walks, went golfing, and even camping together. I was happy again. We began to talk about dreams, and hopes for the future, beginning to realize they included each other. We fit comfortably together, and the spark of attraction from our first meeting grew into a steady flame of genuine caring and love.

My parents liked him a lot. His parents lived just a few streets away from them, and my mom laughed when she told me she recognized him from years before. He was courteous and helpful and genuinely enjoyed my family. My mom thought he was sweet and very handsome, and my dad said he was "a good egg", one of the highest compliments one can receive from my father.

I found Scott's parents and sister to be wonderful as well. As a relationship developed between us, I knew I would be welcomed into their family with open arms.

Scott was amazed when I told him the story of my adoption and reunion, and when I went to Texas the third time in July of 1992, he went with me. We both knew we would stay together, and I wanted him to meet Paula, and her to meet him. They both approved. Scott joined Kenny in his evaluations and head shakings at how alike we were. Paula said, "He's cute and he seems truly wonderful. I believe he really loves you. And I like him for that! At least we know he has good taste!"

He proposed in one of our favorite places—near a lake where we often spent time walking and feeding ducks. It was Valentine's Day, February 14, 1993. When I opened the heart shaped box and saw the ring, and heard his trembling voice ask, "Will you marry me?" I hugged him, laughed and cried and nearly forgot to say "Yes!"

Scott and I drove straight to my parents' house to show my newly adorned finger to my mom and dad, who were both surprised, excited, and happy for us as well. Then we went around the corner to his parents' for another round of hugs and happiness.

We immediately began making plans for an August wedding. It would take place three months after Linda's marriage to Dave. Tracey would be my maid of honor. She had recently asked me to be hers— she and her longtime boyfriend Ryan would be married in October. I was so excited, and happier than I had ever been before. Everything was right in my life.

CHAPTER 37

Paula: A Lifelong Blessing

Kristin started talking to me about Scott soon after they met. When she called to say she wanted us to meet him and asked permission to bring him with her on her next visit, I knew she was pretty serious. Watching the two of them look at each other and talk softly together, it was obvious he felt the same way. I was glad we had the opportunity to meet him and have a few days with them both. Kenny and I liked Scott very much. By the time they left, I knew he was the one. As Scott and I hugged at the airport, I said to him, "Take good care of my daughter."

"I will," he answered.

My life had completely changed in the last four years. I had actually met my daughter! My heart and my soul, my whole being, had always had a powerful connection to her. I had "known" her for eighteen years. I just hadn't met her. Now that I had finally come face to face with my daughter, I found her exactly as I had known she would be. She was not only beautiful on the outside, she was beautiful on the inside as well. The moment she walked into my arms at Bethany, the connection was complete. She not only came into my arms, she came into me. She walked straight into the missing piece of my heart, and filled it to overflowing. From the very start we were open and honest with each other. We could look directly into each other's eyes and see not only the love we shared but also the trust.

It had been so good to have Pam by my side again, leaning on her for support and crying in her arms, this time from joy not sorrow. It had felt so "right" to share this happiness with her, just as we had shared the suffering all those years ago. Pam was just the same as she had been the last time I saw her, but Tracey, that delightful girl, had grown into a beautiful young lady. She had been my daughter's best friend for years. Like mother, like daughter, I thought. It had been overwhelming to see them together, they were exactly like Pam and I had been at that same age. They were as "in-sync" with one another as Pam and I were, and still are. Nothing could please me more. It would be a lifelong blessing for them, no matter how far away from each other they were. They would always have each other, no matter what. Many people live their entire life without having someone like that. I am very thankful that I have Pam, and I am equally thankful that Kristin has Tracey.

It was a pleasure to meet Mary and Bill and the rest of their family. It was very important for me to meet them and learn more about them. I needed this for my own peace of mind, to close another door of the past. I could finally put my mind at ease about the parents God had chosen for her. I had never had any concern about her being abused in any way. I knew God and the adoption agency would see to that. I just felt the need to meet them face to face and talk with them. Now when Kristin spoke of Mom and Dad, I could picture people I knew and could connect with. I was happy to call Mary my friend. We kept in touch, not very often, but it was always good to hear from her. We talked on the phone occasionally and I really enjoyed those conversations.

On Kristin's birthday that following year, I had a phone call from Mary. "Congratulations on your daughter's birthday."

"Thank you, Mary, and congratulations on *your* daughter's birthday," I replied.

Mary had made it a tradition to call every year. I thought it was beautiful. Now, instead of wondering and thinking about each other, we shared our daughter's birthday.

In early June of 1992, Kenny and I were going to Iowa for a family visit. We experienced a delay of about an hour before the plane took off, and we had to sit on the plane and wait. While sitting there I suddenly began having severe pain and muscle spasms in my back. Kenny noticed my discomfort right away, and asked for a pillow for me to sit back on. I thought it must be the uncomfortable seats on the plane, and having to sit there for so long. I took a couple of Tylenol and waited for it to stop. It did not go away or even get any better. I thought, when we got to Des Moines and I had a chance to stretch and move around, surely that would help. But, it made no difference at all. I thought I would feel better the next day. But the pain would not let me sleep or even rest, and I didn't feel better the next day. The pain was just as intense as when it had first started. It didn't ease at all during the time we spent in Iowa. It was terrible.

When we got back to Texas I called my doctor, which started all of the tests, the x-rays and MRI, the orthopedic surgeon and all the specialists, the physical therapy, the trigger point injections, and all the drugs they kept switching around trying to find something that would help the pain. But nothing did. The pain was still intense, and it was also starting in my shoulders and elbows, my hips and knees, and other points of my body. When my doctor ran out of tests, and had tried everything he could, hoping that it was something else, he told me I had fibromyalgia. Fibromyalgia is a chronic pain condition for which there is no known cause and no known cure. All they could do was try to find the combination of drugs to at least ease my pain. I could no longer work. Riding in the car was extremely painful. I was more or less homebound for weeks, sometimes months, at a time. I will always be thankful that I got to travel to Michigan and spend some time there before I got sick.

When Kristin called to tell me she and Scott were getting married, it wasn't a complete surprise. My first thought was, "She's too young," but I knew that wasn't true. I just wanted her to be sure, and she was.

I wanted so much to be there, to have a part in her wedding plans, and to be a part of all the happy excitement. But, it didn't seem it would work that way. Because of fibromyalgia, I just couldn't commit myself. Instead, Kristin kept me up to date by phone. As the wedding was six months off, I prayed that I would feel better so I could go. I wanted so badly to be there, to share that magical day with Kristin and Mary. I wanted to hold my daughter close and wish her and her soon-to-be husband every happiness. As time passed and their wedding day got closer, I knew there was no way I would be able to handle the trip. I was very disappointed. I had missed so much of her life, why did I have to miss this too? I knew how much she wanted me there, and I wanted to be there just as much. I knew I wasn't letting her down because I knew she understood. She had been here and had seen what this horrible disease had done to me. Even though I could not be there in person, I knew, without a doubt, she would feel my love for her on that day.

Mary called one evening about a month before the wedding to see how I was getting along, and if I would be able to come for the wedding. I said, "I want to be there so bad Mary, but there's just no way."

"We're really sorry you can't be here, Paula, but I want you to know, if you feel at the last minute you can come, there is a place for you right beside me." That meant so much to me. What a special person she is, I thought to myself.

Two weeks before my daughter's wedding, Kristin and I talked on the phone. The beginning of our conversation was quiet and filled with disappointment on both sides.

"You really aren't going to come, are you?" Kristin asked softly.

"We've all been praying for a long time that I would be able to travel by this time," I answered, "but for some reason, that's not meant to be. No honey, I won't be able to come, but I'll be thinking about you every single minute of the day. You know that, don't you?"

"I know you will Mom, and I do understand. I love you." I could hear the trembling in her voice.

My own eyes filled with tears as I answered, "I love you, too."

We then both spoke on a much lighter note as we talked about the last minute preparations being made for the wedding. By the time we hung up, we were both at peace with the fact that I would not be there for her very special day.

On the day of Kristin's wedding I was quiet and thoughtful. As I sat in the living room with Kenny staring at the television, I kept thinking about what they might be doing right now. Are they at the church yet? Is Tracey there helping her dress? Is everything going according to plan? Did all the right flowers get there? How was Scott doing? Was he the typical nervous groom? How was Bill? Was he wishing the walk down the aisle with his daughter was over? Through it all I kept thinking "Have a perfect day, little one. Be happy. I love you."

Kenny felt so bad that I couldn't be there for my daughter's wedding. He knew why I couldn't go, and he understood that. Yet he seemed to have a very difficult time understanding why I *didn't* go. I finally told him exactly how I felt. "Kenny, listen to me. Of course I want to be there, and I feel so bad because I can't go. But we have to think about Kristin. I would be sitting there in so much pain, and she would know that. She would feel bad and worry about me, and I don't want that. She knows how I feel, and how badly I want to be there. She knows how much I love her, and how happy I am for her. I don't want to ruin one minute of this day for her. This is her day, let's let her have it." He understood then, and he agreed with me.

I watched the clock a lot that day. Just about the time they were saying their vows, Kenny thought he heard a car pull up so he went outside to check. He came back in with the most beautiful bouquet of flowers I had ever seen. The card read, "Dear Paula and Kenny, Thinking of you this special day. Congratulations on Kristin and Scott's marriage. With love and thanksgiving, Bill and Mary." The flowers were the same as the bouquet Kristin carried. How caring and thoughtful of them. Kenny and I both cried.

I remembered Kristin's excitement when she called to tell me Scott had proposed and, yes, she was getting married. Then she had put Scott on the phone, "You really love my daughter, don't you?" I asked him.

"Yes, I do, very much," he answered, "Why?"

"Because you have two mothers-in-law."

"And I love them both."

"Good answer!" I said as we both laughed.

I could almost picture the look on his face as he would watch his bride come down the aisle. And I knew Kristin would be smiling, her eyes shining love and happiness. It would be as if they were the only two people in the church. I wished them all the love and joy Kenny and I had shared over the years.

I thought back to the first phone call from Mary Sue, to Kristin's pictures and letters, and the phone calls that followed. To finally see my daughter again was an answer to my prayers. I had also been blessed with the opportunity to meet and talk with her parents. Memories of being with Pam and sharing the joy of Kristin remained vivid. Pam and I had imagined a day our daughters would be together, but in our hearts doubted it would ever come. To stand beside Pam and see our daughters together at last was a feeling I can't begin to describe. Many wonderful things had happened, from Kristin's visits, to meeting Scott, and now their marriage. We had gone from all the questions and answers, to special times spent with each other, and now we could look ahead to a future. Just as I had seen her grow and mature, our relationship has also grown and matured. My tiny baby girl was now a grown woman. The past with all its pain and longing seemed to be growing dimmer and the future ever brighter.

I respect and admire Mary very much. I must have seemed like a terrible threat to her, yet she welcomed me into her home and openly shared her life with me. She answered all my questions honestly, without hesitation. She wrote me long letters going back through the years to Kristin's childhood, sending me pictures and sharing with me all of Kristin's "firsts". I know our friendship will continue. We each have our own very special mother/daughter relationship with Kristin that we are comfortable and secure with.

It is amazing how God's plan has brought us all together to close the circle, and how he connected the triangle inside that circle of Kristin, Mary, and me. From the day she was born, and even before, Kristin has made such a huge impact on so many people. So many people love her. Even after all the heartache and pain, all I've been through, and all the hurt I've put my family through, how could I have done anything different? After all, what would life be without knowing and loving Kristin? I can't imagine. I love her so.

To Kristin, my daughter, I say, "The best thing I ever did was you. Be happy, little one. I love you."

CHAPTER 38

Mary: An Open Letter From One Real Mom

I almost never knew you, almost never loved you,
I almost never heard you call my name.
I would've missed the joy and laughter,
And all the love thereafter,
Cause you filled my empty arms when you came.
Yes, you filled my empty arms when you came.[15]

Christine Wyrtzen

Dear Kris,

The first time I heard Christine Wyrtzen's song, I wept. You were only a young girl of ten. We were at her concert together sharing our love for music. Today, a decade later, it still stirs much emotion within me, reflecting on all I would have missed if I never knew you.

Besides music, we've shared another love over the years—reading books. When we hiked down the Grand Canyon, I wondered if you might have been the only kid who ever took a book along to read on the rest stops while hiking down. I think Bethany did a great job of matching the talents and interests of your birth parents with ours, don't you? As Dad says, "We couldn't have done a better job ourselves."

Speaking of Dad, I've been blessed over the past few years to watch your relationship with Dad blossom again and grow. You honored him at Christmas with that wonderful picture you gave him of a father kneeling beside his child's bed in prayer. You know, Kris, even after you left for college and then rented an apartment with Linda, Dad still plods faithfully each night from bedroom to bedroom praying for each of you kids. Thank you for such an expression of gratitude to him. I don't know who shed more tears when you gave it, Dad or you.

We have lived a lot of life together, collecting volumes of memories, and now my dear, we're planning another memory maker, a major milestone in your life, your wedding day. What a wonderful surprise it was on Valentine's Day when you and Scott burst into the kitchen and I heard you say, "Mom! Look what Scott gave me for Valentine's Day!" It was a beautiful diamond ring, representing an eventual leaving of us and a cleaving to another. Who would have guessed that our good-looking paper boy of a few years ago, who rode backwards on the handlebars of his bike, would one day become our second son! He certainly impressed our first son, Brian, with his feats!

It's funny that neither you nor Scott were aware of each other's existence in those days. I guess those were the years you holed up in your room reading books. I remember when you phoned me after you had just noticed Scott at Heaven Connection and asked, "Mom, do we know a Scott from Grandville?" I thought for a moment and then answered, "Kris, I need more clues than that." Then when I saw him at your first concert, I hurried over to you afterwards and said, "Kris, that guy was our old paper boy!"

Kristi, the day is almost here when you'll become the wife of our old paper boy. I have many mixed emotions as the day approaches. Part of me wants the time to fly by so I can resume normal thoughts instead of having a head full of wedding details. Another part of me wants the time to slow down because after the wedding you won't be our Kristi anymore. Dad will give you to Scott, but never forget Whose you really are—a child of the King, Who loves and cares for you more than any of us could.

I've noticed that some moms have a hard time letting go as their children get married. That's something I don't need to worry about since I've already worked through letting go when Pam told us about Paula. After that experience, this is not so hard. I know now that letting go usually leads to more gains than losses. In that case, I learned a lot about God—how much He loves me and that He's 100% trustworthy. I gained a love big enough to share, I gained friends in Paula, Pam, and Mary Sue. Best of all, I still have you as my daughter and now as one of my best friends.

I am really sorry Paula can't come the distance to your wedding. I know that there would have been questions in the minds of some of the guests, maybe some explaining to do about another mom in the parents' row, but I'm thinking that after missing out on all of your growing up, Paula will miss out yet once again. With that in mind, Dad and I have decided to try to help her make it through your wedding day by sending her a beautiful floral bouquet in the same colors you chose for your wedding. I think a note of congratulations will bless her heart so she won't feel so left out, don't you?

You know, Kris, after all is said and done, I just thank God that in His providence He arranged for all of us to meet Paula. I know I had a hard time for a while and some things hurt, but, as usual, God worked it all out for the good of those who love Him.

After the reunion Mary Sue told me, "If you're not adopted, you don't understand the incredible need adoptees have to become complete, to know their roots. By giving Kris permission and freedom to meet and know Paula, you and Bill have given her a priceless gift."

I'm thankful God gave us the grace to give you such a gift.

The only thing that bothered me lately is the question several different people asked me as we were planning the wedding. They asked, "Is Kristin's real mother coming to the wedding?"

I knew what they meant, but I struggled over that word, "real". I asked myself, "Am I not a real mother because I haven't given birth to these kids? What is a real mother anyway?"

After some thought, I found an answer that satisfies me so I can be gracious to those asking questions and still have peace in my own mind.

Now don't laugh, Kris, but I found my answer in the classic children's story, "The Velveteen Rabbit." As you might remember, the toy Rabbit asked the Skin Horse the same question one day. He asked, "What is REAL?"

I think the reply of the Skin Horse describes my experience quite well:

"Real isn't how you are made," said the Skin Horse. "It's a thing that happens to you. When a child loves you for a long, long time, not just to play with, but REALLY loves you, then you become Real."

"Does it hurt?" asked the Rabbit.

"Sometimes," said the Skin Horse for he was always truthful. "When you are Real you don't mind being hurt."

"Does it happen all at once, like being wound up," he asked, "or bit by bit?"

"It doesn't happen all at once," said the Skin Horse. "You become. It takes a long time. That's why it doesn't often happen to people who break easily, or have sharp edges, or who have to be carefully kept. Generally, by the time you are Real, most of your hair has been loved off, and your eyes drop out and you get loose in the joints and very shabby. But these things don't matter at all, because once you are Real you can't be ugly, except to people who don't understand. But once you are Real you can't become unreal again. It lasts for always."[16]

Kris, God has given you two real moms, but each is real in a different way. Paula is "real" by giving birth. I think I must be "real" by the experience of being really loved for twenty-one years, don't you? In less than a week, you'll be given a third "real" mom by marriage. God is a gracious, a generous, an awesome God.

Both Dad and I are thankful that God has given you a Christian man to marry. Our prayer for both of you is that as your wedding day passes and your marriage begins, God will take all the love, the tenderness, the laughter, and the tears and will weave them into a beautiful relationship centered on Him.

Love,
Mom

P.S. Did I tell you that my kindergarten friend, Susie, was the first to R.S.V.P.? She can hardly wait until your wedding day!

CHAPTER 39

Kristin: The Story of His Love

Bright and early on August 21, 1993, I walked out of my parents' house for the last time as a single woman. I had spent the night there, back home—a symbolic last night of childhood under my parents' roof. My mom gave me a hug and a smile of encouragement as I climbed into the backseat of their blue Toyota. She drove off in the direction of the church, stopping at Tracey's house to pick her up. The sky was a deep, clear blue, and there was not a cloud to be seen. The sun shone in what felt like a blessing on this, the happiest day of my life.

On the way Tracey and I talked while I painted her nails the same pale pink as mine. "Are you ready for this?" she asked, trying to push her long dark hair back from her face without ruining her nails.

"Absolutely. Everything is perfect, except for one big thing. Paula and Kenny won't be there. I just . . . you know?"

"Yeah," Tracey always understood. "That I do know. It would have been really neat, your two moms sitting side by side in the front row. My mom's been crying all morning that Paula couldn't come. She says since Paula won't be there, she has to cry for two people."

Paula's back pains had grown worse in the past year or so, and she was unable to travel. I understood this, and knew that she wanted more than anything to be here for me that day. When she had called earlier in the week, I had tried to make her feel better, "It'll be okay. I'll send you a copy of the video. Anyway, I'll be there, and a piece of you is always with me, so in a way, you will be there too."

Since Paula had never spent a large amount of time with my family, and had only met my immediate family and none of my other relatives, part of me couldn't help but wonder if it wouldn't make the day go easier. She was so sensitive to everyone, I would hate for anything to happen that would hurt her or make her think she wasn't completely welcome. I would have liked to have seen her sitting there looking beautiful and proud, but it wasn't to be.

We were real friends now. She had come to see me, and I had been introduced to her home and her world. We had a great rapport, laughing and talking on the phone like we had always been together. She never tried to "mother" me, or move in on territory that she considered taken by my mom. Since her visit to Michigan, I began to call her "Mom", and thought of her as a mother and a friend. It was complicated and simple at the same time. It's hard to describe. She was my Paula. A piece of me in another state. My roots, my history, my recognized soul friend. She was still mine alone, even when she became friends with my mother. Paula always told me she loved me, every time we hung up the phone, got on a plane, or signed a letter. I never doubted it, and grew to cherish the comfort of knowing her.

Meanwhile, my relationship with my mother had grown more than I could have believed. After my engagement was announced, she and I began taking walks around her neighborhood once a week to discuss wedding plans. She was extremely helpful in planning this day, calling the photographer and arranging an interview, finding a florist, a seamstress, and videographer. Once the basics were covered, we began to talk about more than plans while we walked. For the first time in years we shared feelings—about my marriage, finding Paula, and the years in between. As we laughed and sometimes cried together, our bond was strengthened beyond what it had ever been before. I was a grown woman, finding out again that this woman who had always been there for me was an amazingly understanding friend. We had found our way back to trust, and our unique relationship flourished and grew on the memories, love, and future we shared.

The flowers and candles were already being set up in the church when Tracey, my mom, and I arrived. A thrill went through me as I saw the transformation of the sanctuary where I would soon be married. Everything was perfect. A beautiful white unity banner with two rings and a dove hung directly behind the platform. A heart and two fan candelabras stood in the center, framed by two spiral candelabras and our unity candle. Huge bouquets of purple Dutch irises and yellow carnations flanked each one. My mother-in-law (to be, shortly) was attaching a candle sconce and bow to every other pew. It was 10:00 a.m., and we had only an hour until we needed to be ready for the photographer.

My mom began to check on the individual bowls of Siamese fighting fish we would have as centerpieces at the reception downstairs. Tracey and I went straight to the nursery to start getting dressed, so we wouldn't be late for pictures. Another friend, Susie, was ready and waiting to assist with my hair and make-up. I felt like a queen for a day, which is really how you are supposed to feel on your wedding day.

Tracey, Scott's sister Amy, and my sister Sue were in the outer room slipping into their purple dresses and shoes and doing their own touch-ups. Susie carefully put up my hair in its beautiful bow and veil, and just as she began to put the finishing touches on my black eyeliner and mascara, Pam walked in the door.

Pam always told me she thought of me as her third daughter. Because I was close to her heart, and because of Paula. It only took one look at her face to tell me how she was faring on this eventful and emotional day. Her eyes were already red-rimmed, and her lips were pressed tight to keep from trembling. She touched my cheek. With new tears forming, she said, "Oh, how I wish Paula could be here for this day. I wish she could see you now!"

I felt tears come to my own eyes, and, mindful of Susie who still held the eyeliner in her hand, tried to hold them back. Pam reached into her purse for a tissue, pulling out at the same time an envelope with my name on it and a small gray box. My eyes widened and a sharp pang went through my chest. I felt a strange sensation in the back of my knees as, without a word, she handed them both to me.

My hands were not steady as I pulled the pages from the envelope and looked over them to meet Tracey's eyes. She looked from me to her mother, who now let her tears fall freely. I dropped my eyes and read:

Dearest Kristin,

Your wedding day is here. It's hard to believe that the girl who stayed at our house and spent those nights giggling with Tracey is walking down the aisle and beginning a new life with Scott, the man of your dreams. I'm so happy for you.

Remember when you asked me for the rings that had once been Paula's, and then mine? I told you the right day would come to pass them on to you? Today feels like the right day. My heart is full of joy, yet sadness too, because Paula can't be here to share in this special day. So please let these rings represent her for you today.

You already know it represents so much to me, the friendship and pain Paula and I shared throughout the years, as well as my husband's love. It represents many lives drawn together. It truly represents a circle of love, like no other ring I know of.

This ring also represents the wholeness God has brought about in your and Paula's relationship, in spite of the fact the wholeness was broken for so many years after Paula gave you up for adoption. God in His love and grace brought you and Paula together again . . . it has been through Him that the relationship has been made whole.

So please accept these rings today as a gesture of the love and bond I feel for you and Paula. I hope it will come to mean as much to you as it does to me. You will always have a special place in my heart. I love you!

Love,
Mom Teunissen

It didn't take long for me to hold tight this little woman who stood tall, yet was inches shorter than me. Forgetting the eye make-up, I cried along with her. I cried with love for her, and longing for Paula to be there. I was so glad that Pam, somehow a fitting substitute, would be there in her place, "crying for two."

I opened the gray box and gazed at the two silver rings inside. The diamond on the engagement band twinkled at me. "Thanks, Mom. Thanks so much—I know what this means to you, I really do."

Pam nodded. "And I know what this means to you. You know I love you, and I'm so sorry Paula isn't here . . . ."

"Me too . . . ."

"These are very special rings. They've seen a lot of tears and joy, and I know you will take good care of them."

I put both rings immediately on the ring finger—of my right hand. Earlier that week, my pearl ring, the one Scott had given me to celebrate one year of dating, had broken. I had been so disappointed that I couldn't wear the pearl for my wedding. Now, I understood and was somehow not surprised that my ring finger was free to wear these rings that, even before I had seen them, had meant so much to me.

I managed to get control of my emotions, but only after shooing Pam out the door. We could have stood together and cried all day! Poor Susie had to start from the beginning with my eyes, and listen to a thousand apologies from me. She was a new friend and hadn't yet heard my whole, miraculous life story, but she cheerfully got out her make-up again after I promised I'd explain the whole thing later.

Yes, I was late for pictures.

The music started. It was time to begin! Brian, my brother, standing up for Scott, led the procession with Amy. After seeing him in a tuxedo, for the first time, I felt nervous stirrings in my stomach. I stood at the back of the line, clutching my dad's arm while he grinned his huge grin at me. "You can still back out, you know," he teased. "It's not too late—yet!"

Next went my sister, Sue, on the arm of Kevin, a mutual friend from our singing group Heaven Connection. Following them, Linda, my recently married roommate and Mike, a friend of Scott's from work. Finally, Tracey with Scott's best friend Jeff. Tracey shot me a wink and a crooked grin, and I managed a smile back at her.

The bridal march began. Scott stood waiting at the front of the church, looking both solemn and handsome in his dark grey tuxedo. My aunt kissed my cheek, patted my dad's hair, and said, "Now." Dad and I stepped off together, and my confidence returned. It was my shining moment, and I was happy. The whole church stood to its feet, and I saw Pam and Anthony near the back on my side. Pam's whole precious face was contorted into an obvious fight for control, which she seemed ready to lose. I smiled and shook my head. This wasn't a time for sadness, it was a happy moment! A new, bright future was beginning. I wasn't crying now.

Shortly after one o'clock I was married to the man of my dreams. My Uncle Steve performed the ceremony, and Tracey cried through the whole thing. I couldn't see Pam, but I'm sure Tracey wasn't crying alone. My dad, listening intently to every word of my uncle's message, nodded now and then, and smiled encouragingly. My mom sat straight and proud, looking radiant in the pale yellow dress we never thought was her color, until then. I looked at her from on the platform where Scott and I stood, facing the audience. In my heart I loved her and was thanking her—there were no words—for the love, happiness and security she had always given me. The hard times were over, and I now considered her one of my dearest friends. She was always there, always trustworthy, always encouraging. As much as I wished Paula could have been sitting next to her, I was equally grateful to my mom for years of everything I ever needed.

I was called back to attention by my uncle, who began to pray for us. It was our first blessing as a married couple. Music started to play as he said, "Amen,"—but the soloist stayed in her seat. My new husband took both of my hands in his and smiled into my eyes. To my surprise and delight, Scott began to sing to me—to sing a beautiful song of love and commitment he had found and prepared on his own. He sang straight from his heart, and although I tried not to cry (I didn't want to get over-emotional while he was singing and mess him up), I felt a tear of pure joy slide down my cheek. If it were possible to die of happiness in front of two hundred people, Scott would have gone on his honeymoon alone. My uncle never did get around to saying, "Kiss the Bride." I threw tradition to the wind and myself into the arms, right there, of the man I had chosen to marry. Nearly a full minute went by as the music slowly tapered to an end, the candles flickered against the air, and Scott held me in his arms. It was an unconventional ending, as we kissed unbidden and headed down the aisle. Pam and Tracey were joined in their tears by nearly every other wedding guest present.

After a fun-filled reception, Scott and I got ready to leave for our honeymoon. The song my new husband had sung to me floated through my mind. I thought about how wonderful it all was, how wonderful my whole life was. Then I thought of another song—one by Christine Dente, the lead singer in my favorite Christian music group, Out Of The Grey. I sang the lyrics softly to myself while I changed out of my wedding dress and into my jeans:

> *I'm watching You write my life, Lord,*
> *I'm seeing Your hand in all I am,*
> *I'm watching You write my life*
> *as only You, only You can.*
> *Oh, I'm watching You write my life, Lord,*
> *and telling the story of Your love,*
> *I'm watching You write my life*
> *and learning how to trust.*[17]

Christine's words were so true. He had written my life, and it was a story of His love. His hand was in it all.

Before we headed out on our way to Detroit (and on to Jamaica!), I called Paula.

I told her about the ceremony and its surprising and unusual but very successful ending. "It was a beautiful song—you would have loved it."

"I'm sure, baby girl. I just can't wait to see the video." She laughed, half-joking. "Is it in the mail yet?"

"Pam gave me your rings. I got to wear them in my wedding!"

"Oh, I was hoping today would be the day. I had a feeling. I'm so glad for you. For all of us, actually! I mean . . . this is just so amazing!" She sounded happy. Then her voice became wistful. "I'm glad she could be there for you, especially today."

"You were there, Mom, you were there too." I told her I could feel her throughout the wedding, throughout the whole day, and I knew she was there as only she could be. There with Pam, and always, always with me.

All my life I have loved circles. I love to watch things begin and see how inevitably they circle around and end up in the same place. I love how things mysteriously turn up to be related somehow, in the least expected way. I love how my life fit into a series of circles, and how everything ended up being related "somehow".

Paula gave me up for adoption out of love. She couldn't provide what she believed I needed, a stable home and family. I was adopted by love, into exactly the stable home and family God intended for me as soon as Paula's decision was made.

The family He chose enjoyed music. My mom sang with me from a very young age. Through her, God led me into singing and into that special group called MAGI. He led me to Kentucky and straight to Tracey, and our instant friendship was formed—fourteen years after we had lived together in the same home, as an infant and an unborn baby.

God opened Pam's eyes, allowing her to see similarities to her best friend, Paula. She saw them in a completely unexpected place—in the best friend of her own daughter. He painted her many signs and gave her much wisdom. Through Him she knew when to hold her tongue and when to speak the truth, the secret He had chosen to share with her.

God had a lot of fun with this one.

Carefully and tenderly, He set all the details in place. I was gently guided by my parents into the person I was born to become. Through Tracey's unconditional friendship and Pam's motherly love, I was placed in the exact position I needed to be in to meet my birth mother face to face. To fill in the holes. To complete the circle of me!

During these years, Paula was loved and cherished by her family, and guided by God as well. He held her hand as she waited in peace for the moment to arrive when He would pull back the curtain and reveal her daughter to her again.

I thank Paula for giving me life. I am thankful for her dedication to God, her firm belief in the precious sanctity of life, and her love for me. Without these things, I would not be here. I thank my parents for helping me live life—their wisdom, instruction, love, and laughter are worth more than words can ever say. I thank God for his ingenious, creative plan. For watching me so carefully, for guiding me so lovingly, for allowing me to be a part of this awesome story. My life has indeed come full circle.

My mom was right. God gave us this life. And He gave us love— and made it big enough to share.

Twenty-five years saw a lot of life changes for Kristin and her moms. Kristin had the opportunity to experience the mother/daughter relationship in a whole new way when she gave birth to her first daughter, Aiden Beth, in 2005. Fourteen months later, Jamey Elaine was born. These precious babies gave even more dimension to the women's relationships and turned the moms into grandmas! Paula began to visit Kristin, Scott, and the girls for several weeks every year, cultivating connections with them, and expanding her mutual friendship with Mary. Paula and Pam's strong bond continued, as if they had never been apart..

ACKNOWLEDGEMENTS

Mary

We are grateful for Bethany Christian Home which was a well-known adoption agency when this story began. Through the work of Dick Roeters, Harold Wiersma, and others, the adoptive family in this book came together. By the mid-1970s Bethany had expanded their services and their outreach, changing their identity. Bethany Christian Services is now a global nonprofit organization providing a variety of services to children and families around the world.

We thank those at Bethany who prayerfully chose Bill and Mary to adopt Paula's baby girl in a closed, confidential adoption relationship. Without you, there would be no story to tell.

Mary Sue Kendrick was the substitute social worker who filled the place of the vacationing post-adoption worker. She was new to the Bethany staff when this adoptive mom called for help. Her own personal experience and gentle ways were exactly what each woman needed. Beautiful job on the foreword, Mary Sue!

God's timing is always perfect. So, we accepted the fact that about eighteen years ago no publisher was willing to print this book. Thank you for all those who prayed for and encouraged us back then. Thank you to Ron Nydam who encouraged us to self-publish. This is it, Ron!

Thank you to Carrie Kraus back then and now for her quick answers to questions on details about preparing for publishing.

Thank you to Phil Kraus of the radio program Family Life Today who interviewed Mary for her perspective on this story, airing it on April 6, 2002. More encouragement!

Thank you to Mary Ann Boyer of Bethany Christian Services who encouraged us by interviewing Kristin, Paula, and Mary for a beautiful article found in the 2007 September issue of the Bethany *Lifelines*.

Kris Faber, our international friend, how can we say thank you! At just the right time you gave self-publishing a name we could consider. Thank you for sharing your success story with us. We are grateful!

Thank you to Mark and Roxanne deRoo for pizza in 2015 and those encouraging words: "That story has to be published!"

Thank you, Kathy Kroeze, for your help in finding Mary Sue Kendrick after all these years. You went the extra mile!

Laurie Gordon, you were so willing to help find contact information for permissions for lyrics to songs. Thank you so much!

David and Christine Carlson, Dave and LaVonne Yoder. You are a God-send! You were not only an encouragement for self-publishing, but you ran ahead of us, showing us the way! May blessings in abundance be yours! Christine, you took our dream, and made it into a book! Thank you!!!

Paula

Thank you to my parents, Pearl and Herman Vander Ploeg, who gave me so much unconditional love. Because of that gift, I had the love and courage to give my child up for adoption. During my pregnancy and in the "Lost Years" that followed after I gave Kristin up, their love and prayers for me never wavered. My mom started praying for Kristin Roedema Oosterheert long before she was born, and she continued to pray as God revealed the story that only He could write. She was thrilled beyond measure on the day she finally got to give Kristin a big hug. She would have been overjoyed to see this book published.

Thank you to my dear sister Pat Moss and her husband Harlan. They were and still are forever steady in my life—before, during, and after my pregnancy with Kristin. I am grateful for their open arms and open hearts, always ready to hold me when I weep or to hug me when I am happy.

Pam

I thank my husband Anthony Teunissen, who not only walked the journey in this book with me, but prayed, encouraged, listened, dried my tears, and loved me unconditionally as God kept putting the pieces and connections of Paula and Kristin before me. Anthony knew exactly the right way to listen, and the right time to pray, even at 2 a.m., as I bounced things off him, trying to figure where things fit, and WHAT in the world I was supposed to do with this information God was randomly giving me. He and the Lord are the ones that held me up when I needed to step back and just watch as God continued to work. I could not have lived or written my portion of this book without the Lord and this man by my side.

Thank you to my mother, Ruth Hofstra, who loved me and listened to me as only a mom can. She was there for me when I needed her and advised me, in her wisdom, to think about how the choices I made in all of this would affect others. I am grateful not only for her love, but also for the nurturing she gave me as a writer when I was growing up. She would be pleased to see this book in print.

Kristin

Thank you to both of my wonderful moms, Mary and Paula, for giving me the space and the patience to figure out how best to deal with an exciting but confusing situation. Thank you for respecting my needs and trusting me to grow up into the perfect blend of both of you! It was fun identifying what parts of me came from each, and now, so many years later, I can honestly call both of you my very good friends. Thanks for befriending each other and making that part so easy.

Thank you to my husband Scott, who listened to our amazing story and was always there to encourage me as I wrote. He still likes to point out which of my moms I'm acting like!

Thank you to my dad, Bill Roedema, for an amazing amount of painstaking work in tidying up this manuscript and getting it ready to print. Thanks for your suggestions and reassurances, and for keeping us on track. This wouldn't have turned out without your meticulous attention to detail and uncanny recall of grammar rules!

All

As Kristin's soul friend, Tracey Teunissen Westphal played an integral part in the formation of this story, unknown to either of them. Then when the truth was revealed, Tracey used her career skills to put this amazing story together. As a freelance writer, she encouraged the four authors by asking hard, sometimes painful questions. She initially edited the chapters as they were written and placed them in the order presented in this book. It was her desire that the readers see the hand of God moving in His unique, incredible way, showing His love for us all. Thank you, Tracey, for playing well the part God wrote for you!

What about you?

Every writer in *A Love Big Enough to Share* has a personal relationship with Jesus Christ. Each talks to God about her life and credits Him for the answers He provides. Readers have seen the struggles and have read the prayers of each author, ordinary women who trust in an extraordinary God.

If you do not have a personal relationship with Jesus Christ and wish to explore that possibility, we invite you to go online to needhim.org for more information.

The Bible: New Testament

Ephesians 2:8-9 (NIV) "For it is by grace you are saved, through faith—and this is not from yourselves, it is the gift of God—not by works, so that no one can boast."

Romans 10:9 (NIV) "That if you confess with your mouth, 'Jesus is Lord,' and believe in your heart that God raised Him from the dead, you will be saved."

ENDNOTES

CHAPTER 1
1. Children's lullaby remembered from the 1940's. Author: Unknown. Copyright: Unknown.

CHAPTER 2
2. Name has been changed throughout.
3. Name has been changed throughout.

CHAPTER 3
4. PUBLIC DOMAIN. Robert Frost. "The Road Not Taken (1—15)," in *The Poetry of Robert Frost*, ed. Edward Connery Lathem (New York: Henry Holt, 1969) p.105.

5. PUBLIC DOMAIN. Robert Frost. "The Road Not Taken (16—20)," in *The Poetry of Robert Frost*, ed. Edward Connery Lathem (New York: Henry Holt, 1969) p.105.

CHAPTER 5
6. PUBLIC DOMAIN. Johnson Oatman, Jr. "Count Your Blessings," in *Great Hymns of the Faith* (Grand Rapids, Michigan: Singspiration Music of Zondervan Corporation, 1968) p.370.

CHAPTER 9
7. PUBLIC DOMAIN. Anna L. Warner. "Jesus Loves Me," in *Let Youth Praise Him: A Hymnal for Christian Primary Schools, Sunday Schools and Christian Homes* (Grand Rapids, Michigan: Wm. B. Eerdmans Publishing Company and the National Union of Christian Schools, 1964) p.78.

CHAPTER 11
8. PUBLIC DOMAIN. Harriet E. Buell. "A Child Of The King," in *Great Hymns of the Faith* (Grand Rapids, Michigan: Singspiration Music of Zondervan Corporation, 1968) p.279.

CHAPTER 13
9. PUBLIC DOMAIN. William O. Cushing. "Jewels," in *Timeless Truths Free Online Library* (library.timelesstruths.org/music/Jewels) January 29, 2018.

CHAPTER 16
10. Michael W. Smith, Deborah D. Smith. "Friends," Copyright 1982. Meadowgreen Music Company (ASCAP) (adm. at Capitol CMG Publishing.com) All rights reserved. Used by permission.

CHAPTER 21
11. PUBLIC DOMAIN. K. "How Firm A Foundation," published in 1787 by John Rippon in *A Selection of Hymns from the Best Authors, Intended to be an Appendix to Dr. Watts's Psalms and Hymns.*

CHAPTER 25
12. Author: Unknown. "Legacy of an Adopted Child," poem widely known through adoption community, found, among other sites, at Adoption Star and News (https://adoptionstar.com/adoption-poety-legacy-of-an-adopted-child/) on March 1, 2018.

CHAPTER 26
13. Jim Elliot. In *Draper's Book of Quotations for the Christian World*, compiled by Edythe Draper (Wheaton, Illinois, Tyndale, 1992) p.89.

CHAPTER 31
14. Marilee Zdenek. From *Splinters in my Pride*, Quoted in Charles R. Swindoll. *Growing Strong in the Seasons of Life* (Portland, Oregon, Multnoma Press, 1983) Used by permission. All rights reserved.

CHAPTER 38
15. Christine Wyrtzen. "Almost Never Knew You," in *Person to Person*, (Loveland Music, Distributed by the Benson Company: Nashville, 1986) Used by permission. All rights reserved.

16. PUBLIC DOMAIN. Margery Williams. *The Velveteen Rabbit*, (New York: Doubleday, 1991, c1992).

CHAPTER 39
17. Christine Dente. "Write My Life" in *Out of the Grey* (The Sparrow Corporation, Brentwood, TN, 1991) Used by permission. All rights reserved.

Made in the USA
Middletown, DE
09 January 2020

82856284R00188